ROUND TRIP TO HELL IN A FLYING SAUCER

UFO PARASITES -
ALIEN "SOUL SUCKERS" -
INVADERS FROM DEMONIC REALMS

Edited by Timothy Green Beckley & Sean Casteel

With: Scott Corralles - Adam Gorightly - T. Allen Greenfield - William M. Mott
Brent Raynes - Nick Redfern - Brad Steiger - Tim R. Swartz

GLOBAL COMMUNICATIONS

Round Trip to Hell in a Flying Saucer
By
Timothy Green Beckley, Sean Casteel, & Cecil Michael
Additional Material By
Scott Corralles, Adam Gorightly, Michah A. Hanks, Andrew Hennesey,
Thomas Horn, Philip J. Imbrogno, T. Allen Greenfield, William Mott,
Christopher O'Brien, Brent Raynes, Nick Redfern, Brad Steiger, Tim R. Swartz,
Kenn Thomas, Joshua P. Warren

EAN: 978-1-60611-091-8
ISBN: 1-60611-091-1

Nonfiction

Timothy Green Beckley: Editorial Director
Carol Rodriguez: Publishers Assistant
Sean Casteel: Associate Editor
William Kern: Editorial Assistant
Cover Art: Tim R. Swartz

Printed in the United States of America

For free catalog write:
Global Communications
P.O. Box 753
New Brunswick, NJ 08903

Free Subscription to Conspiracy Journal E-Mail Newsletter
www.conspiracyjournal.com

Contents

Taking a UFO Into The Lake of Fire

Introduction by Timothy Green Beckley

It's UFOlogy's dirty little secret. It's something that is better left swept under the rug. Stanton Friedman doesn't talk about it. Stephen Bassett most assuredly would keep the subject at arm's length. The late Richard Hall would have deleted you from his address book. And Steven Greer would never consider it part of his ongoing disclosure program.

To coin ourselves a catch-all phrase that brings together all the negative aspects of the subject, I prefer to call it the DARK SIDE OF UFOLOGY!

It would appear – at least at first glance – that only those who consider themselves Christian fundamentalists have a rigorous drum to beat on the subject matter . . . and it would seem to be almost an exclusive part of their zealous religious belief system that says if they can't find it in the Bible it can't be so – or if it is and they can't define it in any other way then it must be DEMONIC!

When not writing and publishing books on UFOs and the Paranormal author Tim Beckley cohorts with a few demons himself in horror movies he hosts under the monika of Mr Creepo.

The truth is we are not dealing solely with physical craft from outer space occupied by off-world astronauts coming to Earth merely to check out our lifestyle and warn us that we might possibly annihilate ourselves either ecologically or through our warlike activities.

More and more emphasis needs to be placed on the spiritual, occult and paranormal nature of the phenomena seen in our skies and invading our homes and personal boundaries. It's not all "sweetness and light," kiddies. The truth is that there are frequently a lot of negative elements associated with UFO encounters. Some of the entities involved could very well be leading us down the primrose path. You can believe, and the evidence clearly is undisputable, that there are cosmic criminals in our midst who have successfully managed to possess and control the minds of some utterly frightened participants who had no warning that they were to be caught up inside a nightmarish web of confusion and chaos.

There are numerous aspects of this dark side of UFOs that we shall examine closely.

- The connection between UFOs, demons, and possibly Satan himself.

- The fascination for and the link between Nazism, occultism and German-made flying saucers.

- The ghastly exercise of blood draining and human sacrifice throughout antiquity and their relationship to animal and human mutilations and blood letting in modern times, which align closely to the appearance of UFOs in specific theaters of operation on our planet.

- The weird claims of John Lear that aliens are coming here to kidnap humans and not return them. That people are being used for food, and how "they" are experimenting with us – sadistic experimentations – and attempting to suck out our souls and place them in containers for their own use.

- The Islamic belief in the normally invisible elementals identified in the Koran as the Jinn and how these malevolent spirits are able to misrepresent themselves by camouflaging their true identity and traveling around at fantastic speeds.

- Shape shifters who can turn into human looking beings, animals, orbs, fireballs or manifest themselves even as physical "hardware" to fool us into believing they are mechanical devices.

- The casting of magical spells, occult rituals and the ability to conjure upspirits and beings often mistaken for UFOnauts but more closely aligned with the elemental kingdom.

Satan Drives A Flying Saucer

I don't think a week went by when my mail box (not the one that is part of your Windows or Mac, but the one that stands, or used to stand, at the curb) wasn't jammed with a couple of large manila envelopes from a gentleman by the name of William C. Lamb.

To be honest, our "correspondence" was mostly one way. To me, Lamb was a bit of a nutter (that's British for crackpot). He claimed to have photographs of heaven and even God's throne that astronomers had taken on the edge of the galaxy. To him the ole man in the clouds was as real as you or I and the Lord's Kingdom was a place you could actually see if you had a powerful enough telescope. Kind of crazy, right?

Well, the story doesn't end there.

According to Lamb, he knew all about God and Satan firsthand because he had seen Beelzebub with his own eyes. No! It wasn't part of a near-death or out-of-body experience, but a component of a UFO landing.

Lamb had been out hunting in a snowstorm around four or five AM in February 1922, as he explained, when he heard a buzzing sound and saw this huge spherical craft hovering over a nearby field. It was so large and brilliant to his eyes that it blocked out the stars and he found himself mesmerized by its sudden appearance. He watched in awe as a partition

Not all UFOs are "sweetness and light" space visitors. According to the available evidence many are hell bent on causing all manner of alarm and trepidation.

opened on the side of the craft and a gigantic creature with wings flew to the ground and landed in the snow. The being was somewhere between seven and eight feet tall and appeared demonic in its facial features and physical form. Lamb said he hid behind a tree and watched as it tracked through the snow, its hooves – yes, I said hooves – melting down to the tundra as it went along. Eventually it came to a sturdy wire fence and managed to just walk through it, burning through the mesh and leaving it looking red hot.

At the time I had every reason to believe Lamb was totally delusional. It was

obvious that he saw everything through the eyes of orthodox religion. So much so that when he was approached by this ghoulish figure he managed to get it to fly off, using the name of Jesus and commanding it to depart.

The case is known to others besides me. Apparently a letter or two from W.C. was also in the Air Force's Project Blue Book files because astute researcher Jacques Vallee mentions it in his book *Passport to Magonia*. Somewhere, within the depths of 40 file cabinets, I am sure that a couple of Lamb's missives still exist, no doubt more than tattered with age, because if I recall correctly they were typed on onion skin, which was the cheapest paper stock of the day, mainly used for carbon copies and already yellowed when purchased in a stationery store.

Experiencer William C. Lamb claimed to have encountered Satan embarking from a landed UFO. Lamb said his research lead him to ultimately believe that God was a physical being and had a throne in a distant galaxy similar to this.

So much for William C. Lamb. But how about our next character at large? Cecil Michael was certainly one up on Lamb. Not only did he claim to rub shoulders with Mr. Scratch, but he says he went with him straight to hell. Yep, that's what I said – straight to Hell.

Don't believe me? Well, I am willing to share his story in its entirety with you by reprinting in the next section a little tome published in 1955 with the sensationalistic title of *Round Trip To Hell In A Flying Saucer*. Says the flyleaf on a very rare copy:

"Here is one of the most startling stories ever written! The narrator, calmly working in his auto repair shop, suddenly finds himself playing host to a pair of visitors from outer space. From that moment his entire life is changed.

"For weeks the Spacemen practice all types of weird experiments upon their bewildered friend, who is too terrified to protest. Finally, wearying of their ingenious super-games, they decide to take the poor auto mechanic on a trip to Hell. . .And, as you descend with the narrator into a modern Inferno, you will pray, with the auto mechanic who tells the story, that his visit will be a short one."

There used to be a book store in New York City on East 95th Street run by Jim Rigberg. He didn't open until fairly late (like 9 PM after leaving his day job as a short order cook) and this part of Manhattan known as Spanish Harlem was on the rim of a rather unsafe – in those days – part of Central Park. Allen Greenfield and Gene Steinberg and a couple of other kids, including yours truly, must have seemed like teenage thugs from "West Side Story" as we kept a steady gate through the park. Truth is we wanted to get to our destination as fast as possible. Rigberg was the only place where you could get a flying saucer book in Manhattan circa 1967. Actually, he might have had a couple of volumes by Dr. M. K. Jessup or Major Keyhoe, but what stood out in the shop were several stacks of Cecil Michael's "Satanic Verses." I copped a copy for two bucks and read it the next day. Wild stuff. Couldn't take it too seriously. Even now in UFOdom it stands out like a swollen thumb.

The British publication Magonia encapsulates Cecil Michael's bizarre *Round Trip To Hell In A Flying Saucer* in this manner:

"The craft went off into space, eventually arriving at a bleak red planet with a lake of fire into which coffins were cast, the dead bodies inside them then coming to life and burning in agony. He was afraid that he would be trapped there permanently, but apparently he was saved by a vision of Christ that appeared in a beam of white light, and returned to Earth. The trip seemed to have taken four days, but only four hours had passed."

Without further adieu, let us get on with Mr. Michael's story starting at the very beginning of his book. . .

The Screaming Demon of Mexico Does Resemble the Grey Aliens observed with many UFO sightings and experiences

ROUND TRIP TO HELL IN A FLYING SAUCER

By
CECIL MICHAEL

CECIL MICHAEL

Adventure is no novelty to Cecil Michael, of Bakersfield, California, whose entire life has been spent, both on the job and during leisure time, in exciting pursuits.

Born in Webb City, Missouri, on May 16, 1909, Mr. Michael began to contribute to the support of his family at the age of twelve, when he got his first job as a lead miner. At fifteen, he moved to greener pastures in the new field of automotive repair. Mr. Michael worked as a mechanic until World War II, when he transferred his attention and his talents to defense work for the United States Maritime Commission. His duty done, he returned to the automotive repair business after the war. At present he owns his own auto repair shop.

In his spare time, Mr. Michael follows the stimulating will-o'-the-wisp of prospecting for gold. His search takes him from almost inaccessible mountain streams in California to the burning deserts where, he hopes, he may make a lucky strike.

It may have been in the still coolness of a California evening in the mountains that the plot for Mr. Michael's exciting story was conceived, all at once, and, as the author puts it, "served up on a silver platter."

Round Trip To HELL in A Flying Saucer

by

Cecil Michael

I AM WRITING THIS STORY OF FLYING SAUCERS AND MEN from outer space because I feel that the world should know what I learned from two remarkable men. If I am able to express only a portion of my profound admiration for these friendly and happy persons and communicate a part of what I learned from them, I will feel that I have done what they expected of me.

These splendid beings were from another planet. My association with them began in the latter part of 1952 when they walked into my shop. They visited with me six hours that day and on very many successive days.

If these men had not asked me to write this story, I would never have written it. I know many people will doubt what I say. Had I not lived through this episode, I would question that it was possible. But this is a true record of an actual occurrence. It is written so that people can gain some understanding of the supernatural forces that are everywhere around us at the present time.

Their space ship was a magnificent and beautiful sight, illuminated in its interior by a soft yellow light. A bright electric spotlight rotated around the outside of the ship, lighting up the strange designs painted on the hull. It was plain to see that the ship was not from this world, but from another planet.

The two pilots were, if possible, more out of this world than the ship they piloted. As my story unfolds, I will tell you and show in pictures how these men were able to appear from thin air and become creatures with all the characteristics of healthy, happy, intelligent, natural men. I will speak about their magnificent minds and of the powerful magnetic electrical current they control. I will tell of their inserting of the magnetic plate in the human body, of the third eye coming into focus and what a powerful weapon it is, and what its purpose was. I will tell and show what the supernatural looks like in action. I will show you the insides of their bodies; how they are constructed and the beautiful electrical internal display that substitutes for man's natural insides. I will tell of my trip to the planet of Hell aboard a flying saucer, in what direction it is from earth, what the planet looks like, how different the sun is there, what the man that runs Hell looks like, what the people look like that labor for this man, how they do their work, and for what purpose. I will tell of the great fire area and the burning sea. Last, but not least, I will recount the story of how Christ descended upon the outer fringes of Hell, what happened when the two forces of the universe came close together, my forced release from Hell, the long journey back to earth, how earth looks from great distances of hundreds to thousands of miles and at close range, and I will build up to the climax and the end of this story.

The illustrations for this story are as nearly perfect as the local artist and I could get them. These illustrations should give you a good idea of what the two space men and their ship look like, although no artist could do the men justice. In writing this story, I can vouch only for these two men and the two flying saucers. Perhaps all flying saucers and space men do not look the same. I was not the only person to see their ship that night. Many people saw it, and the local newspaper printed a report about it.

I want to offer my humble apologies for taking so long to bring this story to the attention of the public. However, not being experienced along this line, and not having any spare time away from my business, I was not able to get this story written immediately. A lot of valuable time has elapsed since the actual happening I am writing about. I have done my best to tell the story. Now for the beginning.

It was a warm and sultry night back in 1952, only a few days before the terrible earthquake that struck Bakers-

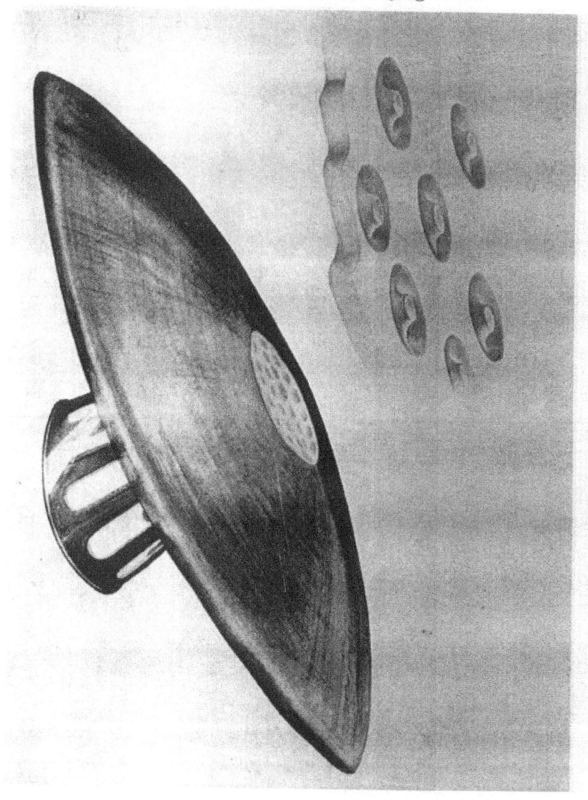

1. A strange spotlight, illuminating the design on the hull, proclaimed it a ship not of this world.

2. The two uniformed pilots showed no concern over the dangerous position of their ship.

field, California, on the twenty-second of August and did so much damage. I had stepped outside on this particular night for a few minutes. It was pitch dark. There was no breeze at all, and it was very warm. At about ten thirty, I looked to the southwest and saw what I thought was a passenger airplane in trouble. I wondered why it was flying so low. It was very low; in fact, just about the tree tops. I could not hear any engine noise at all and wondered why the pilots did not turn it around and try to glide back to the airport, about one-half mile distant. The passengers seemed to be running around in the ship in a panic. Sitting up forward were two uniformed pilots, wearing very odd-looking head gear and uniforms, who were showing no concern over the low and dangerous position of their ship. I listened very hard to pick up the sound of their motor, but the ship made no engine sounds at all. I wondered why the pilots didn't turn their ship around and try to glide back. They stayed on the same course, maintaining the same speed and low altitude.

I conjectured that they might be suspended by cable from a balloon, for, according to all rules of flying, it should have been impossible for them to stay aloft at that slow speed. Then the ship made a slow, gradual left turn, coming closer to me by the second. I could see that the inside of the ship was illuminated by a very odd yellow light, which made it possible to see the inside of the ship very distinctly. Not hearing the noise of an engine, I expected the ship to crash any minute. Instead, it kept right on coming, making a long gradual left turn as it came closer.

I could see what looked like passengers inside. A big black V-shaped shadow was swinging around inside of the ship. It looked as if it started at the bottom of the ship, in the very center, and reached to the top of the cab inside. Each half of the V was about ten inches in diameter, and both halves tapered to a point at the bottom of the ship and spread out at the top of the cab. It looked as if the V was formed by some solid, dark matter rather than by a flat dark shadow made by light reflection. As the V-shaped shadow revolved around in the ship, it swayed and staggered like a drunken person trying to walk.

Just forward, on the outside of the cab and coming out at the hull line where the cab and hull were fastened together, there was a strong electric light, like a spotlight, shining from the bottom of the cab at the hull line up to the roof of the cab. It was quite bright, and looked like any other electric light. This light was rotating around the cab at about five revolutions per minute and turning clockwise. As this light rotated around on the outside of the hull, the big black V-shaped shadow on the inside followed close behind, showing it to be geared to follow at the same speed. As this light passed the window openings on the far side of the cab, the back part of this light looked like blood-red bullet tracers and blood-red traces of bubble streamers. This was the most peculiar electric light I had ever seen in my life. I was hoping that, when it passed around to the far side again, it would slow up so I could get a better look at it. When it did come around again, it not only slowed up, but stopped momentarily. Then it backed up across the window opening slowly and stopped for quite some time, so I was able to really study it.

. I looked up through the window of the cab of the ship in time to see the blood-red streamers and tracers make a long bend in a wide arc and come down upon a large modern city silhouetted in the sky. The city seemed to be approximately two thousand feet directly below the ship. The city was tilted at an angle of about twenty degrees. The big fiery red tracers came from the sky and stabbed down into the large sprawling city to form a perfect pattern of siege over the entire area, and there the beams remained stationary.

Then the city settled down to look level and normal, except that the ground it was built on appeared to be slightly rolling. The fiery red tracers looked to be much larger down in the city. They were perhaps twelve inches or more in diameter. I studied the city very closely. There were blocks of large flat-topped buildings that looked to be five or six stories high. Over to the right of this part of the city was what looked like some sort of park, in which there stood a beautiful, white, square building rising to almost skyscraper height. The top of the lower part of this building tapered off quite abruptly. Up from that portion of the building came a tapering sphere, that was fully half the height of the building itself. At the top of this monumental-looking sphere was a sharp ridge.

I looked back across the city to my left for a distance of about a mile and a half and saw a cluster of tall brown buildings that looked to be of almost skyscraper height. These buildings had more or less flat roofs. There were five or more buildings in this group. Looking past these buildings, in the distance I could see a tall, round chimney with smoke coming from it. This seemed to be the industrial area of the city. I saw a few moving lights down there, coming from the industrial area into the city.

Looking directly out toward the farthest outlying streets of the city, I could see those streets were lined with trees, dwelling houses, and street lights. Deep in the heart of the city, I could see no street lights; the streets looked like deep, dark, narrow valleys among the tall buildings. Directly below were the many square blocks of those flat-topped buildings. I could see a little room on top of each building indicating the presence of an elevator shaft. I noticed that the little house on one building in particular was painted bright yellow. Some of the buildings had some sheet-metal circulating ductwork on their roofs.

I looked down into the darkened streets nearby. It was like looking down into deep crevices. I could not see any vehicles near the center of the city. Some of the higher buildings showed a few lights. From all appearances, this was a city shown in the hours of early morning light. I rubbed my eyes and began to wonder how this city could be shown in the pitch-dark black of night.

I looked back up at the ship. There was still part of the picture of the city showing through the window. I looked all around the outside of the ship, but there was nothing but the blackness of the night to see. So I looked through the cab window. The picture of the city was in view, but the picture was swinging so that it only showed a part of the city. I wanted to get another look at the part of the city in which the tall white building stood. I was standing down on the ground, looking up through the cab window and trying very hard to get another look at that white building, when I got the same sensation as I did before—it seemed to me that I was standing up over this city at about two thousand feet altitude, looking straight down upon the city. The large fire-red tracers came down into the city at about the same places they had before. The part that I had wanted to see again came swinging into view directly under me. I had come to realize by now that this would be the last time I would have the opportunity to see this city, so I gave it one more close look. Then the red tracers faded out, and so did the city below me.

I stood on the ground, looking up at the flying saucer and feeling none the worse from my experience, but feeling somewhat dumbfounded. Actually, this was hard for me to believe even after seeing it all at first hand. Eventually, I brought myself around to believe it and to know it was no effect of my imagination.

I do not feel that the city I saw was a phantom city. I feel that it is a real city, and that it exists somewhere upon the earth, the same as it was when I saw it. It was built and constructed as the people upon this earth build their cities. Should I ever see an aerial photograph of this city, I could, without doubt, recognize it instantly. Then the light continued in its regular rotating course until it came around on the side closer to me. Then the light started to jerk. It made a slapping noise, as if it had jumped out of mesh with the gearing. After some more noise and jerking, it got going again and continued its regular rotating movement. The yellow lighting inside was very sinister-looking. You could get the same effect by lighting several gas burners on an open-range gas stove in a dark room and watching the flickering shadows on the walls and ceiling. This tends to show one of two things —either the ship was powered by some kind of open-jet gas burners or its interior was lighted by giant candles. In these shadows, I could make out some engine mechanism in front of the hull which cast its shadow on the wall occasionally.

By this time, the pilots had gone down below, for they were not visible in the cab. I could not see them any more as the ship drew nearer to where I could see it better. Then I could see that it was no airplane at all. It was clear out of this world. It was a beautiful sight to see, making no noise at all and traveling about fifteen miles per hour. It was close enough to me so that I could throw a rock and hit it. It continued in the long left turn and came in closer. I was trying very hard to look through the cab windows and down into the inside of the hull. Then the ship tilted sideways, and I could look right into the hull of the ship. I could see the plate-glass cover of the center manhole and the brace fastened on to the hull going around with the rotation of the hull. In fact, I saw about three fourths of the inside hull as it rotated around. The inside of the hull was the gray of polished metal.

The ship was something one would only dream about, and had a design one would expect to see 4,000 years before our time. According to the way we build and design ships, this ship would surely date back very easily 4,000 years. It had no markings or scrollwork anywhere on it. The inside of the cab was white, and the outside of the cab and hull were silver color. The hull was about fifty feet in diameter, and the cab was quite large. I would say that it would hold about six to eight men. There was no bottom in the cab. In all of my thirty years of study and work in the field of automotive mechanics, I have never heard of or seen any ship like this one before. I can usually look at a ship or vehicle of any kind and tell quite well how it is constructed and by what it is powered, but this flying saucer is one that I cannot figure out.

It occurred to me that there was something very sinister about this ship, for it maneuvered exactly as I wanted it to move so that I might get a good close look at it and find out more about the ship.

It completed a U turn and went away from me at a very slow speed. I was fully convinced then that there was not any balloon suspending it from above but that it was soaring on its very own power. It was really a magnificent thing to see.

I never at any time had any fear of the craft. Lots of men would give their right arm to see such a craft in flight. I was dumbfounded at seeing it. I could not seem to grasp all that I had seen. I said nothing to anyone for the time being, knowing that no person could actually believe what I had seen without seeing it for himself, and I did not know of any way to get the ship to return just for that purpose. It was plain to see that, wherever this ship came from, time had stood still. Modern-day designing and craft building such as we know it here on earth is surely not known where the ship was built. But, by the same token, their kind of craft construction and propulsion is not known here either. Their method of propulsion is many times greater than anything we have at present time. Just for an illustration—this flying saucer can vanish right before your eyes if it so desires. At a dead stop, it can start up and then vanish instantly before your eyes. Not by magic, but by terrific speed; our best jet plane cannot even begin to do that. I am not running down our jet planes, for they are very good, the best there are.

On the following Sunday morning, at eleven o'clock, I saw what looked like a shiny plane at about fifteen hundred feet altitude and at a distance of about three eighths of a mile. It looked like a silver plate object bristling in the sky. It looked like a gem. It appeared alive. It did not throw off any shiny rays as our metal planes do when the sun shines on them. It was still when I first noticed it. Then the pilot gave it the throttle. For an instant, I could see what looked like dark atmosphere or smoke gather at the sides and behind the ship for a distance of one hundred feet. Then the ship disappeared, as if by magic. I looked straight ahead for about one quarter mile, and there was the ship, dead still. They must have been trying out their fast starts and stops, for the ship was much faster than the human eye. It hesitated for about three seconds and then made another fast run. By this time I had learned to move my sight fast as possible. I did so and caught up with the ship just a split second before it was sitting dead still.

I don't know who else saw this demonstration at this time, but if the pilot was putting on the demonstration for me, he sure was getting a good observer. This was speed beyond the imagination of man. The pilot gave it the throttle again, and he vanished as before. But this time he did something different. After he vanished, I looked straight ahead quickly and saw him coming in from far out in the distance. Then he made a sharp left turn and came to a stop about one-fourth mile straight ahead of the place he had just left. He had made a complete and level U flight on that last run in about the same part of a split second as he had taken to make the straight runs before.

By this time I thought I would be getting speed-dizzy just watching this performance. Now he was ready for another run. There was the same takeoff as on the other flights but this time the ship did not appear again. Probably the pilot got his throttle stuck a split second too long and, most likely, stopped in China or Africa. I have never seen a flying saucer since that time. During all of those fast speed runs and maneuvers that the ship was going through, never once did it make any noise that could be heard by me.

I hope I have explained this in a simple enough way as to give you a good idea of the speed of a flying saucer. The illustrations show the ship about the same as I saw it. The cutaway picture shows the ship as I saw it when it tilted in its turn, allowing me to see down inside the ship. The inside of the cabin was completely barren of any panel board, wiring, or gadgets of any kind. The only thing that I did see in the hull was the brace that I have shown in the picture. This brace rotates around with the ship's hull. I am quite positive there was some engine mechanism suspended just under the cab up forward, for there were light reflections to indicate that. At one time I saw reflections that indicated a narrow, square box with extremely large rocker arms, looking quite similar to our overhead valve engines, but of course judging by a shadow like that is more or less guess work.

If you notice the trim around the windows where the seams join near the top to fit the circular part of the trim, you will see that one of the seams is spaced larger than the others. This is probably a slight misfit. To all appearances, the windows were glassed over with a very clear, clean glass, and the cabin wall was perhaps three fourths of an inch in thickness.

Now look at the glass manhole plate in the bottom of the ship. See how it is made with counter-sinks to reinforce it. This glass plate is about the same diameter as the cabin in its longest width, except that the manhole is a perfect circle around which the hull rotates, leaving the cabin and manhole plate stationary. Also notice how the windows in front of the cab hang out at the roof of the cab and taper in down to the hull line, giving the ship that old-fashioned look.

Now, looking at the rear-view picture, you will notice that the sides of the cabin have almost the same shape. The extreme rear of the cabin is straight up from the ship's hull, making it one of the oddest-looking cabins I have ever seen on a flying craft in my life. It looks as if it could date back to prehistoric times.

I must say that I was not the only person to see this strange-looking flying saucer on that particular night in August of 1952. Our local newspaper also reported it, as did many other people of this city. From all reports, I believe I did get the best look at it on that night. I know the rest of the story will surely bear me out. In fact, this might be why I had to pay the price for observing the flying saucer too closely.

Little did I realize then what would happen in less than two months later. I had been spotted and tabbed for a return visit by those two pilots that would last for a solid two and a half months. Had I known this, I would have taken off for the tall timber for a prolonged time—and I don't mean

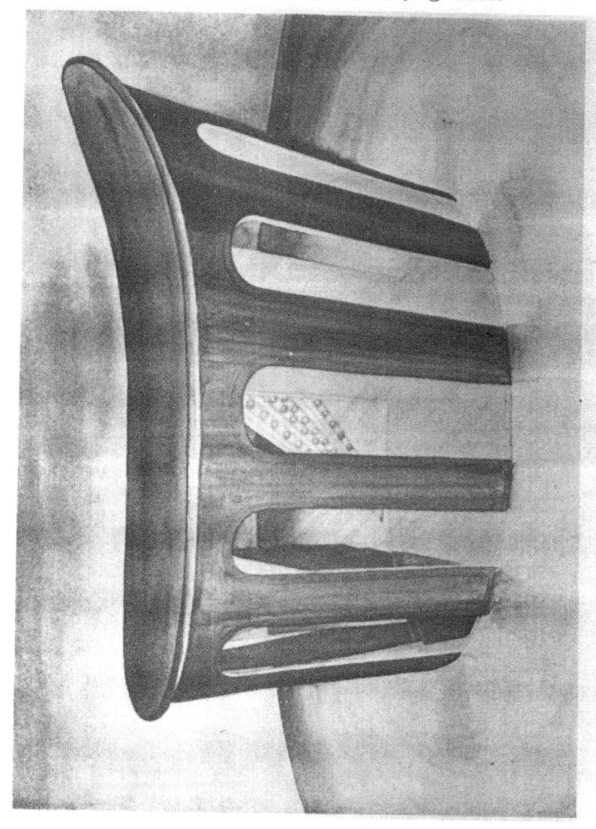

3. There were window openings through which one could see the soft yellow light of the interior.

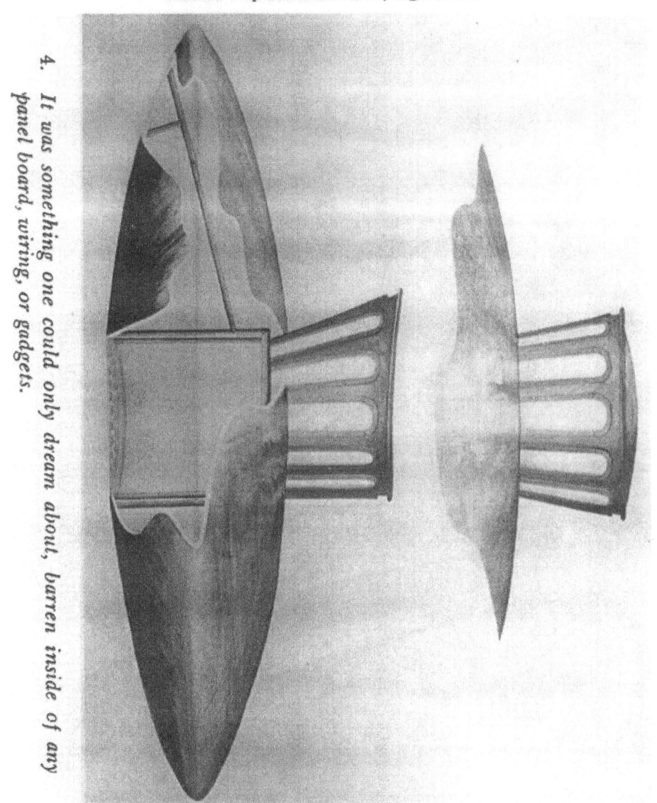

4. *It was something one could only dream about, barren inside of any panel board, wiring, or gadgets.*

maybe! As it was, I was present when the two customers walked into my place of business.

I want to say again that the rest of this story is a true and actual happening and absolutely is not fiction, nor is any of the foregoing. I realize that the two most important questions concerning flying saucers are: Where are the flying saucers coming from? and Why are they here? I hope the rest of the story may throw some light on those two questions.

I am going to tell only what I have seen, what I learned from these men, and what they told me to tell the people to the best of my ability. That is all any man can do or should do. Now to go on with the story. Time went on, and I didn't see any more flying saucers. I thought I was very fortunate to see two of them in such a short period of time.

I want to say at this time that I am in the automotive business. I manage my place and do all my own work. It keeps me busy most of the time. Except for customers coming in and going out, I am alone in the place most of the time.

Things were running along very smoothly until the morning of October fourteenth. I didn't have any reason to think it should be any different from any other day. It was very nice weather that morning, with the sun shining and a brisk cool breeze stirring. It really made a person feel fine. I had a rush job left over from the evening before to finish up, and I had opened up my place of business earlier than usual that morning to get it out of the way before the day's business started coming in. If any man had told me that anything unusual and outstanding would happen on this particular morning, I would have told him he was foolish. On such fine mornings, nothing could go wrong. But I was wrong.

The back of my place is about fifty feet from the alley. Running halfway from the building to the alley is a cement slab. The rear door that opens up on the slab is quite small

—about three feet wide by seven feet high. Just inside this door I have a big test tank full of water. The tank is in one corner of the building, twenty-one inches from the far wall, and extends to within one foot of the rear door. This is where I stand to do part of my work. While standing there I partly block the doorway, especially when I am bending over the tank to do testing. If a fat customer comes in the back door, I simply pull myself against the tank. If a lean one comes in, I just keep hanging out. I don't pay much attention to who comes in, for I have customers coming in the back door very often. They usually bring small jobs from the neighboring shops and want fast service. If the weather is foul, I see them coming in with anything from a newspaper over their heads to blankets around their bodies. Some do it out of necessity and some for pure clowning. When I make it a point to get up early and get a big job finished, I do not like to have any of these jokers come in and start yelling for service.

At nine thirty on this morning, I wasn't quite finished with my job. I had just submerged my work in the water for testing. I looked out the back door and saw two men coming onto the far end of the cement slab, at a fast walk. They were walking almost abreast of each other. They both looked straight at me. Then they both looked down and kept on coming. I figured that here were two more of those jokers who were in such an awful hurry that they would surely stop me on my rush work. I noticed that they were very oddly dressed. When I looked down to their legs, I saw that they were wearing wrap-around leggings on their legs from their knees down, and moccasins that made a shuffling sound as they walked.

I drew myself up tight against the test tank and hoped they would not take the door frame out of the wall as they came in, for they were big men. Then I turned my back on them to go about taking my test on the work I was doing and expecting at any second to hear them start yelling for service. Then I got to thinking that those men looked something like sheep herders. Then I wondered what herders could be doing in my place. They had been in my place about two and one half minutes when my test was finished. I turned partly around to hit the air lift and at the same time opened my mouth to ask what they wanted, when I got the worst shock of my life. There stood a man about three feet from me in about three-fourths exposed form.

I was never so horrified in my life. I felt my scalp go ice cold, and I thought I was going to black out for sure. I started to wipe my face and forehead with my wet hands to keep from passing out, and, at the same time, I turned around the other way for relief. The other man came up from behind me and stepped up on my tank and walked across the water, work and all. Well, this scared me so bad that I couldn't move. I just stood there trembling, with my hair standing straight up. I did have presence of mind enough to hear this man's clothing make a muffled papery sound as he walked past me, as if the garments he wore were made of paper. Of course, both men were only about three fourths exposed now. This man that walked over the tank stepped down into that twenty-one-inch space from tank to wall. He bent his right leg so that his foot came up to about his waist line. His leg seemed to be bent like rubber.

These men were large men and looked as if they might weigh two hundred fifteen to two hundred twenty-five pounds each. One was a little taller than the other. The taller one was about six feet one inch in height, and the shorter one was about five feet ten inches in height. The man that walked across the tank top had quite a time getting turned around in that narrow twenty-one-inch passageway, but when he finally did he stood exactly five feet away from me. Then he drew up his big long arms and folded them across his chest. Then both men came in full form, one on my right, three feet away, and the other just in front of me, five feet away.

I wanted to run out, but I couldn't move a foot. I was paralyzed from fear and the extreme shock of seeing it all. Now that they were fully exposed, they were really nice-looking men, just as natural and solid-looking as any human being could look. I would say they were near thirty years of age and of the white race. Their complexions were medium dark. They were smooth-shaven and had a very athletic carriage. I looked them over for any visible weapons, but there were none to be seen.

I wanted to know what these men were doing here, but, as I looked at them, I began to understand where they might be from. I could not understand why they had come to me.

It looked like they were going to be friendly. They broke out in a big grin, almost from ear to ear. They had more personality than twenty ordinary men have. When I saw they were friendly, I tried to compose myself better and forget about the idea of running out. I pulled out my handkerchief and started wiping the water from my face, feeling much better now. I raised up my hand to stroke my hair back and was not too much surprised to feel my hair was still standing straight out at the back. Then I started stroking it down, and the men started laughing so hard I thought they would burst their sides. I felt so embarrassed that I stopped doing that. I pulled out a smoke, lit it up, and tried to figure out the situation. My scalp felt ice cold from my terrible fear. It seemed that a hunk of ice was running up and down my spine. It was such terrible fear that I just could not get over it right away.

I had wondered why they had not spoken by this time, but I guess they could see that I was in no shape as yet to talk. I felt as if it might be days before I would be able to talk. So we just stood there looking at each other. They were outwardly very pleasant and friendly. I guess I must have been the one who seemed afraid. I was hoping that they would not speak for fear of frightening me further, but I could see that they were getting ready to speak. The expressions on their faces changed gradually from a big grin to a straight, sincere, earnest look. Looking me straight in the face without opening their mouths, they said, "Did we scare you, Red?" These words seemed to register in my eardrums. I was so surprised I almost fell over. I turned around quickly, thinking someone had come up behind me and spoken, but there was no one there. I turned to look at their faces. They nodded their heads, with an understanding look on their faces. Only then did I realize that their way of communication was different from ours.

I wondered how I was going to answer them back when an idea came to me. I would try it out. I would just think the words in my mind but not say them. So I answered them, "You sure as hell did."

Immediately their expressions changed back to a big hearty laugh, and they bent over, holding their stomachs and really enjoying themselves. I thought for sure they would burst somewhere this time.

Please do not think that they were a couple of slap-happy men, for that would be far from the truth. It was plain to see that this was the way they must have lived their lives. They were not just clowning or acting.

I stood there trying my very best to figure out what kind of men they were. It was plain to see that, wherever these men came from, that place was sure a much better place than earth on which to live, for these men were so kind and friendly, and had, from all appearances, been well cared for. Finally, they stopped laughing and looked the place over casually. They seemed to know it just as well as I did, for they immediately got into places where they were out of view of street traffic and open doorways. They stood there looking as if they thought I might talk more, but I was as much frightened of them as they were happy about being with me. They had immediately won my friendship, but I still maintained my safe distance from them. I could not easily get over the sight of seeing them change from three-quarters form to solid form, go all through the natural motions of man, and still not be regular men. It didn't seem possible, yet there they were—just as true and real as anything a person could see in his whole life.

You could travel this whole world over, but you could

never hope to find two men with such nice personalities and such kindness as they showed in their faces. They were simply wonderful, and could not be matched anywhere.

Then I remembered where I had seen these two men before. It was almost two months previous that I had seen the flying saucer. The two pilots I had seen in that ship that night were wearing the same headgear as these men were wearing. They must be the same two pilots I had seen that night.

I turned to look up into their faces. I guess they were reading my thoughts, for they smiled and nodded their heads to give me the understanding that they did know what I was thinking. I came to the conclusion that everything was going to be all right, so I began getting things ready to start up my work. I picked up the torch and fired it up. I noticed that they were watching my every move. I used a steel brush and the torch flame to clean a long tank seam in preparation for soldering. I applied the acids, picked up the solder, and started soldering it up. They leaned over with eager, interested expressions, watching me solder. I stood up to see what they were doing. They were still watching my hands and torch working. I was somewhat surprised to see that they were interested in seeing so simple a task being done. They looked at me and appeared surprised to see that I was watching them and not my work. Then they broke out in big smiles. I surmised that they might be somewhat mechanically inclined, for they acted very interested.

About right then I should have tried to sell them the place, but the idea didn't enter my mind at the time. But there was another question that came to me very fast, and I was deeply concerned about it. What if some member of my family living nearby should enter the building and see these men here? I was afraid that they might not withstand the terrible shock as I had. Suppose a customer should come in and see them standing there? If he weathered the shock, he would probably run out and tell people. Crowds of people would block both doorways and hinder my own work. I did not want that to happen, so I shut off my torch, put it back in the rack, and turned around to look at them. By this time the smiles had left their faces, and they were getting that sincere and determined look again. I saw that they were going to talk again.

They told me that they would not let what I feared happen and also said that I should not expose them. I took it for granted that they did not want me to tell anyone about them as long as they were present. From the looks on their faces, I could see that they meant exactly what they said. I had no intention at all of crossing them up. They shook their heads some, backed up a little, and started smiling again. I was glad that was over and settled, but I could not understand just how they intended to remain unobserved. Then the two men started to vanish gradually. Within about five seconds they were completely gone, leaving nothing at all to indicate that they had ever been there.

It was a great relief to know that they had left. Just then a customer stepped in the front door. Did he get a warm reception from me! I tried my very best to detain him as long as I could, but he was the kind that is always in a hurry, and he left right away. It did make me angry to know that I could not detain him for a little while, but I guess it just wasn't to be that way. I turned around, stepped back to my tank, and started working, thinking back in the past and wondering if I could have hurt myself sometime in a way that had affected my mental processes. I remembered that, the day before, I had a long tough job to put through, but the only injuries I suffered were a cut finger and some scarred knuckles. That is about as bad as I ever get hurt doing this work, and I cannot ever recall getting a bump on the head that might injure a person so as to cause anything out of the ordinary. On the other hand, what I had just seen could not have been a hallucination due to my imagination; it had all the appearances of being genuine and real.

I tested myself in every way that I could think of, even to working out mathematical problems, but everything I tried came out natural and normal in every way. I was about ready to chuck it all out and forget about it when an electrical blue outline of a man flashed in each of the places where the men had faded out. Then the outline turned a rather pale green for the full length and width of each man. Then a brown color formed over the green color, and faint features of the men started appearing on the brown color. Then, in one second, they snapped to solid form and had all the features and the natural color of ordinary men. If you think that this would not chill the blood in your veins, then you should come face to face with them sometime.

There they stood, directly in front of me, with big grins coming over their faces. I stopped work, racked up my torch, and stood there in bewilderment. Finally, I pulled out a package of cigarettes and, after taking one for myself, I stretched out my arm to offer them each one, not knowing if they would accept one or not. They looked at me, then at the package I was holding. Then they looked at each other, shaking their heads negatively. I reached over to light up my torch. I started back to work, being fully convinced by this time that they were genuine and real. Now I fully realized what they meant when they said that they would not let other people see them here in my place of business. So long as they would keep it that way, it would be perfectly all right with me.

As the morning wore on, I wondered if they were going to talk by voice. It did not seem possible that they could not make vocal sounds, for they could do anything else that man does, only much better. The way they performed before that customer came in proves what wonderful brains they possessed. They were far superior to average men in everything they did, and they looked just that way too. They were very clever in all their actions. At one time, when they were laughing, I noticed that short beams of light came out of the eyes of one of the men. He was standing sideways to me. The beams shone out about four inches from his eyes and looked like flashlight beams. I immediately stopped what I was doing, walked up close to him, and looked him in the eyes. By this time, the beams had stopped. His eyes looked natural enough, except that the whites of his eyes seemed much darker than a normal person's would look. This made his eyes seem all the

5. Their way of vanishing took about five seconds. Anyone would have to see it to believe it.

6. *As he came slowly into view, I saw the amazing cluster of weird light-green bubbles inside his body.*

blacker and more piercing. I had seen enough by this time to realize that these beings could not possibly be constructed the same as we are, and that they probably would never make voice sounds. But it was not necessary for them to do so. They were very good at using expressions and had a telepathic way of communication.

I began to study their clothing. It looked old in design, as did their ship. You could see the seams sewn in their complete outfits. The garment that covered them from the shoulders down was made of rather coarse and porous gray material. Their headpieces were sewed to their garments. The moccasins they wore were very crude-looking. The only seam in them was on top of the foot in front, and on the heel. The design on the moccasins resembled the design on the headpieces. Their wrap-around leggings looked very crude indeed. They looked to be about a half inch thick by two inches or more wide. They were wrapped around their legs from the ankles up to the knees, and were black.

At noon, it was time for me to stop work and go in for lunch. The men had faded out completely. My noon hour relief was coming across the slab to enter the building. I did not dare to tell him what I had seen and put up with that morning. I went to lunch and hoped that they would not be there when I returned.

The first thing I did when I got home was to look in a mirror to see if my red hair had turned gray from the terrible shock of seeing the strange men. I was relieved to find that it was still its natural color; but my face was somewhat pale and white. "Well," I thought, "I sure came through that epsiode in good shape."

I took a full hour for lunch that day, and hoped, when I returned, that the men would surely be gone. I entered the building, sent my relief out, and started back to work. I thought my visitors had gone. But that was not to be. They flashed their thin blue outlines. Then it seemed that gas exploded from the thin outlines, toward their centers, and turned green, moving slowly like fog until the forms were fully covered with this pale green color. Dark lines appeared under the green. A light brown gradually spread over the green until the forms were completely brown. Faint features appeared. Then they snapped into solid form. There stood the men, as natural-looking as could be, with smiles coming over their faces. It was very plain to see that these men possessed a tremendous power that no man of earth could possibly have. It was not long before I had realized how real their power was.

I have told you some already, but I will give another example. If a customer was coming down the street in his automobile at fifty miles per hour, the men would start to fade gradually. By the time the customer had stopped his automobile at my front door, the men would be completely faded out. They would stay invisible until the person in question had gone. They never left for good until their time was over for the day. I will explain this further along in the story.

If you think you have learned a lot about men from space so far in this story, just hold on, for I am going to take you through seventy-five days of strange sights I was shown. Also, I will show by pictures, all that I can. There are some wonders that I will not attempt to show.

So far, I have told you things that no earth man could ever hope to comprehend—of men coming up from thin air and disappearing in the same manner. These men never failed to do so.

At about three forty-five that afternoon, they simply faded out. That thin blue outline was the last to disappear. I looked up, expecting someone to come in the front door, but there was no one around. I thought that perhaps they had messed up their timing, but they didn't come back that day. I hoped that they would never come back.

I was getting over my fear of seeing them the rest of that day and hoped that they would not return in days to come. Although they were remarkably wonderful men, a strong barrier of fear developed on my part when they were in my presence. I could not penetrate this barrier, no matter how hard I tried.

Around nine thirty the following morning, the men returned. But they did not walk in as they had the morning before. They simply appeared in about the same places from which they had faded out the evening before, going through their same electrical and lighting commotion as they had the previous day. However, when they snapped to solid form this time, they looked somewhat more refreshed and still more friendly. But I was feeling the fear coming back fast, so I started moving the tools I would use for the day clear out on the far end of the slab, intending to stay out there all the time I could. I would be able to do at least half of my work out there, but still I would have to come in to the tank and do the other part of my work. But I felt that would be better than staying with them all day long. I did not feel much fear of them when I was out there working, but I just could not get around to doing the other half of my work inside in their presence.

In about a half hour, I looked inside and saw that they had faded out. I thought that they had left. After a few minutes, I stepped in through the rear door to get a special tool that I had to use. They flashed their blue outlines once to let me know that they were still there. It made me angry to think that I had moved out while they stayed there. I got to going inside on purpose every few minutes. Each time I entered they flashed on, until they had enough of that and would not respond each time. To test them more. I went in and lingered for short periods of time, trying to get them to come on in full form. But the more I tried, the less response I got from them. Then the time came for me to go in for a long period of time. They appeared in full form, without any hesitation at all. They knew of my movements even before I had decided them myself.

These fellows were plenty smart. In fact, they were too smart for me. Thinking that I could outsmart them was foolish, as I was to find out later. I did not know how to get them to leave.

I decided to call in the sheriff. I started to walk over to the phone to make the call. Then I just happened to think that, sure as I would make the call, they would fade out completely, as they had done before when any other person approached the building. This would make me look like a fool to the sheriff. I decided not to call him. I remembered that they had told me from the start not to expose them. I thought the whole thing out and decided not to tell anybody. I had stayed with this situation this long and I would stay with it to the finish.

I turned to walk back to my work and looked up at them. They had a very understanding look on their faces, for they understood my decision already. But I was still in mortal fear of them. If they were ever aware of this, they didn't show it.

I noticed that they were conversing. They nodded their heads a little. The man on my right (the taller one of the two) turned and walked toward the front door. As he did so, he started dimming out gradually. Within one step of the front door he completely faded out. Where he went from there I do not know, but I expected, at any time, to see one of the nearby merchants pass by in a dead run, screaming at the top of his voice. This didn't happen. I assume the man didn't expose himself elsewhere, for I would have heard about it.

After about three quarters of an hour, the men reappeared, going through the same electrical commotion as usual before assuming solid form. The men looked at each other and nodded their heads. Then they reduced to one-half exposed form. The man who always posted himself on my right side never stayed in full form, because he stood between the front- and back-door openings, where it was easy for anybody to see him. This position also put him in plain view of the street traffic going by the front door. A queer thing about this man was that, although he was just as friendly and polite as the other one, he was not so much interested in me or my surroundings as the other one was.

When I tell of him cutting down to a half-exposed condition, I do not mean that he showed only the lower section or the upper section of his body. In all of their exposures, these men were always full width and full length. What I mean by half exposed is that they could simply fade their bodies away to a dark gray (almost smoke black) color to fit emergency conditions. For instance, if street traffic was light, the man to my right would come up to about three-quarter form, in which you could just distinguish the features of his body. If the street traffic was heavy, he would fade out to a point of being just barely visible. If people were walking by, he would be invisible. There were times when I was not sure where he was standing. I would look at him for a few seconds. Then he would expose a portion of his body so that I could see for myself. In this and many other ways, they were very obliging.

These men looked enough alike to be brothers, but definitely not twins. Little did I know on this second day of their visit here to earth that they would be with me for a period of two and one half months. If I had had any way of knowing, I would have taken a long vacation. It is hard for me to say this of these men, but it was still harder for me to tolerate them in my presence, even though they were fine and wonderful men. I doubt if there are many men who would go through with what I have been through without cracking up completely.

I thought they would not return after the second day. They gave no reason for being here, and I could see no reason for them to linger. The second day ended about like the first. At about three thirty in the afternoon, they simply faded out gradually. Then they were gone completely. I was glad to have them gone. I summed up the events of the past two days and realized that they definitely were friendly and that they were much interested in what I was doing and in my surroundings. They had done me no harm.

If I told people what I had seen they could not believe it, so I decided to tell no one. When I remember how, during those two days, I tested them out in my own simple way to see their reactions, I feel a little foolish. Once, I swore at my work, watching their facial reactions to see if they heard me. They didn't respond. Another time, I whistled a song for quite a long time. I looked up occasionally to see what their reaction was. There was none. I thought that either they were not hearing any voice sounds at all or they already read my thoughts and were playing dumb. Whatever the case was, they showed no reactions.

I thought over a lot of things that evening after they left, but the main problem was why I, of all men in this world, should be paid a visit by these men. Of course I had seen them in their ship at very close range that night. But that was the only reason I could think of. I also wondered why these men were down here on earth among flesh and blood people, scaring the daylights out of them. They were fully aware of my questions, but they stayed right on. I did not know the answers, and considered that I could not hope to know the answers.

On the morning of the third day, I was subjected to a completely new surprise—the magnetic third eye. It was another fine morning. Everything was going along just fine. I was working out in the back, clear out on the end of the slab behind my building, where I had moved the day before because of the two men from space. I did not like it too much, but I was playing it safe, for I did not like the idea of moving back and forth every day. I decided to stay out there a day or two longer, just to be sure. The morning was getting well along. I looked in through the window to see the clock on the wall. It was already past nine o'clock. I sure did hate to see nine thirty come around on the clock, but I decided not to worry about it. Those men had no reason to come back this morning, so far as I knew. But I was wrong again in my judgment of these men. They were determined characters.

I looked in the back-door opening and, sure enough, there they were. I glanced up at the clock. It was a few minutes past nine thirty. I looked back through the door opening and saw them close together, crouched down at the far end of my tank. Each man had one foot on the floor and was sitting back on his leg and foot. They were bouncing together and just laughing their fool heads off about something. In the position in which they were sitting on the floor, they might have been having a dice game, but I did not see any dice. I thought, "What have those two bums got up their sleeves now?" Then I heard one say, laughing, "Shall we let Red in on it?" That is all they said.

This made me rather angry. I came almost to the point of turning the water hose on them, but the thought of having to sweep the water off the floor kept me from doing this. A few minutes later I was to realize what they meant. I had walked over to the job I had just finished, picked up my tools, and started to take a few steps back to place them on a nearby tank top when, all of a sudden, a shock hit me. I felt it on the top of my head. I jumped back to see if I had stepped on my electric light cord, but there was no electric cord on the slab. I looked up overhead to see if any electric wires had broken, but they all looked all right to me. I could not imagine where the shock had come from. I looked back in to see the two men still laughing their fool heads off.

I was getting angrier, but I thought, "I will try to hold out back here until noon before I go into that building, just to spite them." I thought they had, in some way, caused the shock. I stepped over to another job, picked up the tools and was going over to put them on the tank when, all of a sudden, I felt as if a very tall person had come up behind me, placed his two hands very gently on my head and, with his finger tips and the forefingers and thumbs of both his hands, inserted a thin magnetic plate right in the center and down toward the front of my head. At one time, when it seemed as if the plate was being forced through the roots of my hair, I felt some pain, it was very slight. I tried several times to brush the top of my head during the operation. That was impossible, not because I did not have the strength to do it, but simply because some unseen force that I could not even feel with my hand warded off my hand each time I threw it back to brush off whatever it was. At first I tried to pull out of its grasp, but this was to no avail. I felt considerable pressure from the hands on my head. Those magnetic shock waves, or currents, really felt good during the short operation, which lasted perhaps only fifteen or twenty seconds.

I must have passed out momentarily. When I started coming to, I felt some unseen force supporting me on either side. Then I felt this force diminish very gradually, until I could support myself. Then I staggered three or four steps, leaned on the tank for support, and said, "What is happening to me this morning?"

After about three or four minutes, I felt as good as ever and turned to see where the men were. Then the inserted plate seemed to turn a half flip over in my head, with a magnetic shock. Then I realized the power of the magnetic third eye coming into focus.

I looked in through the doorway at the men. A strong unseen light beam seemed to come from the plate inserted in my head. It made a humming sound. I could feel rapid vibrations from it each time it made positive contact. Each time that I looked at the place where the men should have been when they were invisible, the plate would contact and one man's form would be outlined instantly. If I continued to look at him, he would continue to come into solid form. If I moved my gaze off him, he disappeared. This held true as long as I was not in the building with the two men. When they knew I was coming in for any length of time, they were only too glad to pop right up in solid form and were very courteous about it.

I realized what a real weapon they had hung on me. I thought I would play with it and use it on them to good advantage, so I stepped back from the door opening and started raking it back and forth across the inside of the building, like a soldier using a machine gun on the battlefield. I raked it back and forth rapidly, and I had them jumping all over the building. Each time it hit them, they would flash their blue electric outlines, and it began to seem as if a lightning storm was going on in there. This went on for about ten minutes.

Then they began to tire and would not respond each time. I gave them a rest. I had had my fun with them for this time and felt satisfied.

I want to say that, along with the humming and vibration of the beam, there was a strong drawing sensation of feeling coming off the plate and going to each man's form. When I swung the beam on them, I could feel positive contact on the inserted plate instantly. When I swung the beam away from them, the power stopped instantly. It worked as fast as any electrical current between two connections, but this beam had no wires. Bear in mind that I could not see them with this beam. I could use it only to detect them.

If they were willing, they would show themselves so I could see them with the naked eye. If they were not willing to show themselves, I always got the positive contact anyway. Therefore I was always able to pinpoint them when they were not visible because other people were present. I dared not tell of their existence, for they had warned me of this at the very first. I did want to tell others about them and show them to other people, but I was caught between two fires. I decided to make the best of it.

The magnetic current, in some ways, felt as strong as a two-hundred-twenty-volt electric potential, but, when the beam came on, it felt many times stronger. Although it was a powerful thing, it did not feel as if it would injure the human body in any way. In fact, it felt as if it had a soothing, healing effect. It felt so good one would think it could cure all diseases in a human body in a very short time, including leprosy and broken bones. It is hard to explain this current to any person, but I have brought in all the facts. Figure them out for yourself, if you can.

The days went on, and the men kept coming back. Things moved along much more smoothly, but I was still very skeptical about them. With the third eye, I did not have to wonder if they were around; I could detect them any time I wanted to. This made things much better. In fact, the eye seemed to settle a lot of differences among the three of us. Many times I wanted to step up, slap them on the back, and tell them what swell guys they were. Yet there remained a barrier of fear between us that I just could not penetrate myself.

I thought that perhaps I should not get too friendly. I should know them longer and study them more thoroughly. After all, this was the most unusual thing I had ever heard of on earth in my whole life. No matter what I thought about it, I could not be too cautious.

Well, I guess you readers think you have learned all that there is to know about flying-saucer pilots and their ships. But hang on. We have hardly scratched the surface. This story will get more weird and sinister as it goes along. Please remember that all I talk about actually happened.

The taller man had the habit of going out for a stroll two or three times daily. One day the weather turned cold. My little dog came in to get out of the cold, ran over to get into my waste-paper box, and started to go to sleep under my writing desk. I had this dog trained to be a very good fighter. It was nothing for him to put big dogs, two or three times his size, on the run. The dog had been in the box only a short time when the big fellow walked over to him and leaned over to pet him. Ordinarily, any man is his friend. He plays with anyone who will pet him. But not this man. My dog sat up and let out the loudest, longest, and fiercest growl I ever heard a dog utter. It sounded like the growl of a lion. He let out a second big growl before the man straightened up and walked away from him. The dog's growls did not sound as if he would fight. They sounded more as if he had total fear of the man. After this episode was over, the dog lay down and slept. This goes to show that I was not alone in my fear of these men. Their effect was the same on a beast as it was on a man.

These men kept regular hours while they were here. The men were present four and one half days a week and were never present on a Sunday. That left them absent one day during the week, but I never knew in advance what that day would be. I thought several times of having some friend of long years' acquaintance come with me some day and try to see these men. But, never knowing what day they would be absent, I found this difficult to arrange. All the old friends I knew were very busy at this time. I was not sure if the men would expose themselves to anyone else. However, some time before this, an old man came into my shop. I gave him my chair to sit down in, as he was very old and not feeling well. The men were present. I thought, "I will keep a sharp eye on the old man and see if anything happens." I watched him very closely as he sat there talking, looking out over the tank, through the back window and directly toward where the men usually appeared. The men were invisible at the time. As I stood there watching the old man's face, I noticed that he jerked to one side a little and then turned back. I looked up to see one space man against the wall, faintly visible. Then he flashed his outline and faded out. The old man turned to look again, but, not seeing anything at this time, turned around to look at me with a surprised look on his face. Then his expression became normal. I could see that the old man had just thought he had seen something and let it go at that. I would have liked to have been able to tell him that he was not just seeing spots before his eyes, but I just could not do so at that time.

I saw the old man several weeks later. I tried to make him remember that day and hour. I asked him if he remembered seeing anything unusual at that time. But his memory was as old as his body. I did not press him any further but, when I told him what he missed seeing he almost had a fit because I hadn't told him when it happened. That, of course, was impossible.

I can well understand why the space men did not appear for the old man. He would not have been able to stand the shock.

The space men kept coming back. I was beginning to think they were never going to leave. They were the most determined men I had ever run up against. Yet, I would never have entertained the idea of ordering them off the property. In the first place I could not get up enough nerve to do that. Also, I would never have attempted to do so, for they were too fine and good for me to harm in any way.

I began to wonder why they were very fine images of men and yet were not men at all. It just did not make sense to me. If someone else had told me this was possible, I would have said he was crazy. There they stood, looking just as hardy and healthy as any men could look. As long as they were about, they never touched a thing purposely, and they were cautious not to be in the way at any time.

One day my oxygen tank ran dry, and I had to change tanks. I had to wait until a customer came in and one of the men faded out so I could roll the tank along that narrow passageway to make the changeover from an empty tank to a full tank. I felt as if I was walking on a slick bar of soap on a wet floor. I sure was glad when that changeover was done. I might add that it was made in record time. When the customer left and the man came up to full form, he gave me an understanding look, as if to say that no harm had been done. That made me feel better.

They never partook of food or anything I offered them. It would look very funny to see sandwiches and glasses of water standing in space with no support under them when the men faded out. You will learn why they would never have accepted nourishment a little later on in the story.

A few more days passed by, and the men were still here and as happy as ever. I had given up hope of their leaving. I still could not understand the reason for their being here. They made no attempt to explain. What they had shown me so far was a marvelous thing. Were it calculated in dollars, it would be worth plenty of money for any man to see what I had already seen. They spoke very little in words that I could hear. When they did speak, it was in questions. But they were always willing to communicate by facial expressions. If you had stood up in front of these men as I did, there would have been no question in your mind as to where they had come from. The main question would have been why were they here on earth. It would make no difference how tall, how wide, or how big you were, or how much wealth you possessed. You would still have felt very humble in the presence of these men. You can take my word for that.

Next, I am going to tell you about the internal expose sight. The next morning they came as they had before. They looked very refreshed and very happy. I was expecting something a little out of the ordinary might happen. They looked a little too cheerful for it to be just another routine day. I knew, from past experience with them, that there was no use in trying to avoid whatever trick they had in mind to play on me. I was quite busy and didn't pay much attention to them, but I turned to see the tall man go walking out the front door. I looked over at the other man. He was all smiles. I thought, "He is extremely happy this morning."

I did not stop my work. After a few minutes, I looked over to notice the man who had stayed behind. He was acting very strangely. It seemed that he was not sure about whether to dim out or stay in full form. I guessed that he would snap up in form or fade out and I continued to work for another ten minutes. Then I looked up again and noticed that his head had disappeared. The rest of his body was in full form and natural-looking, with the exception of his arms, which were almost snow white. They looked as soft as velvet. The hairs on his arms were silky-looking and waving very slowly, as if a slight breeze were blowing against his arms. This breeze would have had to be a two-way breeze, blowing from the wrist toward the elbow of each arm. His arms were folded across his chest and seemed to be illuminated with a phosphorescent light. I turned my face both ways trying to detect a breeze. There was none.

His head appeared again. There was something very sinister-looking about his head and neck. They were dark smoke color. As the head came up to normal height, it turned a few degrees to be straight in line with me. Then his eyes opened to look me straight in the face. His eyes were much different-looking now. The parts near his nose were about normal size, but the eyes tapered back to the side of his face in long pointed slits. His eyes seemed full of gray matter. Their large dilated pupils were hardly visible. This was a weird sight, but it did not frighten me, for I was getting used to such sights. I stood there, observing it all. The eyes closed and the head turned back a few degrees so that the face looked straight forward from the body. The head started to go down slowly into the body. As it did so, I noticed that the color was thinning out between the outside of the neck and the center. I could see the silver-painted wall of the building directly behind him. This thinning portion looked as if it were dark, swirling smoke, moving very slowly and going down into his body at the neck opening. None of the smoke escaped or floated away as natural smoke would have done. The head and neck gradually disappeared completely.

I stood there watching this go on for another ten minutes. By this time, the head was coming up and going down more frequently. The last two times it came up, I thought he was going to scream out at me and tell me to come over to him. One reason for this scene was that he wanted to attract my attention.

The reason that he stayed headless was that he knew I would be less afraid of him that way. He looked less invulnerable to me in that condition. If I was able to read his expressions correctly, he wanted me to come over quickly. Nevertheless, I took my time getting over there. I had it in mind to rub his arm to test it for softness. Had I known then what he was going to show me, I would have bounced over there without delay, for what he showed me was really something to see. As I started coming up to him, an opening appeared in the front of his body, just below his folded arms. A green glow of light appeared inside his body. This light attracted me, took my attention at once. I looked in through the opening down to where the stomach should be and saw the most weird yet beautiful lighting arrangement one could imagine. The whole inside of his body had a dark black lining. From the belt line up, all was hollow as an empty barrel. The whole lower section was filled with big light-green bubbles, about two inches in diameter. Smaller white bubbles were below the green bubbles. Below the whole mass of bubbles was a complete lighting display that was simply beautiful. There was a small cluster of lights in the center at the very bottom. Just above that, a light-pink tube about one half inch diameter lay crosswise. This tube was grooved, or slotted for three inches from each end. Each slot was about one-eighth inch wide. Out of these slots came bright light beams, white to golden in color. These two beams of light revolved slowly clockwise under most of the mass of bubbles. The white light would stab through here and there. Where the light came through the thinner portion of the bubbles, it shone all the way up to the inner top part of the body, exposing the whole empty shell.

I stood there looking this thing over for several minutes. Then I looked up to see where the head went when it disappeared into the body. When the beam of light from below shone across my face, I could not feel any heat radiate from it. I decided that the head was dissolving into the black inside lining of the hollow shell each time it disappeared. I tired of seeing the inside of the body. I straightened up to see if the head had ever come up, but the body was still headless. I looked at his arms. They were still white. I tried to see where the breeze that waved the hairs on his arms came from and decided to rub his arm and feel if it was smooth as it looked. I raised my hand to stroke his arm when, quick as a flash, he snapped into solid form with a horrible look on his face that put me to flight. I ran around to my side of the tank and didn't look up for the next ten minutes.

When I did look over at my visitor, there was a faint smile coming over his face. I heard his body make a slight sound. (I do not think it was my teeth clattering.) It was not too long before he was his natural happy self again. I never did get to touch his arm as I had intended, and I shudder to think of what might have happened if I had done so. I made it a special point after that to keep my distance. I believe that the least a man could expect, should he touch one of them, would be to get knocked colder than a wedge, or perhaps worse.

The scene we just came through was brought on purposely by him to show me his body structure. Had I been an electrical scientist, it might have been educational to me. As it was, it looked very pretty in one way and very mysterious in other ways. It seemed to me that these men took great pleasure in frightening me half to death whenever the opportunity arose.

You have read of the expose test. Now look at the cutaway picture and see for yourself that all that I have said looks very much the same as I have explained it in the story. In the picture, I made the opening bigger and lower so that you can see more of what I am talking about. Even so, you can see and understand only a small fraction of the scene that took place. Notice the black inner lining inside; this lining is what I presume the head and neck might have dissolved into each time they submerged and disappeared. Also, note the light beams shown on the black lining. The light shining on the lining looked just as solid as anything might look. I could see why the bubbles were a milky-white color near the bottom of the whole mass; under them was a very strong white light. But explaining the big light-green bubbles on top of the mass is more difficult. I saw no green lights anywhere. The two rotating golden-white beams did not penetrate the large bubbles too much. However, when the men took form from thin air, this pale-green color was one of their forming colors.

If a man here on earth could build a mechanism such as this he would have the world by the tail in a down-hill pull; but, take it from me, he probably never will. The insides of these men do not depend upon material things that come from earth. If man were brillant enough to decipher the contents of the magnetic plate and to find out what form of matter draws its contact out of thin air when nothing is visible to the naked eye, he would be getting close to the solution of the problem. Although it has been very interesting and educational to see all these things at close range, it still leaves me ignorant of the scientific facts. The structure of these men is one of those things that are beyond the knowledge and imagination of mankind.

After this last episode, I decided to stay on my guard and not get in any more close brushes with my visitors, who took delight in frightening me occasionally. I believed that they could be feared as well as liked.

Everything settled down to a regular routine. The men from space were always happier and more refreshed-looking after frightening me. This angered me to some extent, for I thought they might be gloating about being able to frighten a man with their weird ways. But perhaps this was their natural way of life and they did not mean any harm at all.

One morning I was very busy. My visitors seemed very friendly and contented. As the morning wore on, they were very pleasant and cooperative in their actions. At one time, it seemed as if they were going to speak. I turned to go about my task, thinking I did not have to look at them to hear their words. But they did not speak. I remembered that they had acted this way before, when they were getting ready to do something unusual, and I began to worry. I had not forgotten the last strange incident and I did not want to get involved in another episode like that if I could help it. The men faded out several times that morning for people entering on business, but came right back when all was clear. At noon, they faded as they always did. I felt somewhat relieved that nothing had happened as yet. I thought I might have blocked them somehow this time. I was tired of being frightened by these men and their unearthly doings anytime they took the notion to frighten me, and I hoped that somehow I had developed a kind of resistance to their pranks. But I was wrong again in thinking that I could prevent anything they cared to do from happening.

After lunch I started back to my work. I kept very busy, never looking up much. In the early evening, the phone rang. I walked over to take the call. When I turned to go back to my work, I saw that the men had followed right behind me. I was startled to be so close to them. One of the men spoke. "You shall tell the people of our visit here," he said.

I took a few steps away from them and stood looking at their faces. I was quite sure I had heard them, and I was not going to try to get them to repeat what they said in words. It was an easy matter to find out if I had understood them by watching their facial expressions. Their remark sounded as if they were ready to leave. At least I hoped so.

I asked, "Are you going to leave?" They responded negatively. Next I asked if they wanted the dog back. As I expected, this also drew a negative response. I asked, "Do you want me to tell people about your ship?" Big smiles came over their faces.

I said, "I will tell people all about your presence here." They were very happy now.

I thought several minutes. I knew that few people would come into my shop. How would I let large numbers of people know about these men? I looked up at them and asked, "Do you mean to have me write a complete story of all that I have seen and know of you men?" They were very happy and all smiles. It looked for a minute as if they were coming over to shake hands. Had they started to, I would have started to back up. But they just stood there, nodding their heads in answer to the question I had asked. They looked very pleased.

I wondered what proof I would have for the people, so I turned to them and asked for a picture to show the people. At the same time, I went through motions of taking their picture. They did not like this idea at all. The smiles left their faces. They looked at me very sincerely. Each man raised one arm up and drew his hand across his chest, tapping a forefinger lightly on his chest. They were trying to tell me that they were proof enough, standing there in person right in front of me. I thought back to the first morning they came walking into my place and remembered that they did not want to be seen by any other person. At least, that was the understanding among the three of us at that time. I wondered if it was possible that they might have misunderstood me, so I turned the palm of my hand up and made motions across it with the finger of my other hand. I pointed to myself. I repeated the same motions and then pointed to them and to the outside. In this way, I tried to make them understand that I simply wanted pictures for the people. They knew I was after a picture, but they were determined not to consent to my getting one. They backed up a few steps, looking displeased at my suggestion. One man took a step forward and tapped his chest again, trying to make me understand that the fact that he was standing there should be proof enough. That response was final with me. I would not go any further for a picture. I had learned, by this time, never to try going against these men, for I had never prevailed over them.

Although I was not able to photograph my visitors, they did not expressly prohibit me from drawing pictures of them. This I have done. However, no artist could do justice to such fine men as they were.

When my visitors had made me understand that I should tell people all about them, about their visit here on earth, and about their ship, I told them that it would be a pleasure for me to do so. In order that people can and will believe in what I have told them in this story, I have had illustrations made of what I have seen. I hope that these pictures serve, to some extent, in convincing people I do know all that I have written about. I realize that what I have written and shown is not from our planet as well as you do; I admit that I cannot blame any person for being skeptical to a certain extent. This visitation from space is something new to us. Perhaps such events will become more frequent and better known in the immediate future.

When I looked up at these men and said that I would try to get the story written, they smiled from ear to ear. It was plain to see that this was the way they wanted it done. However, writing a story is not in my line. I could not see how I was going to do it, or when I would ever get time enough to write. In fact, I could not see myself ever going ahead with the story, but I kept that to myself at this time, hoping this would be their last day here. Once they had told me what they wanted done, they were very nice and almost over-friendly for the rest of that evening. I almost hated to see such a pair of wonderful men leave that day. But, thinking back over the past several weeks, and the weird capers they had gone through, I was glad they were going.

As I have said before, these men were a very determined and thorough pair. They left no stone unturned to gain their ends. They left at their usual departure time that evening, for which I was grateful. I felt that at last I could go back to my routine way of life without any interference. I would forget about the men and the story I was to write. But this was not to be.

The very next morning, my visitors came back, much to my surprise. I wondered what they wanted this time. They looked very happy and refreshed, yet they seemed different. Every time I looked up at them they looked me straight in the eyes. I looked up into the face of the space man standing directly in front of me. I looked into his big, black eyes. They looked different. This time he looked me square in the eyes, not saying a word. I could see that there were hurt and sorrow in his eyes. I almost wept. The only way I could keep from doing this was to turn my face away from him. How was I to understand at this time that they had known what I would do? I had no thought as to why they had returned. I kept my eyes looking down, feeling ashamed for a reason I could not fully understand as yet. Before, they had been more interested in what I was doing than in my expression. But I did not let this change worry me. I felt somewhat irate now that they had come back. I guessed that there must be something on their minds, for they were behaving in an unusual manner. I decided to be on my guard and keep my distance from them.

They returned each day as they had before. It was late in the morning of the third day after they had returned that the phone rang. I stopped what I was doing, walked over to the desk, and took the call. As I turned around to go back to my work, there they stood, right in front of me, looking sincere and anxious. They wanted to say something, but it looked as though they did not know how to say it. From what I could make out of their actions, they wanted me to go somewhere with them right away. I stepped out in the middle of the floor and thought over their actions. This was the first time that I could not understand what they wanted. For me to go someplace with them would be physically impossible, or so I thought. I remembered the close brushes I had with them and definitely decided not to fall into any more of their weird traps. I decided that I had a chance to try to out-maneuver them this time.

I extended my arm and pointed my finger straight down to the floor. I told them that I would go with them so long as I did not leave the building. They looked at me as if they did not understand what I had meant by the indications I had just made. They looked me in the face and then looked at my hand and looked at the floor. They did this several times.

I dropped my arm and walked back to my work, leaving them standing there. I thought that I had surely stumped them and there would be no more scenes from them at this time. I fully realized that if a person ever did go out the door with them, it probably would be in knocked-down shadow form. I was not ready for that experience just as yet.

They walked over to where I was standing, smiling strangely and with narrowed eyes. I thought for sure I had beat them to the draw this time. I was just as wrong this time as I had been all the other times before. For these men were bound and determined to fulfill their mission before they left for good, as I was to realize fully after it was all over.

I looked up to see what they were doing. They still had a queer look on their faces, so I turned back to my work. All of a sudden I fell off into a solid dream.

Before I continue on any further with this story, I want you to understand that this next scene was brought to me by these men in some kind of hypnotic form or dream. What

I experienced did not interfere with me in my work or my business in any way. It is difficult to explain it all, but I will try to tell you how it worked out in as few words as possible.

For instance, if the phone rang, it would be up to me to take that call. In some way, they were able to get me out of the dream instantly and bring me back to my own conscious form and normal being without putting a hand on me. When the business transaction was over and I returned to my work, I dropped back into my trance instantly.

In my trance, I went on a trip. What I saw on this trip was terrible and awful, so I will not show any illustrations of it. It is bad enough to read about these experiences, not to mention seeing and hearing it all as I did.

I had just dropped off into a solid dream. I was out bird hunting with my older brother. We were out east at the foot-hills of the nearby mountain range at about noon. We hunted all afternoon. Late that evening, we were going back to our car and talking over the day's take. We had seven or eight birds between us, and we talked of all the walking we had to do for the small amount of game we had shot. Within one hundred yards of where our car should have been, there was an abrupt rise. I could see the top of an old tree just past the rise. I said, "Let's go up there. We might get more birds." So up we went.

In a clear spot near the base of the tree beyond the rise was a flying saucer. It was quite a big thing to see out here.

The dream stopped. The space men had jerked me out of it. The phone rang. I took the call, completed the business transaction, and then walked over to my bench to start work. I stopped to light up a smoke and try to figure out what was happening to me. I remembered everything about the bird hunt, but I could not remember anything about business while I was gone. I looked at the work I had been doing. It was progressing well. I reached over to pick up my torch. I lit it up and was ready to start work. I looked over to the men and saw them pushing the palms of their big hands toward me. This meant that they wanted me to keep going. I started to balk. I wanted to know why there seemed to be two of me. They gave me no satisfaction on this question. I remembered that I had told them that I would go anywhere with them just so I did not leave the building. It was a fact that I was still here. There was no reason why I should not go along with them on this scene.

While out there hunting, I suffered the same feelings that I would normally feel. Here I got tired of walking, hungry for food, and hot from the sun beating down.

I looked over to them and they started pushing their big hands in my direction and telling me to keep going. Wham! I was back there in the hunting scene, holding a shotgun in one hand and birds in the other hand. Remember, I had a torch in my hand when I left the building. You see what I mean when I say this is some kind of a dream yet not a dream at all.

The flying saucer looked quite big. It was resting on the after part of its hull. A manhole plate was open in the center of the bottom of the hull. We went over and looked in. There was nobody inside. We had seen nobody around when we approached. It was quite apparent that there was nobody in or around the ship at this time. But I thought I felt the ship vibrate just a little when we were looking inside. I told my brother so, and he agreed. About then, the ship jerked again. I told my brother that this ship was getting ready to take off and that I was going with it to find out where the flying saucer came from. I asked him to tell my folks goodby for me. I told him that if I returned I would know from where these flying saucers came.

We had a fast argument to thrash out just which one of us would go. It was finally decided in my favor. My brother told me that the fast acceleration would tear me to pieces. I told him that I would take the chance. We looked around inside the ship and decided to lash me to the main post at the after end of the cabin that ran down to the bottom of the ship. There was not a thing to sit on, so we picked up two pieces of old tree limb outside and took them inside the ship. We tied one with sash cords to the main mast post about one half way up from the bottom of hull, with it sticking straight forward. The other piece we tied to the first piece. We brought it down on an angle and tied it to the post. That made a seat, after a fashion. We knew time was running out, and we hurried to get these preparations made. I sat down on the slat. He lashed me to the post as best he could, and then lashed my arms and hands back to nearby smaller posts in spread-back fashion, with my legs tied securely to the center post.

My brother said, "That might help some toward holding you together."

"Well," I said, "considering the amount of time we had to do it in, it isn't bad."

We had used up all the ropes and cords in our car to do the job. It was very warm inside the ship, and I began to wonder what I was going to do for air. My brother shut the manhole plate. The ship gave another big jerk. I knew she was ready for flight. I told my brother to get out through the hole and slam the plate quickly.

No sooner had he slammed the plate shut and got clear than the ship righted itself up on the plate, started to spin slowly, and rose. It drifted up very slowly for about three hundred feet. Then it stopped gong up. It started to spin at about sixty revolutions per minute. The ship got cooler inside —just about right for comfort. The rotation slowed up to about half speed. Then the ship went due south, climbed up at a seventy-degree angle, and immediately increased speed to perhaps two hundred miles per hour. I looked down and saw my brother waving goodby. I watched all the scenery below growing smaller by the minute. I saw the nearby rough mountain ranges getting smaller and smoother-looking, and the glassy-looking ocean with the evening sun setting across it made a wonderful scene. The curvature of the earth started to show. Every minute it became rounder, until it looked like a huge round thing with a big white cap on either side of it. As the minutes passed, the earth became smaller, until it was no larger than a basket ball. I looked forward to see the atmosphere getting hazy to foggy-looking and getting darker by the minute.

Then I noticed two small rods coming up from the bottom

of the hull and going through a bracket at the bottom of the cab where it joined onto the hull. One rod handle was pointing to the port side, the other to the starboard side. What a simple, crude steering device this was to operate such an advanced ship!

I looked back to see where the earth that I had left a few minutes before was. It was getting very small, way back down in that haze. I heard a noise up forward, and I turned around. I saw that two pilots had come aboard, and they were looking very sad for some reason. They were just standing there, looking out to starboard and forward. This was the first time I had seen them without their big smiles. I did not feel afraid of them, for I was completely in their care now and I thought that they would take me to their planet. I could think of no reason why that should make them so sad-looking.

I had just turned to look back to earth and see if it was still visible in the haze when I heard a commotion up forward. I turned around and saw the pilots pointing to starboard and up. I did not see anything, so I turned to look back aft. There was another commotion, and I heard them telling me to look. I sighted off in about the spot to which they were pointing to see what they were making all the noise about. This time I saw a tiny red speck no larger than a pea, out in the inky blackness. I wondered how they had been able to spot it so quickly. They looked very excited over seeing the red spot, but it meant nothing to me. They didn't explain what it was. I presumed that it might be their planet. One of them turned the center lever handle hard to port and turned the starboard handle the same way. Then the fast acceleration pinned me tight to the main mast and the back of the cabin. I felt as if I were flattened against the cabin wall like wallpaper. The pressure began to ease up, and then it stopped. I knew we had left the gravitation of earth. The pilot brought the ship to bear straight for that tiny red spot. We must have traveled several thousand miles in that long sweeping turn. We were traveling due west. If my calculations were correct, the ship's hull was spinning at a rate of thousands of revolutions per minute. The hull was making a slight humming sound. The lighting inside the hull looked like a huge transparent bowl of yellow light.

We traveled on wide-open throttle. I thought that it shouldn't take long to reach wherever we were going at this terrific speed. Then, to my discomfort, both pilots bent down and went up forward to their quarters in the hull of the ship, just as if they were turning in for the night. I guessed that they knew what they were doing. I was in an awkward position for a long trip, with no chance to lie down and rest.

Everything went well for the next two hours. The tiny red spot had grown very small. I was thinking of how far away it must be when one of the pilots came into the forward end of the cabin. He opened a slide panel, exposed a bright, metal-colored box about the size of a man's hand, and started making adjustments on it. Then I heard a man's voice come from the box and ask the pilot, "Have you got him aboard?"

The pilot answered, "Yes."

Then the man's voice said, "Put him on." The pilot motioned for me to talk with this man.

The voice said, "I am sure glad you came along, for I have a good job for you."

I told him I did not want any job, but he went on to tell me how good this job would be. I still refused to accept, but he insisted that it was a good position. This talk carried on for about a half hour. I finally shut him up by saying I would help him in a pinch for a short time only. I had no idea of the identity of the man to whom I was talking or where he was at that time. I thought that I might meet him at our first landing.

I remember two things I bore in mind on the whole trip. They were that I was from earth and that I must return there, regardless of where the pilots might take me. I was in hopes that a pilot would come back and turn off the communication system, but he did not. Everything quieted down for another two hours. Then the man's voice came over the speaker system again. There was the same old "yak yak" talk again. The only way I could shut him up this time was to tell him that I would have to see what he wanted me to do before I could accept his offer of a job. That shut him up this time. But not for long. About two hours later, the old "yak yak" voice returned. This lasted all through the night, at about two-hour intervals, and I was getting tired of hearing it. By this time the red spot dead ahead looked like a big, red orange.

At this time I was jerked back to make a business transaction. After it was completed, I hurriedly looked over the works. Things were going along well, and I looked over to the men. Instantly they shot me back aboard the ship. I was never conscious of any traveling time from earth to ship, but I do remember shrinking back into my tied-up position aboard ship.

We were getting closer to our destination by the minute. After many hours, the red ball was about fifty feet across. The two pilots came forward to look at it. For about twenty minutes, they cut the ship's speed down, stood watching, and kept braking the ship's speed in preparation for a landing. We went through a clearing in what looked like dark heavy fog all around the ship. There was a clear path straight ahead; it was about the width and height of the ship. At the far end of the cleared path, a flame that looked like a huge forest fire was burning. The pilots landed the ship just short of this flame. Then they raised the forward part of the ship up at an angle of ten degrees. They reached down, unsnapped the manhole plate, and dropped it open. Bright sunshine was reflected up through the opening. I could see that we had landed on ground, but I did not know where. Then I heard the voice of the same man who had "yak-yaked" so much on the trip. In a commanding tone, he asked the pilot, "Did you bring him along?"

The pilot said, "Yes, he is tied up now."

The man's voice said, "Cut him loose and get him out here."

After they had cut me loose, I rubbed the circulation back into my arms and legs. The pilots motioned for me to go out. I dropped down on the plate to walk out onto solid ground and bent over to walk from under the ship. The man with the voice took me by one hand to guide me forward. I stopped to look over the place. I knew from the first look that I was not going to like this place. I looked back at the ship to see if the pilots were coming out, but they had not stepped out. I had been hoping that they would not take off and leave me here. I started to look over the planet. It was very dry-looking with a few small hills in the distance. The ground was very rough; it seemed to have been torn up by earthquakes. In some places, the ground would protrude up thirty feet, exposing dry, broken sandstone and clay formations. Apparently there had been a drought for years and years. There was no vegetation of any kind, and no signs of there ever having been any. The sun there was much different than on the earth. It was too bright to look at with the naked eyes. It cast thick, yellow rays to within a short distance of the ground. The temperature was near a hundred degrees fahrenheit.

I noticed a large fire burning ahead of the incline in front of our ship. That fire accounted for the high temperature. A dozen yards in front of the ship, I noticed a small weather-beaten shack, with a doorway near one end of it and with one small window in each side of it. It had a sloping roof. I turned back to look at the ship. I realized why I had not been able to see out. The pilots had never permitted the cabin to come through what looked like pea-soup fog. Only the front of the hull and the belly of the ship with the hatch open were not covered by this black wall of stuff.

I looked in through the open hatch and saw the pilots lying down in the ship's hull. They made no attempt to come out or take off with the ship. This made me feel better. I turned to see what kind of person had talked about the good job he had for me. He looked like a tramp. He would not let me look him in the face. He always managed to keep his back partly turned to me, and did his talking mostly over his shoulder, never looking back. He was wearing an old, dirty, beat-up black hat with a wide brim and a tall rounded crown. He wore an old blue-serge suit that had never been cleaned or pressed. It was out of style. He wore run-over ox-fords. He wore an old, dirty rag poked up under the back of his hat to hide the back of his neck and his ears. This rag came down to his shoulders. There were more dirty rags poked up each coat sleeve to cover the top of his hands. An old, dirty, brown piece of material was tucked under his trousers and hung down to his heels in his rear. His coattail hung down and flapped over this rag. He was about seven feet tall and of slender build. This was certainly a sight to see.

Had I not been so tired and worn out from the long trip, I would have hauled off and kicked him in the pants then and there. He was the old bum who had pestered me all night over the speaker system on the ship, and for what reason I did not know. Just then he asked if I was tired from the trip. I told him that I was tired and worn out from the trip. We walked up to the small shack in which he was staying. I thought that he might bring out some chairs for us to sit on, but we sat down on the ground. I was propped up against the shack, and he was sitting out forward from me, with his back to me. The more I looked him over, the more I wondered why he had tried so hard to conceal his identity. But I decided I was not going to ask him about it, because it was none of my business. I noticed that his skin was white (what little I could see from where I sat), but it was very dirty. His skin looked as if he had not bathed in years—perhaps not since the droughts had set in. He sensed my close scrutiny while we were sitting there.

He started to talk again about giving me a job. He was a good talker, but not too highly educated. He didn't use slang in his conversation. I became tired of listening to him talking and paid him little attention. I looked out over the wide terrain to the south and noticed some small, black people pulling and pushing large packing crates and pulling logs across the broken ground. One person handled each log or crate. These people seemed to be as strong as mules. I wondered where they had found the logs and crates in this land where there was not even a tree stump in sight or a blade of grass to be seen. Each time I looked at the workers, they scampered behind the loads they were dragging or hid behind rises in the ground. The more I looked, the more of them I could see. Even far in the distance, they were dragging their burdens to the west and stacking them in neat rows along the great fire-area line. I could spot the workers most distant from me for a second or two before they became aware of my gaze. Then, sure enough, they would stop working and run to hide behind whatever they were working on.

I thought these people were very strange, so I turned to the old bum and asked him who the people out there were. He told me that they were working for him. There must have been several thousand little black men out there, and they were working for all they were worth.

It was so hot there and I was so tired that I leaned back against the shack and fell asleep. When I awoke, it was early evening. It was beginning to get dark. A group of the small dark men came walking up to within forty feet of the old bum and me and formed a half circle around us. They did not appear to be hostile at all. They acted as if they were curious to get a close look at me. There were about forty of them in this group. As they approached, the old bum walked out to meet them. They talked in low voices, so I could not clearly hear what they were talking about. From all appearances, they were discussing me. The old bum turned partly toward me while talking to the little men. They had a short rather quiet giggling confab among themselves. Then they quieted down. It must have been strange for these little men to see another big man similar to their boss man come visiting upon their planet. They stayed around for quite some time, some sitting down, others standing up, and still others leaning against upheaved ground. Never for an instant did they take their attention from me.

Finally the old bum spoke a few words to one of the black men, and this message was passed from one black man to the other. Then they all started to file past me and walk back toward the great fire area. Some stopped to have a few words with the old bum on their way. It was plain to see that he was their master. My companion asked me if I was hungry. When I said that I was, he motioned to one of the little black people to come up. The little black man was so shy of me that I did not get a good look at his face. The rest of his body did look human enough. He was about the size of a pygmy and very black-skinned. He was clothed in a very short skirt that reached only to the middle of his thighs. A wide strip of cloth draped over his left shoulder was fastened to his skirt in front and in back. His clothing was made of heavy light brown material. The garments looked clean.

The old bum told him to wait on me. He told him to get us something to eat. The little black man ran into the shack and came back out in about a half hour with a biscuit on a dirty plate and an old dirty jelly glass half full of water. I looked at this food and thought, "They sure have bad rations on this planet." But the worst was yet to come. When I started to bite into the biscuit, I found it to be as hard as iron. Biting on it was clear out of the question. But I was very hungry, so I ran my teeth up against it and worked them very fast. In this way, I was able to wear off a little flour dust. It took me what seemed like hours to get the biscuit consumed. Even though this food stopped the pangs of hunger, I was completely worn out from the ordeal of eating it. My little black serving man found a small piece of board that he used to rig up a seat for me. He placed a big clod of dirt under each end of the board and put it against the shack so that I could sit on it and lean up against the shack. We sat there and watched the big fire light up the sky far into the night until I dropped off to sleep. I awoke the next morning after the sun was up to find I was still feeling tired and worn out. In fact, I felt worse than the night before. It had been just as hot at night as it was in daytime. It was absolutely hopeless to try to get any rest at all.

I hoped that the old bum would mention something about breakfast, for I was feeling hungry. But all he could talk about was the good job he had for me. I put up with this talk until about midmorning. Then I stood up and shook myself off. I felt a little better now. I looked over to him and said, "Just where is this good job you are talking so much about?"

"Well," he said, "come with me and I will show you."

We started walking up the incline to where it stopped almost at the edge of the burning area. Flames were leaping up all over this burning sea. A hundred yards off shore and farther out, the fire was burning bigger. But closer to shore, the fire was thinned down to scattered wisps of flame dancing here and there over the sea's surface. I stood at the top of the incline, where it stopped just short of the narrow strip of beach at the edge of the burning sea. I looked down the thin beach strip to my left and saw neat rows of crates and logs stacked up; the stacks extended farther than the eye could see. I looked closely at the stacks of crates and logs and discovered that they were not crates and logs at all. They were stacks of coffins and rows of human bodies, piled up along the beach for perhaps miles.

The coffins were somewhat old-fashioned-looking and were stacked one on top of the other, three in a stack. The stacks were in pairs. About ten feet away, there were stacks of twelve human bodies each. Some bodies were fully clothed and some were only partly clothed. About twenty feet farther down the beach, there were stacks of the same kind. For just as far as the eye could see in each direction, there were stacks.

I was still standing there trying to grasp it all when the old bum stepped down onto the beach strip and walked over to one of the casket stacks. He said to me, "See, this is all you have to do."

He put his right hand under one end of a box and raised it up a little. Then he took his left hand and slipped it under the box and picked up the box. Then, with a forward heave, he slid the box out into the sea. It went about thirty feet and then burst open, not from impact of the sea but from human force; for the man inside suddenly came to life. He came out screaming, fighting, and trying to swim ashore. But the more he tried, the farther he drifted away from shore. He was a nice-looking man, about forty years old, with black hair, dark eyes, and a white skin. He was smooth-shaven and wearing a new green suit.

This was only one scene. There were many more out there, and no two were alike. I looked out over the sea. There were people all over it, screaming and pleading to get back. But the undercurrent of the sea just carried them out farther, slowly but surely, to where the flames were burning bigger and higher, all the way to a solid mass of flames that was thirty feet high.

I noticed a woman about forty feet from shore. She was perhaps thirty-five years old. She was very white-skinned, had black hair, and was dressed in a new sleeveless pink silk dress. She did not seem to belong there. Nevertheless, there she was. She was having the same troubles as the others. A little dancing flame played around her a minute. Then it jumped up on her shoulder. She tried to submerge quickly to get away from it. When she came up, I could see that her hair was burned on the side where the flame had been and one of her arms and shoulders was badly scorched. I noticed that the fluid from the sea on her white skin looked like a colorless, thin, oily substance.

I had seen all of this I cared to see, and I started to back up. I waved my hands at the old bum, telling him that I would not have anything to do with this kind of a job. I could see by his sudden actions this turn of events made him very angry. He said to me, in an angry, loud voice, "Man, this is your chance to get up in the world. It's a chance of a lifetime." But I kept backing down the incline and toward the ship, telling him I would not have anything to do with this sort of thing. Then he showed his face for the first time, in his anger over my refusal to help him in his tasks. He had a long, slim, wrinkled face with a large, long, prominent, ugly nose and dark, piercing eyes that looked very wicked. His face was caked and dirty-looking. He followed me back to a very short distance in front of the ship, talking in a pleading and reassuring manner, trying to get me to come back and reconsider the whole thing. But I was determined not to do so, and I told him so.

We sat down a short distance in front of the ship, and he gave me the same talk about how good things would be up here. But I paid no attention to him. I looked in the ship and saw the pilots lying on their backs, taking it easy. Once in a while they got up on their elbows to see how I was making out with the old bum. They talked for short periods and then lay down. But never once did they attempt to come out. It seemed to me as if I had to have the old bum's permission before I could leave. The pilots were not helping me at all. I could not figure a way out as yet. It looked hopeless to even try. But I was not going to give up. I would keep on trying until a break came my way, and then I would grab onto it. I felt that I did not have the power to get out of this situation. After all, this had been strictly a one-way passage for all the other people here. Why make an exception just for me? However, there was a ship waiting for me, if only I could get aboard. But how?

While I was thinking, I heard the old bum's voice. He was getting more determined that I stay on. The arguments grew hotter and longer until about midafternoon. Then I looked up. Just over the top of the ship, there appeared a thin streamer of white light. The portion of this beam that was closest to me seemed very small, but back in the distance it funneled out, revealing a clear sky and sunshine. In the middle of the light, Christ appeared in plain view. This was a most welcome sight to see.

I turned to the old bum and, pointing my hand to the light, I said, "If you don't let me go, He will send for me."

He raised up to see what I was pointing at in the light and then dropped his head down and said, "Yes, He is always interfering." Then, breaking off his sentence with low, grumbling noises, he shut up for the time being.

For the first time, I realized I had a chance of outwitting and outtalking him. I hoped to get his permission to leave this awful place. But, in a very short time, he started his same old talk. I pointed up to where the light was and told the old bum that if he did not let me go, He would send for me. But the old bum was very persistent in his arguments. We argued until it was almost dark. Then it was chow time again. I got the same old meager rations.

I knew that I would escape soon, but I did not know just when. Therefore I ate the meager rations so as to sustain my strength. By the time my rations were consumed, I was exhausted from the terrible exercise of eating them. Here I was jerked back to earth and normal conditions. I felt relieved to get out of that hot hellhole and back to earth. The black men faded out and I saw a customer. It was only a short business transaction and the customer soon left. I was alone again, except for the two pilots, who had come into full form immediately. I decided to rebel and not let them send me back to that awful place. I was just getting ready to open my mouth and tell them what I thought about it when all of a sudden—wham—I was back on the red planet. The old bum turned and saw me. I lay down on the ground for another night of sleep. I had no rest. I awoke the next morning, and the old bum continued his arguing. I began to get angry. He kept it up until almost midmorning. Then I decided that I had heard enough of his talking, and I told him so. I pointed over to the ship and to the light and said, "He will send for me." Then I turned back to look him in the face.

He looked very meek and, turning his head to one side, said, "You can go."

I turned and went to the ship. The pilots were up and ready to go. I walked under the ship, climbed up on the manhole plate, and jumped in, without looking back. The pilots reached down and snapped the plate shut. One pilot took the controls, leveled the ship, and then spun it around to put it on course. Then he gave it full power. He stayed at the controls for a few minutes so as to be sure to get the light beam coming in the front cab window on dead center. Then both pilots leaned down to go up forward. I looked back and saw nothing but inky black space. We were absorbing the light streamer as the ship proceeded.

I was tired, so I stretched out on the plates for much

needed rest and sleep. Hours later I awoke. I felt the ship being braked. Both pilots were standing forward, at the controls. I got up, hoping they were not making another stop as unpleasant as the last one we had made. Far in the distance, I could see the light streamer bending gradually to our port side. Down there, we would enter the earth's orbit.

The pilots were very thoughtful on this return trip. I felt very grateful. They went much slower coming down than they had gone on the trip coming up, when they had been quite excited. I guess they remembered how the fast acceleration and earth's gravitation had flattened me to the cabin wall.

It was not long before the heavy, dark space had begun to thin out to a lighter gray color. The long sweeping turn had been completed. I could see a very small ball, far past this heavy atmosphere. The small light streamer was leading directly to it. I supposed that this small ball was our planet, earth. But I could not recognize it from this distance. As the minutes and the miles passed, it became easy to see that the small ball was earth. It was a relief to know that they were bringing me back to where I belonged. There had been times on this trip when I had not known where we would go or where they might leave me. But I always bore in mind that I was from earth and that I must return to earth.

We came in closer. The earth appeared to be a big smooth ball, with white caps on two opposite surfaces. We were traveling rapidly. I felt gravitation holding me snugly back against the cabin. It gave me a secure feeling to ride in this ship and know that it flew safely, even though it did not have a hardware store full of gadgets to make it fly. The earth grew much larger and rougher-looking. I could see mountain ranges and dark, smooth ocean surfaces. At this distance, earth looked dead. I could hardly believe it contained life of all descriptions.

Yet it was very pleasant and peaceful to look upon, especially after having left the planet of Hell, which was surrounded by blackness and had no moon or stars in its sky.

The only illumination in hell after darkness was the big eternal fire. As we came closer to earth, I could see thin ribbons of silver twisting between some of the mountain ranges and crossing over smooth surfaces. These ribbons were rivers. Between the ship and earth were flat smoke spots, that I recognized to be clouds. The nearer we came to earth, the thinner and less visible our light streamer became, until it completely vanished. It had been a wonderful beacon. One pilot cut down the ship's speed. The other pilot started tinkering with the ship's communication system. He gave me a small silver disk, about one-half inch thick by three inches across, with a small switch on it. He motioned for me to use it. I flipped the switch and was surprised to hear a ringing sound, much like a telephone ringing. After a few rings, I was surprised to hear my brother's voice. I could see him as well as hear him. I could see his family sitting down to their evening dinner. Although I had disturbed them right in the middle of their meal, they were glad to hear I had come back safely and wanted to know when they could see me. They were somewhat shocked to learn that I was calling from aboard ship. I told my brother that I thought I was coming down to land in about the same place from which I had taken off and that I would be there by the time he could drive out there. I asked him to come at once. I flipped the switch off and handed the disk back to the pilot. He replaced it in the metal box and slid the panel closed.

Both pilots went forward, leaving me alone in the cabin. It felt good to look down and see the mountains slowly rising up, exposing valleys and cultivated fields. I could see that the sun was very low. I wondered if the ship would land near the spot from which it had taken off. The nearby terrain looked very familiar. Coming closer, I could see an automobile coming down a dirt side road at very fast speed. It was going in the same general direction as the ship. The ship slowed down and landed within fifty yards of the original taking-off place. It came down as light as a feather and tilted to aft. I pressed on a small catch on the edge of the glass manhole plate. It sprang open. I dropped down through the opening and turned to raise it back shut. I was surprised to find that it was so light in weight.

I walked out from under the ship, and immediately it started to rise up and rotate slowly. Then, with great speed, it disappeared to the east and over the mountain range.

My brother had just driven up. He asked me why I had not tried to detain the ship so that the two of us might try to take the ship over. I told him that a person should never attempt to harm a space man in any way, for he might get hurt or killed. We got into the car to go home. I asked him, "How long have I been away?"

He was very quick to answer that I had been gone four days, almost to the minute. He was curious to know where I had been and all about the trip. I told him that I was very tired and hungry and it had been a long trip. In the near future, I would tell him. He drove me over to my place of business and let me out at the front door. I waved goodby as he drove off. I turned to walk in the front door and over to my tank. At last, after the terrible four-day trip, I felt my full natural self again.

Just then the phone rang. I walked over to take the call. I could feel myself getting angrier every minute with the two pilots for taking me on that trip. I finished with the phone call and turned to go back to my tank. I saw the pilots in front of me. With smiling faces, they asked, "Red, how did you like your trip?"

I was so angry then that I believe I would have wrung their necks if I had dared to touch them. I snapped back, "I didn't like it worth a damn."

They were quick to answer back. "We did not think you would like it." Then they broke out in a big laugh that lasted for several minutes.

I turned to leave them standing there laughing. I walked over to my bench and started working, feeling very bitter toward them. Soon they came over to me, trying to be friendly with me again. But I could not forget this episode so easily. I looked up at the clock on the wall. It would not be long before they left, if they were regular on this day. I began checking the time. This whole trip had taken, from start to finish, about four hours' time. The whole four-day round trip to hell had taken place in four hours' time. It was a mystery to me. I looked up at the men. They were experts at reading a person's thoughts and really had wonderful personalities. It was very hard not to like these men yet I did not like them. I did not know what else they might do to me. They were capable of anything. I had left earth at near sundown, traveled all night, spent two and one quarter days and two nights in hell, suffered from the heat and hunger, and returned to earth all in a matter of four hours' time. It is a true mystery and yet it actually did happen.

Soon they left for the day. What a day! I was sure glad to see them go this time and hoped they would never return. Should they come back, what could they show or do that they had not already shown and done? I started to think up ways and means to get rid of them, just in case they did return. I knew that I had no chance to combat them by physical force, for they were too big and husky for me. I would have to think up some way other than force. This was a problem. A thought came into the old bean. "Why not just ignore them completely and see if it will work out?" I would give it a good try. Anyway, they might not come back any more after all they had done. I believed that they had just so much to say and to show on their mission to earth. This was the way it had been planned out at the very beginning, and nothing I could do would change or have any effect on it whatsoever.

As I said at the beginning, they knew more about me and my surroundings than I knew myself. If the men should return after this day, they would have a lot of nerve and brass. To think what they might pull off the next time really made cold chills run up and down my back. They possessed a lot of power that people of earth know nothing about.

I would like to mention at this time I am very thankful to the Almighty that the men never once entered my dwelling or returned after dark, for either might have been very frightful and tragic. The space men did juggle one day during each week to discourage any planned arrangement that I might make. They always kept regular hours for their arrival and departure, and were always very courteous and men of their word in every way. It was easy to understand that they were men of the very highest culture. By the fine manner in which they conducted themselves, and by their wonderful expressions and actions, they tried not to offend me or interfere in my business in any way. They were very cautious in this respect. By the same token, when they saw I was up in my work and coasting along easy, and they had another caper to perform, they did not hesitate to put it through, regardless of how I felt about it or what I did. It was quite obvious that the men were here for important reasons, and they had to show and tell them to some person on earth so as to get certain information to all of the people. These men showed a lot of patience while here on earth with me. They showed me the kind of men they were and the complete construction of their bodies. They showed me the place from which they had descended.

Any planet that can produce men such as these is surely a much finer place than earth could ever be. I hope that this story has explained where the flying saucers come from and why they are here. As to what our future destiny will be, men who possess more knowledge than I have must supply the answer. All I can do is to guess at the correct answer.

In writing these last lines, I feel I made a terrible mistake. But all men make mistakes. Here goes.

The next morning I had high hopes that the men would not come back another time. I could see no reason for their returning. I had definitely made up my mind how I was to handle them if they did come. About nine thirty that morning they returned just as they had in days past. They looked very cheerful. I gave them a quick look and turned to look away. I did not look higher up than their waistlines, keeping my eyes down. But that did not keep them from bending down occasionally to look up at me with their smiling faces, trying to win my friendship. Again it was hard not to like these men, even though I was determined not to. But I had made up my mind, like an elephant, and I did not intend to change it, no matter what happened.

Occasionally, I would take a quick look at them when I knew they were not observing me. I could see they were not pleased with me for the change in my attitude toward them. They looked dumbfounded and puzzled by it all, and I could see it hurt their feelings. They didn't know how to take it. They stepped away from me. They spoke to each other about the situation, the same as two ordinary men might do in similar circumstances. I felt that I had won round one with them. I wanted to keep giving them the cold shoulder and not look their way, hoping against hope that it would discourage them.

To my disappointment, the men came back every day for the next two and a half weeks. I was becoming frightened of them by this time. I worried about the decision I had made and was following out, but I felt I could not change it now. I expected them to tell me just what they thought and would do.

They were fine men and did not want to do me any harm. I believe now that the only reason they came back was to gain back my friendship before leaving for good. But I did not give them a chance to do so. The last four days of their stay was a time of really rough going. I could see by the looks on their faces that they were going to be hard to handle. There were no smiles on their faces. They were very sincere, but almost mean-looking.

On the morning of the last day, they came within four feet of me and just stood there for more than an hour. I was using a small hammer at the time. I made it appear that it was too small for the job. I walked over to another bench to pick up a one-and-one-half-pound mechanic's hammer and took it back. I pounded on the same work to make it appear that I had to make the job right. I did not want to arouse their suspicions, but all I could think of was that I had a handy weapon with which to defend myself.

I put the hammer down on the rack, where I could get it quickly in case I needed it. I was completely forgetting that they could read my thoughts. The men backed up a few steps and did not venture closer for the rest of that morning. But I was very frightened of them now, for I had no way of knowing what they were thinking of doing. Noon finally rolled around, and the men faded out as they always had at lunch time. I was sure glad to be able to take one hour away from them. Upon my return, they came right back. They stood at a distance from me, conversed and looked at me. But I was as determined to keep them off as they were determined to break me down. I expected the men to get rough at any time, but they stayed at a distance.

In the early afternoon, they stepped up close again, making more commotion than before. I was keeping as close a watch on them as I could as I worked. I lit up a smoke and was going along fine. Then I turned partly around to look for a tool. There the men were, almost right on top of me. They startled me so much that I let out a cough of smoke in their faces. I reached out for the hammer. I was surprised to see them step back quick from the tobacco smoke. They could not stand the smoke at all. They were making a lot of commotion and talking between themselves.

I realized that the situation would be less complicated from here on out. I was sure glad to find this out. During the rest of that day, the men tried several times to come in closer. Each time they did, I blew tobacco smoke their way. That backed them up, but it made them very angry. I chain-smoked the rest of that afternoon until the men left. At their departure time, they just faded out and disappeared, never to return.

Many times during the last two and a half weeks they were here I felt ashamed of how I was treating these two men. But I felt I could not change once I had started this way of acting, so foolishly and stubbornly carried out my plan to the end. It might have been very interesting and important to hear their final words before they left earth for good. At this time, I cannot say that I would openly welcome another visit by these men. By the same token, I surely would not turn against them again as I did at the end of their visit. I value all the things they showed me and told me more than money. Where can you go purchase even a tiny portion of what they possess, even if you have all the money in the world?

In bringing this story to its end, I rise before God and man to swear that this story I have written began in the latter part of nineteen hundred and fifty-two A.D., and ended in January, nineteen hundred and fifty-three, A.D.; it is a true account of an actual happening and of the flying saucers of today and the supreme supernatural. I have written the story just as it was shown to me by two men who, urgently and persistently, against my own will, asked that I write it for the people. Perhaps men of great knowledge and wisdom who read this story can decipher the true advanced meaning of it and translate it so that all people, the world over, may benefit from it.

CECIL MICHAEL

Bakersfield, California
October 30, 1953, A.D.

U.F.O. occupants confront excavator

Meanwhile, according to "O Dia" October 5, there has been yet another very interesting happening at Lins, Rio de Janeiro, Brazil off late 1968.

At 6.20 a.m. on October 2nd, a 41-year-old employee of the Lins Municipality named Doribio Pereira was about to start his morning work driving the caterpillar-type mechanical excavator assigned to him. As he was standing on the caterpillar tread, engaged in putting oil and water in the engine, he was astonished to behold suddenly, right in front of him, at a distance of only a few feet and no more than a foot or so from the ground, a strange cigar-shaped craft, of a most beautiful golden colour.

The next minute he caught sight of a strange person who in reaching into his sleeve drew out a weapon shaped something like an electric drill. He aimed this weapon at Doribio Pereira, there was a sudden bright flash (like from an electronic flash). The emission from this unexpected discharge totally immobilised the witness, who felt himself glued as it were to the spot where he was standing up on the excavator, unable to shout or speak.

He was however able to watch the strange beings and their craft. On the underpart of the "cigar" craft there was a platform, on which three of the crew were standing, and he was able to see into the conveyance (as its roof was of glass). Inside he could see one being operating a sort of type writer, using both hands. Of the beings on the platform outside the one positioned in front of him, was looking at the engine of the excavator while another on the right from where he stood was preoccupied using a conch shaped object (shaped like a shell) to remove a sample of soil from the cut about where the excavator had recently been working, and he was doing this without leaving the platform.

They were working as though automatically, without gestures and, so far as he could detect, without speaking to each other, and from time to time they entered the object through a doorway in its front part, through which the witness was able to see four backless stools set apart, from each other. The craft was now making ready to leave, and flashed an intense vivid light, three times, the platform below was taken in, as well as another cone-shaped device, there then appeared underneath a thing (like a sort of giant electric polisher) revolving at great speed. The machine making a slight sound then took off, in the direction of Guaicara. Its flight was said to be somewhat like that of a duck, very smooth and low at first, and then putting on great speed, climbing rapidly was soon lost to the sight in the sky.

Doribio Pereira now felt himself able to move. But he found it impossible to run, as he wished, so he had to walk as far as the nearest road, where he was soon picked up by a passing motorist who surprisingly enough happened to be his friend Ezequiel, who seeing the shaken condition he was in drove him straight to his home. Doribio's wife was shocked by his pitiful expression and apparent paleness and to relieve him made up a cup of mint-tea which he then drank. Still in a very nervous state he decided it was his duty that he should report the matter to the Town Council offices. The Municipal head, Rubens Furquim, hearing from his staff about the case, came out of his office and, seeing him in this condition, ordered that he be given a glass of milk and a sedative, to calm his nerves. It was alleged so we were led to believe in appearance his complexion in whiteness exceeded that of a corpse.

Returning to the place where his excavator was, he found that the soil there had been moved by someone. Five of his workmates (all named in the "O Dia" report) had seen some marks left there supposedly by the cigar-shaped craft, but these marks were now no longer visible (they were scrape marks on the face of the hillock of earth that he had been removing).

When questioned by the authorities as to the sort of clothing that the strange beings were wearing, Doribio Pereira said that they "had clothing like a saint, down to the knees, on their heads a hood (capuz)", "the sleeves were loose, and the colour of the clothing was blue with sparkling reddish reflections". On their feet he said "they wore sandals open at the front so that their toes were visible. The colour of the sandals was dark brown, and they had narrow bands tied round their legs up as far as the knees, like the ancient Romans".

He said the beings had eyes, noses and mouths. He did not see whether they possessed teeth, as they were working in total silence and did not once open their mouths. . . . G.C.

Penang, 22/8/70. Today.— The gates of an English school near here were locked yesterday to keep out hundreds of people curious to meet six pupils who claimed they saw a flying saucer land packed with spacemen three inches high.

The pupils story made headlines in the English language Press yesterday and detectives went to Stowell school, at Tukit Mertajam, to question the children.

Two boys, aged 10 and 12, said they were prepared to swear in a temple their story was true.

One boy claimed he saw five spacemen one in a yellow uniform with horns on his head, and the others in blue uniforms. "When I tried to catch them, the one in the yellow suit, apparently their leader, shot my right leg. See, you can see the mark", he said pointing to a red spot. . . . A.S.

Another incident which occurred during January 16th 1968, the man concerned received a strange phone call urging him to be at Heavens Gate, on the Longleat Estate owned by a Lord Bath, at 9 p.m., exactly in three days. On that Thursday a few minutes past the appointed hour the female companion of the man spied a U.F.O. overhead, it was tilting from side to side apparently attempting to draw their attention which undoubtedly it did, then flew straight in their direction towards Heavens Gate, where it dropped with the suddenness of a stricken bird.

Our two companions raced from the neighbouring parking lot opposite, over the fence and tore to where the saucer had landed to find a craft which was literally no bigger than a soup plate. Then a golden ladder, thread thin appeared from the base of the miniature spaceship, down which climbed tiny figures no more than four inches in height, roughly there was about two dozen in all. Stepping away from the landed craft, which was now quite blacked out, each in turn zoomed up to the height of the man and woman standing there, dumbstruck, aghast and refusing to credit the testimony of their eyes.

They shook hands with our two companions, all was perfectly normal and friendly as though they had known them from before (previous encounters presumably). After much small talk, our male friend was invited to take a journey with them in their machine to see what unsuspected wonders lay awaiting to be yet uncovered, to this he agreed. The woman was left behind, lumbered with his personal effects. To her further amazement, all were again dwarfed in size including her companion, this time. They ascended the ladder, cobweb fine, a whistling noise accompanied the lift-off, rising and spinning in a slightly agitated manner until gradually it settled into free flight, all the time as this was occurring the ship was growing larger stage by stage then finally it soared upward and vanished.

The woman was so taken back, frankly she said "I could have stooped down, and plucked the saucer up from the ground and actually held it all in one hand, thats how small it was. When I saw my companion reduced in size, the same as the others, before he went up the ladder into that machine, my heart simply broke in two, almost so that I couldn't help shedding a tear or two."

During the journey he allegedly was supposed to have seen buried cities, communities and mountain chains lying deep under large oceans, and something about seeing the inner core. . . . A.S.

Round Trip to Hell in a Flying Saucer

The Dero closely resemble the Dover Demons, or are they one and the same?

The *Dover Demon* is an alleged cryptozoological creature sighted on three separate occasions during a 25-hour period in the town of Dover, Massachusetts on April 21 and April 22, 1977. It has remained a subject of interest for cryptozoologists ever since then. Cryptozoologist Loren Coleman was the initial investigator and the individual who named the creature the Dover Demon; it was disseminated by the press, and the name stuck. Coleman quickly assembled and brought into the inquiry three other investigators: Joseph Nyman, Ed Fogg, and Walter Webb. All were well-known ufological researchers in eastern Massachusetts, with Webb being the assistant director of the Hayden Planetarium at Boston's Science Museum. Coleman did not feel he was necessarily dealing with a ufological phenomenon, but he wanted to have seasoned investigators with good interviewing skills to do a comprehensive examination of the eyewitnesses and their families, as well as law enforcement, educational, and community members.

The Dover Demon was first sighted at night by three seventeen-year-old boys who were driving through the Massachusetts area when the car's headlights illuminated it. Bill Bartlett, the driver, reported that he saw what he thought at first was a dog or a cat, but upon closer inspection realized that it was a bizarre, unearthly-looking creature crawling along a stone wall on Farm Street.

Bartlett continued to watch the creature, and he reported it to have a disproportionately large, watermelon-shaped head and illuminated orange eyes, like glass marbles. It had long, thin arms and legs with slender fingers, which it used to grasp onto the pavement. It was hairless and had rough, flesh-toned skin, described as tan and sandpaper-like. The creature's appearance was very plain, with no nose or ears, and no mouth was seen. The witness drawings portray its head as having a skull shape, forming the contour of a circle on top with a more elliptical ending projecting down to include where the nose and mouth would be.

Other witnesses have claimed the creature had green eyes and seemingly smooth, chalky gray toned skin, three feet tall, and made a bloodcurdling noise, similar to a hawk's screech combined with a snakes hiss. But all witnesses say it had no ears, mouth, nose, or known sex.

The creature was sighted again an hour later, by John Baxter, 15, and Pete Mitchell, 13, as they were walking home. He said it was bipedal and ended up running into a gully and standing next to a tree. The next day, Abby Brabham, 15, and Will Traintor, 18, driving down Springdale Avenue, claimed to have seen a similar-looking creature from Traintor's car, on the side of the road. Brabham's description matched Bartlett's and Baxter's descriptions, except this time the cryptid had illuminated green eyes. She approximated its height as "about the size of a goat". Investigators attempted to shake up Ms. Brabham by noting she said it had green eyes reflected by car headlights, while Bartlett mentioned orange eyes were reflected back to him by his automobile's lights. Ms. Brabham was steadfast in her description.

Bartlett, Baxter, Brabham, and Traintor all drew sketches of the monstrous sight shortly after their sightings. On the piece of paper that includes Bartlett's sketch, he wrote "*I, Bill Bartlett, swear on a stack of Bibles that I saw this creature.*" From Wikipedia.com

UFO Possession and Mind Manipulation

By Timothy Green Beckley

"UFO behavior is more akin to Magick than to Physics as we know it. And modern day UFOnauts and the demons of past days are probably identical."

Dr. Pierre Guerin,
senior researcher of the
French National Council for Scientific Research

There are mounting indications that UFOs have a long-term plan of operation in store for Earth and its inhabitants. Data, meticulously collected in a worldwide research effort, would seem to support that stunning theory.

UFO literature is filled with hundreds of cases in which unsuspecting observers have been subjected to continuous harassments following an encounter with a flying saucer. Many times the witness finds his home plagued by a host of inexplicable phenomena. In other cases, eerie, mechanical-sounding voices, purported to be "messages" from an alien source, begin emanating from their radios, TV sets, or telephones. In addition, mysterious strangers dressed in dark clothing, commonly referred to as the Men-In-Black, or MIBs, visit the often confused eyewitness and warn him not to speak about his sighting to anyone.

The late French researcher Dr Pierre Guerin concluded that "UFOs behavior is more akin to Magic than to Physics as we know it."

Many observers, however, endure far more harrowing experiences than these. As terrifying as these incidents may seem, they are no comparison to the instances which appear to be actual cases of *UFO possession.*

Often, while interviewing a UFO eyewitness or contactee, I find myself face-to-face with an individual who is convinced he is slowly – but surely – losing touch with reality. Having come that close to the unknown, the individual feels his very existence is being threatened by an alien force bent on gaining total control of his body and soul.

Some witnesses persist in believing that they are being "haunted" day and night by an invisible specter whose main objective is to capture their free will and make them the "property" of someone – *or something* – else.

Cases of UFO possession are actually quite common! Yet very little is known about it because of the scarcity of research into the subject. Investigators have remained extremely cautious about digging too deeply into this particular area. Their hesitancy, however, may be justified.

An exhaustive study of my own shows that accounts of UFO possession are almost always identical. Frightfully so! The following patterns have emerged, again and again:

- After a close encounter with a UFO, the eyewitness goes through a period of anxiety, during which he is unable to consciously remember certain aspects of the incident.

- Within months – sometimes weeks or even days – the personality of the observer actually changes. Eventually, it may alter to the point where he finds it impossible to get along with workers, close friends or even family. Personal tragedy seems to strike many of those who have had ground level encounters with UFOs. Much could be written about individuals whose entire personal world crumbles around them following such an experience.

- In some cases, the eyewitness discovers he has developed certain "gifts" or abilities. Though they may appear to be beneficial at first, too frequently this is not the case. Among these unusual abilities are extraordinary powers of ESP, precognition, or psycho-kinesis. In addition, a heightened intelligence level or an unusual increase in physical strength may be noticed. Such peculiarities will often manifest themselves shortly before a person a person is about to be possessed. Shortly after this, he may begin slipping into a "trance," during which time it appears as if an alien intelligence has "taken over" his body and is using his brain.

It was during my in-depth investigation of an extensive UFO wave in the U.S. Southwest that I met Paul Clark, a tall, slimly-built man in his mid-20s. (Because of the seriousness and the possible repercussions this article may cause, we have decided to change the names of those individuals involved.)

His story is one of the most believable accounts of alien possession that I have ever heard. And I'm convinced it is *not* a hoax.

During the course of three rather lengthy conversations with Paul, I felt I learned much about him. Like so many other American boys, he spent his teenage years playing baseball, listening to music, and chasing girls. Paul never paid close attention to his schoolwork, with the result that his grades were "just average."

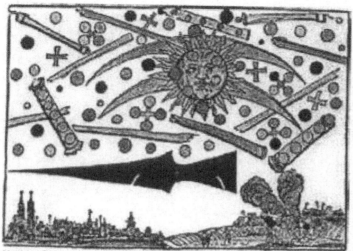

Many of our ancestors came to realize the dark nature of the UFO phenomenon as they portrayed them in art.

Nevertheless, he was well liked by his fellow classmates and also managed to get along amicably with his elders.

Now, at 25, this same "average young man" feels destitute, as if he doesn't have a friend in the world. Nearly a total recluse, he shuns any activity which might expose him to public scrutiny. He is divorced from his bride of four years, and has quit or been fired from numerous jobs.

Of course, these radical changes in his life did not occur overnight, but rather were a painfully slow period of moral and physical deterioration.

Paul was more than willing to tell me the details of his ordeal. As we talked, it became apparent that he was anxious to get the matter off his chest. The problem had obviously been weighing him down for too many years.

"For the longest time, I thought I was going insane," Paul said. "Often my best friends would accuse me of behaving irrationally and I wouldn't have a clue about what they were referring to. My mind, on those occasions, was an absolute blank. I found myself going to doctors and psychiatrists, but even they couldn't offer me an explanation that could account for these amnesia attacks."

Whatever the cause of his trouble, it was obvious that it was rooted in an eerie confrontation with a visitor from outer space! The even took place on a Friday night in August 1967. At the time, Paul lived with his parents on a rather secluded ranch near Waco, Texas, which was surrounded by trees, dense thickets and bramble. Here is his personal account of what happened on that fateful summer evening.

"The weather had been unbearably hot all day, with temperatures soaring into the 90s. I got permission from my folks to spend the night outdoors, camped in back of our ranch house with a couple of friends.

"We set up a makeshift shelter, turned on a portable radio, and proceeded to shoot the breeze. The sky was as clear as I'd ever seen it, with stars twinkling against a background of absolute blackness.

"Around 10 p.m., the air began to gradually get cooler. In the distance we could hear an occasional rumble of thunder, and once in a while the sky would light up with a flash of lightning. It was a great sight."

Unfortunately, the beauty of the night was short-lived. It was shattered less than two hours later.

"Shortly after midnight, we lowered the flame on our kerosene lantern and retired," Paul Clark continued, a slight trace of tension building in his voice. "Immediately I turned over and closed my eyes. Before long, however, a peculiar high-pitched whine woke my up. The nearest I can come to describing this would be to say it sounded like a million bees buzzing."

Sitting up, Paul peered into the darkness and saw nothing. Within a few moments, however, he managed to pinpoint the source of the noise. It was coming from the woods near the ranch. With his curiosity now aroused, Paul decided to investigate.

Are aliens coming here from other worlds -- or are they the minions of Satan himself?

"I didn't want to wake my friends, so I tiptoed over to the area, hoping to catch a glimpse of whatever was causing the noise. I recall wandering aimlessly farther and farther away from our backyard camp, as if I was being pulled by an invisible rope. All around me, the whine continued to grow in intensity until finally it encircled me on all sides."

At this point, Paul sighted his first UFO.

"Up ahead of me, between the trees and bushes, was a glowing light the size of a basketball. As I approached to within 25 feet of it, I could see the light was actually a pulsating sphere."

In an attempt to block out the loud irritating noise that now was growing in intensity, Paul put his hands over his ears. This had little effect, however.

"My head began to swim, and my eyes started to water. Next thing I knew, I was on my hands and knees – somehow I must have fallen without realizing it – crawling on the ground, trying to get back to the safety of my friends."

He was unsuccessful!

Upon "coming to," Paul found himself in his parents' living room. His head was pounding from "the worst headache I've ever experienced." Standing around him were his mother and father and his two friends.

Paul says he found it difficult to understand what they were trying to tell him.

"It was as if they were talking to a complete stranger," he said. "I had, for all intents and purposes, lost my identity. I had no idea who I was or where I was."

Round Trip to Hell in a Flying Saucer

While he tried to calm his nerves and gather his thoughts, Paul's friends filled him in on what had happened.

"They said they had suddenly been awakened by a brilliant flash off in the woods. They noticed that I wasn't in my sleeping bag nor did they see me nearby, and they became worried. Considering all the possibilities, they felt I might have wandered off in my sleep and fallen into one of the many ravines in the area," Paul said.

Using a flashlight to guide them through the underbrush, Paul's friends began calling out his name. Their worry grew into fear because he did not respond to their cries.

Five minutes later, their search ended when they found Paul stretched out on the ground face down.

"Lifting me to my feet, they explained how I seemed to be in another world, dazed and looking right through them. My eyes, they claimed, were rolled back in their sockets and my skin had turned white as a sheet. In addition, they said my flesh felt ice-cold, like that of a corpse."

On the way back to the house they noticed something else. Paul's head had swollen like a balloon. His forehead appeared enlarged and extended several inches beyond normal.

"It was 'puffed up,' as if I'd been stung by a mass of bees."

This condition rapidly disappeared and Paul's head returned to normal by the time the three boys reached the safety of his parents' quiet ranch house.

For weeks afterward, Paul Clark felt worn out, "as if I'd been drained of all my energy." He found it extremely difficult to concentrate long enough to do even the most mundane chores. All he could do was mope around the house and he spent a good portion of the time sleeping.

As the months went by, Paul regained his strength. However, even as he returned to normal, physically, he couldn't help but wonder about what had really happened on that late summer night.

"My friends came up with a rather logical explanation. They concluded that I'd been walking in my sleep – I'd never done that before, to my knowledge – and that a thunderstorm had come up in the middle of the night and I had barely missed being struck by lightning. They figured a bolt had struck near where I stood, and after traveling over the surface of the ground had reached me. Along the way, the lightning must have lost a great deal of force. Otherwise, they theorized, I would surely have been instantly killed."

Though their explanation seemed reasonable, Paul couldn't shake the persistent feeling that a lot more was involved.

"I recalled the bright light dancing about, and the strange buzzing that literally ran through my skull."

He knew there had to be another answer – even if it was an unpleasant one.

After several years had passed, Paul became engaged to and later married his high school sweetheart, Irene.

"After we got married, I took a job as a ranch hand near Calvert, Texas. And though the week was tiring, it paid pretty well. Each week, I was able to put some money in the bank, figuring someday I would have enough saved to buy a small place of our own, and perhaps even start a small cattle business."

Since that night in back of his parents' house, Paul suffered both mentally and physically. Dizzy spells, headaches and fainting became common.

"I'd be seated at the kitchen table and all of a sudden my wife would be applying cold compresses to my forehead. I'd pass right out reading the newspaper or eating."

Gradually his condition deteriorated.

Christian fundamentalist groups maintain that UFOs have opened a portal to hell from where demons can emerge into our world to cause disasters and mass murder.

During this difficult period which followed his UFO experience, Paul became keenly fascinated with science and began reading books on physics and engineering, subjects which he had never before showed even a mild interest in.

"It was as if I were furthering my education," he insisted. "I didn't know why I found these topics so fascinating. My mind seemed to be developing – expanding – at a rapid clip."

Coinciding with this heightened curiosity and intelligence, Paul found himself growing extremely moody. As the months passed, and after discussing his suspicions with his wife, that ufonauts were trying to control him, it became more difficult for Paul to be around other people – including his wife, parents and coworkers.

"I had a hard time keeping my thoughts together."

He started showing up late for work, and then not showing up at all. Finally, he quit, not wanting to wait until he was fired. A string of lesser paying jobs followed, but they all ended the same way.

Then things went from bad to worse!

Round Trip to Hell in a Flying Saucer

"My mind was incapable of thinking straight. It was always a million miles away, toying with some advanced mathematical formula or scientific equation. The funny part of all this was that I still didn't know the reason I was so hung up on these things. After all, I wasn't a scientist or an engineer, just a simple country boy."

During this period, personal tragedy struck the Clarks. Their year-old son suddenly died. Doctors diagnosed that the infant had succumbed to a cerebral hemorrhage.

In early 1973, Paul's wife left him and filed for divorce. One of the reasons she gave was that she felt the boy's death was somehow related to Paul's condition. She felt that the UFO issue had broken up their previously happy marriage. The same pattern is often repeated as UFO witnesses have found their formerly happy lives turned into nightmares.

Paul didn't even bother to contest the divorce action.

"Even though I loved Irene dearly, she didn't matter that much to me anymore. It was as though I had a special mission on Earth. It was 'beyond me' to lead an ordinary existence!"

Irene's decision to leave came after Paul's second encounter with mysterious unidentified objects. Not knowing what to expect – or what he husband was capable of doing – she decided to leave.

"Again, I must tell you what happened as seen through another person's eyes. My mind is almost a total blank when it comes to the events of that night."

Paul and his wife were driving home from Belmont, Texas, where they had spent the evening with relatives.

"It was around 1:30 a.m., and I was speeding along the darkened back roads to avoid traffic, when suddenly a large, yellowish ball of fire appeared on the road ahead. Immediately I slammed on the brakes because otherwise I would have collided head-on with the object."

The UFO slowly lifted from the road top position a few feet above the pavement and began drifting toward the side of the road. About 30 seconds passed before it stopped and hovered next to a grove of trees.

It was then that a frightened Paul Clark insists that he was directed, as if by magic, to leave his car and walk toward the UFO that now remained stationary. Just as in his first UFO experience, the nighttime air was now filled with an eerie loud whine, similar to a shrill scream.

"My wife pleaded with me not to leave the car, but I was no longer in control of my movements. It was as if my body was being *made* to react, pulling me in the direction 'they' wanted."

Walking toward the light, Paul says he heard a voice inside his head. This "inner voice" demanded that he walk straight ahead and not look back.

Meanwhile, inside the parked car, Irene Clark was almost hysterical.

"She considered going for help, but was afraid the police might think she was daffy," Paul said. "So, in desperation, and because there wasn't anything else to do, she decided to 'sit tight,' hoping I would return soon."

When he did, havoc followed.

"Somehow, I wound up back in my car. Opening the car, my wife says I looked like a 'monster' – that's exactly the way she put it! My face was more 'alien' in appearance than human. My features had changed grotesquely, eyes bulging out of their sockets."

She compared his face to the creation of a master makeup artist on the set of a science fiction movie.

Shaking nervously, Mrs. Clark tried to get Paul to climb into the back seat where he could lie down and remain calm while she drove to the nearest hospital. Irene thought a wild beast, or perhaps a poisonous snake, had attacked her husband. Instead of complying with her wishes, Paul pushed her aside with a "violent shove" that sent her sprawling against the opposite door.

Paul slid into the driver's seat and grabbed the steering wheel in a rage.

"Supposedly I was talking incoherently, as if in a trance."

When he gripped the wheel, *it bent out of shape like it was made of putty.*

Within a minute of this remarkable feat – one that would require extraordinary strength – Paul slumped against the dashboard, with his eyes shut and his forehead dripping perspiration.

To Paul, it was all a dream.

"I don't remember a damn thing after leaving the car and hearing the hypnotic sounding voice and seeing the lighted object. If it wasn't for the steering wheel being twisted, I'd say my wife probably made up the whole crazy story."

Since his second meeting with a UFO, Paul feels more strongly than ever that he is being influenced by alien beings. Following his last encounter with ufonauts, Paul Clark's life has stabilized somewhat. He has learned to cope with the "force" trying to control him. At this time, this "average student" is on the threshold of obtaining a degree in electrical engineering!

While Paul's narrative is intriguing in itself, Clark is by no means the only person to have been selected to receive such "special" treatment at the hands of ufonauts. Even high-ranking government officials have received "communications" and been "manipulated."

Somewhere in a locked file cabinet, hidden in some obscure office in the Pentagon, is a two-inch thick file that contains perhaps the best-documented UFO possession case of the decade. The episode actually involves an Air Force officer, the Office of Naval Intelligence, and the CIA.

Until just a few months ago, this manila folder was closely guarded – stamped "Top Secret." Its contents were finally leaked to an enterprising scriptwriter, Robert

Emenegger, on assignment from Sandler Institutional Films, producers of a syndicated documentary on UFOs. The source of this "leak" was, surprisingly enough, Lt. Col. Robert Friend, U.S.A.F., former head of Project Blue Book and well-known UFO debunker for the government.

Now retired, Friend seems to have done an "about-face" on the question of UFOs. Not only does he think they exist, but he also seems to give serious consideration to the even more puzzling UFO contactee cases.

A most revealing interview with Friend appears in the book *UFOs, Past, Present and Future*. In this interview, the former Blue Book spokesman describes a case in which contains all the typical elements of a "UFO possession."

While head of the Air Force's UFO project, Friend says he was informed as a "matter of courtesy" that a well-respected Rear Admiral was especially interested in a woman living in Maine who claimed to be receiving highly advanced and technologically correct information from extraterrestrial beings. These entities were said to contact her while she sat in a trance-like state. The admiral, with the approval of the Air Force, sent two of his most responsible and trusted men to investigate.

Relaxing in a chair before them, the woman expressed her willingness to answer any questions they might have. At this point, she no longer seemed to have control of her physical self. Her body was ostensibly "taken over" by members of an intergalactic organization referred to as the "Universal Association of Planets."

A few minutes into this unprecedented "conversation," one of the officers present, a Navy commander, was told that further answers would be directed *through him*. The officer was instructed to hold a pen lying on a nearby table. The "spacemen" then took control of his hand and proceeded to respond to questions through a process known in parapsychological circles as "automatic writing."

Colonel Friend notes that news of this highly provocative experiment reached Washington almost before the man returned. Top officials at the Central Intelligence Agency also heard about the episode and demanded to know more. It was Friend's duty to find out what he could.

"It was in 1959," he told researcher/scriptwriter Emenegger, "when I was invited to attend a meeting in the security section of a government building in Washington. I was briefed on an experiment that had been conducted with this same Naval commander before a group of CIA members and military personnel. It was described how, after going into a trance, the commander contacted a supposed extraterrestrial being. Several questions were put to him, and answers came back such as: 'Do you favor any government group or race?' Both were 'No.' 'Can we see a spaceship?' The commander, still in a trance, told the group to go to the window and they'd have proof. The group went to the window, where they supposedly observed a UFO. I was told that when a call was made for a radar confirmation, the tower reported that that particular quadrant of the sky was blanked out on radar at that time."

Round Trip to Hell in a Flying Saucer

Friend says that after being briefed on all the details he asked if the officer could attempt a contact for him personally. While he watched, the commander went into a deep trance.

"Questions were put to him, and he printed the answers in rather large letters, using rapid but jerky motions very unlike his natural handwriting. During the course of the questioning, we were told the names of some of the so-called extraterrestrials. One was 'Cril,' another 'Alomar,' and another 'Afta,' purportedly from the planet Uranus."

The former head of Blue Book admits that he was puzzled.

"All those involved were found to be highly credible and responsible professional government men."

After turning in his report, Friend was told by a superior to forget the entire affair. He was informed that the CIA was making their own study and therefore the Air Force had been instructed to "lay off."

What was his reaction to this command? As might be expected, it was a military one.

"Well, when a general tells a colonel to forget it – you forget it!"

Friend later discovered that every witness present in that government office on the day the Naval officer went into a trance was relocated or transferred to other duty.

"To this day," concludes the ex-Air Force officer, "it's an unresolved incident to me. I just don't know what to make of it . . . It seems totally unique in all my experience with investigations of UFOs."

Had he cooperated to any degree with civilians, Colonel Friend probably wouldn't have been so awed with this case. For many years, private organizations have patiently gathered and investigated similar cases. Indeed, whole sects have been founded, based on similar "trance" messages.

There are hundreds of so-called "mental contactees" who claim to receive information and data of a highly advanced scientific and philosophical nature. In fact, during the 1950s and 60s, this method of communicating with UFO occupants (better known as "channeling") became so popular that entities calling themselves "Ashtar," "Agar" and "Monka" were heard from daily somewhere in the world. As far back as the 1920s, the "I AM" religious movement gathered a tremendous number of supporters. Their entire doctrine was derived from messages purportedly delivered through their leader from a "higher" source. And even earlier, around the turn of the century, Madame Blavatsky founded the Theosophical Society. Her "guide" was a long-deceased Tibetan master. Today, Madame Blavatsky might find that her white-robed monk was a silvery-garbed "Venusian." The "source" appears to be the same; only the "messengers" have changed.

There is no doubt that this phenomenon is widespread and it is by no means limited to the U.S. Cases of mind-altering UFO possession seem to be occurring on a global scale and at an alarming rate. There have been reports of entire towns being placed under a strange "spell," *with the simultaneous appearance of flying saucers* in the area.

A large-scale attempt to invade and seize the minds of human beings occurred on April 29, 1967, when a coastal village on the outskirts of Rio de Janeiro became the target of a strange aerial visitor.

For approximately one hour on that day, the hundreds of citizens of Barra de Tijuca, Brazil, were literally forced into establishing contact with an unearthly intelligence, which quickly subdued every single person in town.

The series of disturbing events began at noon, when an emergency telephone call reached Dr. Jeronemo Rodriguez Morales, chief physician at Barra de Tijuca's general hospital. An excited voice explained how a man in his late 60s had fallen unconscious on the beach near town. The caller seemed alarmed because he felt certain the man had suffered a heart attack.

Apologizing to his waiting patients, Dr. Morales immediately drove to the scene. Upon arriving, he found the man brushing sand from his clothes. He was standing and talking quietly to a crowd of people who had gathered to offer help.

"I was merely walking about the sand dunes," the man explained. "I had been watching the birds high above the water when suddenly I blacked out."

An on-the-spot examination, conducted in the hospital's old ambulance, ruled out the possibility of a heart attack, and Dr. Morales decided that the man had suffered a mild case of sunstroke. Knowing he was needed back at the hospital, the physician headed back to his waiting patients. Within minutes, however, the ambulance's shortwave radio blurted out the disturbing news that a fisherman had been discovered in shallow water beneath a nearby bridge and was said to be trembling from shock.

Dr. Morales quickly drove to the area and arrived just in time to see the "stricken" fisherman casually drying himself off and inquiring what all the excitement was about. When the doctor explained that he had blacked out, the man seemed insulted.

"I'm not sick," he argued. "I feel perfectly well."

He assured Dr. Morales that he had been tossing his nets into these waters every day for 20 years without any difficulty and would do so for 20 more.

Within a short while, Dr. Morales received word of six other "stricken" individuals. All followed the identical pattern: people "keeling over," then reviving themselves without aid, and, after a flurry of excitement, vehemently insisting that "it was absolutely nothing."

The next episode, which occurred a little after one p.m., involved a young woman who had been innocently strolling along the beach with her three-year-old child at her side. Suddenly they *both* "passed out." Because of the child's age, Dr.

Morales insisted the youngster be taken to the hospital for an extensive vaccination. The worried mother readily agreed.

While carrying the young boy into the emergency ward, Dr. Morales happened to glance skyward. High above, glistening in the sun, was a tremendous elongated object – a UFO. He watched as the shiny craft wobbled back and forth. It went through an entire series of gyrations. Several times it dropped lower in the sky, offering a better look at its metallic surface. Then, just as rapidly, it would dart back to its former position high in the clear blue sky.

During lunch, several other physicians and nurses on the hospital staff excitedly commented on their own sightings of a "cigar-shaped" craft which they had noticed suspended over the town that day since noon.

Coincidental? Most unlikely. Three days later, the same craft appeared again. Once more, a number of people dropped unconscious to the ground. During these two days, many other individuals were treated at the hospital for headaches and dizziness, no rational cause being found for their illness. From the evidence we have uncovered, the cause seems apparent.

Individuals in the grips of UFO possession often behave irrationally and have even been known to commit criminal acts.

Former NASA Mars mapping expert, Dr. Jacques Vallee, in his third book, **Passport To Magonia**, writes of a chilling account of UFO possession that occurred behind the Iron Curtain.

"In the Soviet Union," Vallee reports, "not very long ago, an eminent scientist in the field of plasma research died under suspicious circumstances – he was murdered by a mentally disturbed woman who pushed him into the path of a train which was speeding into a Moscow subway station. The accused claimed that a 'voice' from space had instructed her to kill this particular man, and she felt unable to resist the order."

Furthermore, the French-born scientist says he has heard from "trustworthy sources" that Russian criminologists are disturbed about the recent increase in cases of this nature.

"Quite often," Vallee maintains, "mentally unstable people are known to run wildly across a street, protesting that they are being pursued by Martians, but the present wave of mental troubles is an aspect of the UFO problem that deserves special attention . . ."

We have long known that UFOs show no political preferences or respect for national boundaries. Aggressive acts have been committed worldwide by individuals who insist that they are in contact with extraterrestrials. Once contact has been established, they are doomed to do what is asked, whether they approve or not!

Here in the U.S., Brad Steiger, a respected former English professor turned author and parapsychologist, has been diligently gathering volumes of pertinent data. In the last few years, he has managed to amass an impressive collection of material dealing with the many peculiar side effects experienced by flying saucer eyewitnesses. He has gathered statistics on all sorts of "UFO oddities," including episodes involving instantaneous teleportation of observers; cases of enhanced psychic abilities; and information pertaining to the bane of all UFO researchers, the Men-In-Black. These areas all contain elements of the UFO possession syndrome.

A short time ago, Brad told me he had talked to a young serviceman who complained of hearing "beeps" inside his head. The loud and annoying noise began immediately after a UFO flew directly over him. Steiger was further convinced of the man's credibility because, "as another researcher and I sat with the young man in a motel room hundreds of miles away from my home, I heard him describe every room in my house and correctly identify objects within each room."

Another victim of UFO possession, a veteran of WWII, told Steiger how he was walking up a street in Italy one night shortly after the Allied occupation, when he heard a buzzing noise above him.

A long time researcher of the paranormal, Brad Steiger warns of the possible dangers one can be confronted with like this apparition that is trying to unscrew a light bulb during a seance.

Round Trip to Hell in a Flying Saucer

As a team Brad and his wife Sherry Hansen Steiger have written dozens of books and are without a doubt the most articulate of both the light and dark sides of the esoteric. Brad is always a welcome guest on talk shows including Coast to Coast AM and Jeff Rense.

The next thing he knew, *he was in northern France.* Not only had he traveled by some unknown means, but *four months had elapsed of which he had no recall.* As if to compensate for the loss of time, however, the soldier found that he had suddenly developed clairvoyant abilities, which he did not possess before the incident occurred.

"Today, he lives in a large Midwestern city," Steiger said, "more disturbed than elated by his 'gift' from unknown donors."

In the July 1975 issue of "Probe the Unknown" magazine, Steiger talked about the morbid experience of a young married couple, Sam and Mary, who, in their spare time, had been attempting to track down and verify sightings of humanoid creatures made in their home state. They made it a regular policy to notify Brad of their individual findings.

One evening, after returning home from an interview with the witnesses of a humanoid sighting, Mary began feeling strange. A terrific headache sent her off to bed early. Once asleep, she was visited in her dreams by "grotesque entities" who told her that they wanted her and that she must leave her husband. They threatened violence if she did not obey. In subsequent "dreams," the confused woman saw "grim, dark-complexioned men beat Sam to death." Here, again, UFO researchers have noted many similar instances where space entities have shown they are able to manipulate the dreams of earthlings. Their "hold," once obtained, is enormous.

Mary's experience didn't end there, however, and the torment continued, becoming more oppressive with each day. Shortly afterwards, her telephone became – as Steiger so aptly phrased it – "an instrument of fear." Mary was awakened late one night, in the middle of one of her bizarre nightmares, by the ringing of the phone. Answering, she heard a cold, calculating voice ask in a mechanical monotone, "Now are you ready to come over to our side?"

According to Steiger, Mary was later visited by a man who appeared at her front door flashing impressive-looking telephone company credentials. He was anxious to know about her "problems." Sam later checked the man's papers and found his "impressive credentials" to be fakes. The man didn't work for the phone company – in any capacity.

Round Trip to Hell in a Flying Saucer

Immediately following the stranger's appearance, Mary began falling into deep, coma-like trances. These trances were usually prefaced "by a headache, a pain in the back of her neck, then a lapse of consciousness," and she seemed powerless to prevent their occurrence.

Needing assistance, the young couple contacted Steiger. He suggested they minimize the situation in their minds.

"The important thing is not to play their game," the author warned. "In many ways, their effect [that of the MIB] is like an echo. Cry out in fear and they'll give you a good reason to fear them."

They took Stieger's advice and were greatly relieved to find that the phenomena came to an abrupt halt.

Sam and Mary were left in peace – but other individuals have not been set free so easily.

Take the case of Hans Launtzen. A trained engineer, Hans is not the type of person to be easily frightened or duped. Writing from his home in Copenhagen, Denmark, this reliable UFO witness filled me in on the details of his December 7, 1967, encounter with two disc-shaped craft.

"At the time, I was on a walking tour with four friends in a wooded area not far from Hareskoven. Because of a severe case of hepatitis, I found it difficult to keep up the brisk pace of my associates. I had to stop several times, because I was so tired. At that time, my liver was extremely distended."

As the group passed a clearing, Launtzen asked his friends if he might rest a few minutes. They of course said it was okay.

"Suddenly, we all saw two great yellow globes about 50 yards from where we were standing. For some reason, at this point I asked if I could walk into the woods for 10 minutes. My friends agreed. I had no intention of walking toward the UFOs, as we could not see them anymore. I seemed to be walking in a trance – like one who is being guided. I just walked. Then, I felt the presence of something above, but could not see anything."

At this point, Hans began to feel a throbbing pressure in his head, which seemed to bring on a telepathic conversation with whoever was "guiding" him.

"They told me that I should *give* – and not *receive*. And that I should not be alone. And they said, 'You are only standing here by the help of your friends.' Then whoever was doing the talking seemed surprised and said, 'This is the first time.' I don't know exactly what he was referring to, except that he probably meant that it was the first time they had met anyone quite like myself. They told me that I had a very strong power and that it would soon become even stronger."

Hans asked the invisible voice "to make it so this power could not be misused."

With this final request, the conversation ended. For some time afterwards, Hans continued to walk in a trance. Eventually, he found himself at the place where he had first seen the yellow globes.

"There was an open area which I decided to cross. I don't remember walking across it. All of a sudden, I heard my friends calling for me. I looked at my watch and saw that more than an hour had elapsed."

Returning to his friends, Hans was told that they had been searching for him during this period.

"They thought I had gotten lost."

Strange things then started to happen. Hans found himself running to their parked automobile. Only an hour before, he had barely been able to walk because of his liver condition.

"I realized that I had been cured of my otherwise chronic hepatitis. On my next visit to the clinic, the doctors told me that my liver had returned to its normal size. Blood tests showed that it was functioning as any healthy liver should!"

The medical experts could not offer any explanation for the change in Hans Launtzen's physical condition.

"I didn't dare tell them about my contact," he admitted.

The oddest part of the story remains to be told. Soon after the experience, the Danish engineer found his entire life and personality beginning to change.

"I felt something spreading inside my body. Something was actually moving up along my spine from my lower back to my neck and the back of my head. This movement was accompanied by a pleasurable feeling. It made me stand up and make strange movements and turns."

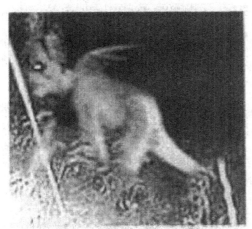

A monster made in Photo Shop or a real demon let loose upon the land?

He explained that he was in a trance state much of the time.

"I just had to follow whoever was pulling the strings. Afterwards, I became extremely frightened as to what might be going on. I began to imagine all sorts of weird things!"

As it was, the "feeling" began to spread throughout his entire nervous system. After several months, pain would frequently shoot through his arms, chest, back and neck.

"I had never experienced such strong pains before in my life," Hans declared.

Gradually, however, the effects of the pain began to subside.

Then Launtzen found that he was frequently becoming overwhelmed by the most pleasurable states of mind.

"It was so wonderful," he stated, "that it cannot be described."

On other occasions, the contactee said he felt a strong fear and anxiety, so much so that he was afraid to leave his apartment.

"I went through periods of extreme sorrow, depression and desperation. I have never experienced such severe mental suffering in all my life."

It was at this point that he began to realize he no longer had any free will to think and believe as he wished.

"I would converse with people, voicing opinions on a wide range of topics. Later, I discovered that whatever I had heard, I had to believe and act accordingly. Of course, this created great confusion. Strange thoughts started to come into focus. I knew they did not originate inside me because they were often of a very negative and destructive character. It was not possible for me to stop these thoughts or overpower them, although I tried – believe me, I tried!"

The cover of one of Brad Steiger's most recent offerings on the subject of monsters. He has written over 150 books with millions of copies in print worldwide.

Hans said that he had never before thought it possible that such a chaotic state of affairs could possibly exist in one person's mind!

Eight years have since passed and Hans finds himself once again leading a normal existence. When asked for his comments on the entire episode, he replied, "It has been the most wonderful and pleasurable experience of my entire life. On the other hand, it has also been the most painful, horrible thing that has ever happened to me. Before, I had a bad liver. Now, I am strong and healthy again. I am most thankful to the UFOs for having cured my otherwise chronic hepatitis, without which I would never have been able to resume my work and other normal activities."

Obviously both positive and negative factors have been experienced by those who have come within close range of these strange craft.

Realizing that something most peculiar is manifesting itself, we are still left with a gnawing question: Is an invasion force poised at our atmospheric doorstep? And if so, is their proposed takeover being done for our own welfare, or for some as yet unknown, and perhaps sinister, reason?

Round Trip to Hell in a Flying Saucer

Logically, we would like to believe that the metallic ships described eons ago by the pharaohs as "celestial sun discs" are manned by a super-race of benevolent "space brothers" who harbor genuine concern for our world. But, then again, is this really the case? Are we actually being aided in our moment of need by "interplanetary wise men," or is some devious scheme unfolding as we ponder this very question? Could it be that an interplanetary battle is being waged by rival starmen to gain control of Homo sapiens? Maybe, as some outspoken researchers have stated, a "war of the worlds" is being waged, not here on the physical plane, but in some other dimension.

Veteran investigators of the paranormal will undoubtedly recognize that attempts to gain mastery over the human race are nothing new. As intriguing as cases of UFO possession may be, a direct comparison can easily be found in the lore of the occult. Indeed, spirit and demonic possession has been written about for centuries. It is almost a commonplace phenomenon in theological and psychic circles. Only recently, because of the immense popularity of the motion picture "The Exorcist," has the subject come to the attention of the general public. Many moviegoers found this picture uncomfortably realistic.

Like the hideous demons of old, it would seem that at least some UFOnauts have developed the ability to control certain individuals they have selected to do their bidding. Many times, I have sympathetically looked on – much like the young priest in "The Exorcist" – as a UFO observer undergoes a dramatic change in character and personality. It is uncanny – and difficult to explain rationally.

There is, however, another school of thought regarding this phenomenon.

Individuals such as Paul Clark, whose story we detailed earlier, insist that any direct manipulation of humans by space people is being done for our benefit.

"I've been led to believe," says Paul, "that there is a grand event slated to occur in the not-too-distant future. I have no idea when this event will transpire, or what it will consist of, but I do know that it will be earthshaking and will affect almost everyone."

Another good example of what seems to be a "positive" case of UFO possession involves none other than Uri Geller, the extraordinary psychic. Reportedly he is able to accomplish a variety of astonishing feats, including the bending of metal by means of psycho-kinesis; interfering with, and rendering inoperable, various electrical and mechanical devices; and beaming in on the telepathic thoughts of others. Geller has recently been linked with extraterrestrials. He openly acknowledges that his powers originate from a source "outside" himself.

Dr. Andrija Puharich, the man responsible for bringing Uri to this country several years ago, admits that his gifted protégé is an agent for inhabitants of a planet located in another time-space zone. All the remarkable things that go on around Uri are, he says, directed by these "solar beings."

Though it has a definite Space Age twist, Uri's biography contains all the ingredients found in a suspenseful occult or gothic novel. During the occasions he slips into a hypnotic trance, Uri's features are said to change. In addition, a strange voice – definitely not his own – is heard from the psychic's mouth. Regaining consciousness, Uri has no recollection of what has transpired. And although Puharich has attempted to record these "foreign" tongues for posterity, he has constantly run into problems. When the tape is replayed, it is frequently blank. Other times, the cassette itself will vanish right out of the recorder!

Both Uri Geller and Paul Clark are adamant that there is a specific reason why they have been "called" to represent this unearthly power. They agree that some monumental event is slated to happen within a short time, and it's essential we be fully prepared for it. Geller and Clark also agree that the ufonauts are using them for the good of Mankind. We are told that they have a definitive plan and have simply decided to utilize human agents to get the job done faster.

Whatever the answers might be, an exhaustive study of the UFO puzzle shows "higher powers" are at play. They are attempting to systematically guide or influence our destiny. A sufficient number of strange occurrences have been reported which prove beyond a reasonable doubt that at least *some* of these "other-world travelers" are out to control the course of our civilization – *if not by physical force then by the direct manipulation of human minds!*

Priest Performs Blessing at Location of Imp Sightings

Inexplicata
The Journal of Hispanic Ufology
January 6, 2005
Source: El Once Digital
Date: January 6, 2005

Residents of Parana's Antartida Argentina district requested the presence of the parish priest of the Our Lady of Guadalupe church in order to receive spiritual assistance after the alleged apparition of imps.

Under these circumstances, Father Eduardo went to their homes, performed several prayers, blessed the site and sprinkled holy water in the homes and trees where the strange figures were seen "with the purpose of calming the spirits seen."

Neighbors said: "Following the manifestation of the imps and their exposure in the media, we began to feel fear. For this reason we asked the parish priest to assist us."

Once the subject became widely known, "many people came by and notified others. There were even mentalists or parapsychologists who gave their opinions on radio and in other media," said one of the spokeswomen for the group, who swears to having seen seven imps on Friday, December 30, who attacked personnel from the Fifth Sheriff's Office with stones during the moment of greatest tension.

The fact [of the imps' appearance] itself was not confirmed by the authorities, but they did agree to note that something threw stones at them from the dark.

The local parish priest, who requested that his name not be published "due to hierarchical matters," remarked that "One must be careful with the things that are being said. Some remarks must be taken with a pinch of salt and, without saying that anyone is lying, it can be understood that there is a great deal of fantasy in these remarks."

"The subject of imps has no logic and cannot be rationally explained. I know that some people came to church asking for spiritual assistance," he summarized.

He made it clear that, "It is very strange [for people to say] that they flew and turned up everywhere. [But I know] they will continue to believe in this, which borders on fantasy."

On the other hand, he cautioned that "no one has requested an exorcism, but this can only be authorized by the local bishop when faced with definite proof of the Devil's presence. From what we were told, there is nothing diabolical or related to evil in this place."

Along these lines, he differentiated between "assistance to souls in purgatory, which must be aided through prayer, but to go from there to say that those souls can turn into imps is another story."

Another resident told Diario Uno that in the canyon area "men and women can be seen involved in strange things, such as practicing some sort of rituals like Umbanda, which request the presence of spirits for doing good and evil."

Translation (c) 2005. Scott Corrales, Institute of Hispanic Ufology (IHU).
Special thanks to Christian Quintero, Planeta UFO.

A possible Satanic - Uncle Sam collaboration has not been missed in the amazing occult art of David Dees (www.DeesIllustration.com)

Satanic Influences Inside The Pentagon

By Timothy Green Beckley

Everyone loves Nick Redfern. He is both a serious researcher and an easygoing sort of guy. The time passes quickly when you're in his company – along with that of a Guiness Beer. Like the foaming brew, Redfern hails from across the pond. But since his marriage to an American gal, he has transplanted his British roots to the State of Texas. Indeed, I've done several interviews now with the smooth-domed investigator who has written more books that anyone in the field, with the undisputed exception of Brad Steiger.

Round Trip to Hell in a Flying Saucer

In September 2010, Anomalist Books published Nick Redfern's latest book, *Final Events And the Secret Government Group on UFOs and the Afterlife*, which looks at the history of a hidden think-tank within the US Government that believes that, rather than having alien origins, UFOs are really a tool of the Devil. We recently sat down with Nick and spoke with him about his *Final Events* book, and the beliefs of those in the Government who hold to the "aliens are demons" theory. Redfern might have ruffled a few feathers among the top brass of UFOlogy, but his dealings with this group inside the corridors of the Pentagon give us cause to believe that Uncle Sam is waging a cosmic war, at least on some level, with the great pretender Satan himself. Nick's answers to our questions opened a flood gate – better yet, a tidal wave – of valuable information on a subject that for so many years has been predigested.

BECKLEY: When did you get wind that there was actually a think tank or secret group in the government who took seriously the idea that demons and UFOs go hand in hand?

REDFERN: The lead came from a man named Ray Boeche. Ray is an Anglican priest and he is a former State Director of the Mutual UFO Network (MUFON), for the state of Nebraska. In late 1991, Ray was contacted by two physicists working on a secret Department of Defense project to contact – and to try and exploit the mental powers of – what they called "Non-Human Entities," but that are more commonly known as the Grays. Ray met the guys for a clandestine discussion in Lincoln, Nebraska, in November 1991, and that's how the story started. It was as if there were people in the official world that wanted to see if the mind-power of the Grays could be utilized as a form of mind-weaponry by the Pentagon. In other words, it was something along the lines of a next-generation Remote-Viewing type program.

But the idea was that instead of training the mind to psychically spy on the enemy, it would be to psychically assassinate them using powers of the mind, gleaned from the Grays. But, the DoD physicists told Ray Boeche that the further they got into the project the more they came to believe that the Grays were highly deceptive, and they also came to believe the Grays were actually – and quite literally – deceptive demons from Hell, who were here to deceive us about their true agenda, which was to bring people over to the dark-side and prepare things for Armageddon, but to do it under the guise of a faked alien appearance.

The DoD physicists wanted Ray's opinion on all this, because he had a background as a priest and as a MUFON State Director. And it was when I began to investigate Ray's story in 2007, after extensively interviewing him about it, that I got on the trail of the think-tank group behind all this – that calls themselves The Collins Elite – and managed to get some interviews with them, and copies of their files too. And, when I had enough data, that's when I decided to write my book on the subject: Final Events *And the Secret Government Group on UFOs and the Afterlife.*

BECKLEY: What evidence did they offer you that there is a relationship or a link that would prove their theory?

REDFERN: The Collins Elite did not offer any evidence at all. Like all worldwide religions, Christianity is faith-based, which essentially equates with the idea of belief without demonstrable evidence of literal existence. So, they had a lot of belief-driven ideas, theories and conclusions.

But, all of them were lacking in terms of having actual evidence to support the notion that the UFO presence on Earth was a Satanic deception, but it is what they believed. So that people will not be in any doubt at all as to where I stand on all this, my personal view is that the conclusions/beliefs of the Collins Elite are wrong. I think the whole idea that this is all Satanic and that only Christianity has it right is far too simplistic. How do they know other religions are wrong? The answer is simple: they don't know. They just believe all other religions are wrong. How do they – or we – know that any religion is correct? I would agree with the Collins Elite on a couple of things, however: I actually gave up on the E.T. hypothesis a long time ago, and I suspect we're actually dealing with extra-dimensional entities, and they may not have our best interests at heart. I do believe that they might be malevolent and deceitful, and that we're not seeing the full picture. But that doesn't automatically mean they are something that stepped straight out of a Hell that no one can prove exists. I don't personally believe in the whole Heaven and Hell concept. I think it's far too simplistic, and is a scenario created to control people via fear and guilt. But, the fact that there are several groups within the Department of Defense and the Pentagon that do believe this is what makes it a fascinating story. And that's why I decided to write my *Final Events* book.

BECKLEY: Did they offer you up any specific cases?

REDFERN: Yes. They claimed that the whole modern era of Ufology was the work of Aleister Crowley and Jack Parsons. From January to March 1918, Crowley received a series of visions via his "Scarlet Woman," one Roddie Minor; this is the infamous Amalantrah Working. Throughout his life, Crowley had a number of these Scarlet Women, all of whom essentially acted as channels or vessels for the transfer of messages perceived to be of angelic and/or demonic origin. But Crowley was interested in more than mere messages; it was his deep desire to invite, or to invoke, the entities behind the messages into our world and to engage them on a one-to-one basis. Crowley was certainly no fool and he was fully aware of the potentially hazardous and disastrous implications that might very well result from his planned door-opening activities. This did not, however, in any way dissuade him from enthusiastically pressing ahead.

Researcher Nick Redfern tests the waters (and a few other things) when he recounts in his recent Final Events book his dealings with a a mysterious government think tank that believes ufos are demonic in scope.

And, it seems, he succeeded beyond his wildest dreams – or nightmares, maybe. It was during the Amalantrah Working, which included the ingestion of hashish and mescaline to achieve an altered state of consciousness, that Crowley made contact with an inter-dimensional entity known as Lam, a large-headed figure that could have quite easily passed for a close relative of the enigmatic being that stares eerily forth from the cover of *Communion*, Whitley Strieber's alien abduction book published in 1987. The Collins Elite also focused, as I mentioned, on the brilliant, maverick rocket-scientist Jack Parsons, who died under controversial circumstances in 1952. Parsons, a devotee of Crowley, undertook in 1946 the infamous Babalon Working. Like Crowley, Parsons was fascinated by the notion of opening dimensional gateways, and this is precisely what the Collins Elite believe happened – that Crowley and Parsons opened the doors to this demonic deception in a fashion that allowed for (in the Collins Elite's view, at least) these entities to confront us in a build-up to the final battle between good and evil, but under the guise of aliens.

As for other cases, the Collins Elite also came to believe that the whole Contactee/Space Brother movement was demonic. For example, the fact the 1950s Contactee George Hunt Williamson made some of his contacts via Ouija-boards was seen as evidence by the group that he was being deceived, because the Collins Elite concluded Ouija-boards are tools that demons can exploit. On this same issue, when they began to research George Adamski, they found that his co-author on his first book, *Flying Saucers Have Landed* – an Irishman named Desmond Leslie – had a very interesting background. Desmond Leslie's father, Sir Shane Leslie, was a big student of the occult, and had a deep fascination with the teachings of the aforementioned Aleister Crowley. So, the Collins Elite was putting together strands like this to support their theories and beliefs.

BECKLEY: Were all the members of this group Christian fundamentalists, or did the group include atheists and agnostics as well?

REDFERN: They were all, or came to be, Christians, and some of them were indeed full-blown Fundamentalists. So, in other words, their investigation that concluded UFOs are demonic was hardly what we could call an unbiased investigation and conclusion.

BECKLEY: Are any of its members famous?

REDFERN: As far as I can tell, all the members were regular people in the military, government, intelligence world, and Department of Defense. However, it does appear to be the case, from the story I uncovered, that they deeply influenced the mindset of none other than President Ronald Reagan, who was highly interested in UFOs and who also had a very disturbing interest in "End Times" scenarios, both of which, of course, are central aspects of the beliefs of the Collins Elite.

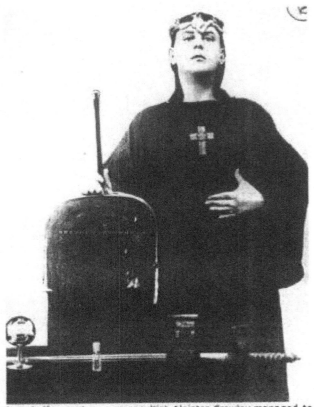

Over half a century ago occultist Aleister Crowley managed to conjure up a variety of demonic forces some of whom look remarkable like the UFO entities seen today.

BECKLEY: What exactly is their concept of a demon? Are we talking Satan's henchmen here?

REDFERN: Yes, that was their conclusion – that these things are the literal manifestation of Satan's hordes. However, they believe that such demonic entities lack physical form. In other words, their natural appearance is not of the typical horror movie image of horns, glowing eyes and a fork-tail, etc. Rather, they believe these entities are essentially non-physical, and along the lines of pure energy. But that they can create deceptive imagery with which to deceive us that looks physical, but really isn't. In other words, they believe the whole UFO phenomenon is illusion-based, and they believe abduction stories are actually nothing more than solely illusions projected into the minds of the abductee to further instill this alien imagery. The Collins Elite do not believe that any abduction experience has ever taken place outside of the confines of the human brain – partly due to these entities not having physical form as we understand it.

BECKLEY: What is the weirdest idea they laid down to you?

REDFERN: That these demons farm human souls, as a form of energy, as sustenance, an answer I'll get into deeper with the John Lear question below.

BECKLEY: Are they shape shifters? Do they abduct humans? Experiment on them? Cut them into little pieces?

REDFERN: No, the Collins Elite do not believe that these entities have any physical interaction with us – at least not in the way that we understand the term. They believe the whole alien abduction scenario is a scam, a series of brain-induced hallucinations provoked by these entities as a means to reinforce the idea that they are aliens here to experiment on us, etc. In other words, for the Collins Elite, abductions are a way for these creatures to deceive us further. So, there's no actual physical interaction with us at all, the group believes. But they can provoke hallucinatory

Maverick rocket scientist Jack Parsons was fascinated by the notion of opening dimensional gateways. He is said to have opened the doors to the demonic deception that will end as the final battle between good and evil.

imagery in the mind: aliens, goblins, Bigfoot, etc., to make us believe we're seeing something physically and externally, the Collins Elite concludes.

BECKLEY: The always controversial John Lear has said that aliens are sucking human souls. Did anything like this ever come up with the group you are in touch with?

REDFERN: Yes, this was one of the central themes of the beliefs of the Collins Elite. They came to the conclusion that the Earth is a farm, and that we are the cattle. They came to accept – based on interviews with a number of people who had Near Death Experiences, theologians, experts on Demonology, etc. – that these entities essentially harvest and feed upon a poorly defined "soul-energy" upon our deaths. In essence, the Collins Elite thinks that because these demonic creatures are basically energy-based, that our energy feeds and fuels them. The group interviewed a number of NDE witnesses who claimed to have seen vast, never-ending "soul-factories" while in a near-death state, and who also claimed these Gray-like entities process us, slaughter-house/farm-like one by one, and extract energy – rather like the idea of a demonic vampire.

BECKLEY: Any tie in with human sacrifices or animal mutilations?

REDFERN: Ray Boeche was told about human sacrifices connected to the project, but the information given was literally just that, and not expanded upon. I do have information on animal mutilations, however. I didn't put this in my *Final Events* book, so this is a bit of a scoop for you! One of the things that a former member of the Collins Elite told me was that there were several groups in Government that believed in the demonic angle. But, whereas the Collins Elite were supposedly trying to keep these entities at bay, groups like those that approached Ray Boeche were trying to enter into Faustian-style pacts with them. And one of the things that I was told was that there was a group buried very deeply in the U.S. Army that was involved in the cattle mutilations, but that had nothing to do with aliens, but that did offer an explanation for the whole "Black Helicopter" angle. Supposedly, this Army group doing the mutes were actually killing the cattle and taking blood and organs as sacrificial items, that would then be used in ancient rites and archaic rituals to both appease and summon up these "Non Human Entities" as they described them, in an effort to try and engage them and use their mental powers.

BECKLEY: So were they at any point looking to tell the public of their findings?

REDFERN: Yes, they were. This was a very controversial area, because they were unsure for a while how to do this. Whether their belief-system has any merit to it or not, they did recognize that telling the public the truth as they saw it, would be a fraught task, and one that could lead to the collapse of society, when the realization sunk in that we are essentially living on a farm that is designed one day to allow for the reaping and "digestion" of our souls. They came to the conclusion that subtly, bit by bit, government and the intelligence world should be infiltrated to a greater degree by Christian extremists and then combine that with trying to almost create like a fascist-Christian government that would rule the nation with a rod of iron, instill this belief system about UFOs in the population, and tell them that a strong denial of these beings can actually hold them at bay. That's what the Collins Elite believes – that if we deny their existence or deny their power, it actually has a way to lessen their ability to interact with us. But the Collins Elite concluded that, for the entire population to hold such deep beliefs, it would require the nation being placed in literal lock-down status, and near-totalitarian indoctrination of old-time religion. And, if we look at the world today, we do see more and more people (some of them quite insane people, too) trying to make the Government and the military more and more dominated by religion. So, maybe they really are beginning this process.

BECKLEY: Do they believe an actual day of tribulation is at hand?

REDFERN: Yes, they do. They believe these entities know they are doomed when the final battle between good and evil, God and Satan, comes to pass, and they believe these demons, as Judgment Day draws near, will create a worldwide, faked, UFO sighting wave all across the planet, and that we will be deceived into thinking these are friendly aliens come to help, when in reality – the Collins Elite believes – these will really be the demons, seducing as many millions as they can with their ET-driven lies, as a means to take as many of our souls as possible with them when the final battle arrives. At least, that's the Collins Elite's conclusion on it. Personally, I'm always very wary of prophecies, future-predictions, etc.

BECKLEY: What did they figure would be the reaction of religious leaders and of the average guy in the street? Isn't this likely to blow the minds of everyone? I know it would blow mine, probably yours as well?

REDFERN: The sheer fear of learning that we are basically cattle whose whole existence is geared so that these demonic entities can feed on our souls after death – in the form of ominous, never-ending soul factories – was deemed as being too terrifying to tell people, at least right now. Which is why the Collins Elite concluded the best way to do this would be by spending the next 10 or 15 years, basically, secretly building up a kind of Christian dictatorship that would have an iron-grip on the population and then when we're under their vise-like control, even if there was mass panic the Government would invoke the worst parts of the Patriot Act and lock-down the country with martial law, curfews, etc., and have constant indoctrination in schools, on TV, etc., until people came to accept it, and came to believe that they could hold these creatures at bay with deep, fundamentalist belief. But the problem, as the Collins Elite sees it, is how to get the population into that mindset – and that's where this whole religious "New World Order" plan comes into play.

BECKLEY: So is Satan real? Has he or is he paying us a visit in a flying saucer?

REDFERN: My personal view is that, no, Satan and his minions are not paying us visits in flying saucers, or under a deceptive guise of aliens. Ironically, for someone who has written a book about how a group in the Government really does believe this is going on, I'm personally not a religious person at all. I have never been to church, aside from weddings and funerals. And, I find it hard to understand how anyone can say with confidence that this religion, or that religion, or any religion is definitely wrong and that someone else's religion is definitely right.

I'm not saying there's definitely no afterlife. But, when we have countless religions all across the world that have varying beliefs – sometimes wildly varying beliefs – then I don't see how anyone can say for certain their view is right, without hard evidence. And as for the Collins Elite, their conclusions lack hard evidence and are based solely on belief and faith, which is never a good thing. If any religion could provide me with proof – not deeply held beliefs or deep faith, but actual proof – that they're right, maybe my personal views might change. But, no religion in the history of the planet has ever proved anything, and the Collins Elite can't prove that demons from Hell are visiting in flying saucers. They can only offer their beliefs that this is going on, and that's not enough.

BECKLEY: Wouldn't you say this sounds pretty outlandish? Certainly Stanton Friedman isn't likely to add your theory to his lecture program. Do any serious UFOlogists accept this theory?

REDFERN: It certainly is outlandish! I think that what the story I relate in *Final Events* tells us is that the government often secretly funds think tank groups with unusual ideas and theories. And the reason the government does this is to try and determine if there is any intelligence/espionage or national security issue that has a bearing on the work of the group, and if any sort of advantage can be gained in these intelligence and national security areas by looking into things along the lines of the Collins Elite. Yes, there are a number of UFOlogists who do believe the demonic theory for UFOs is correct. There's the aforementioned Ray

Boeche, who was a State Director with MUFON, and who did a lot of work in the 1980s looking into the famous Rendlesham Forest, England UFO landing case in 1980. Michael Heiser, author of the book, *The Facade*, is a strong believer in the demonic angle. As are authors/researchers Guy and Nicole Malone, and Joe Jordan, who works at NASA's Kennedy Space Center, and who is heavily involved in researching alien abduction cases in relation to the demonic angle.

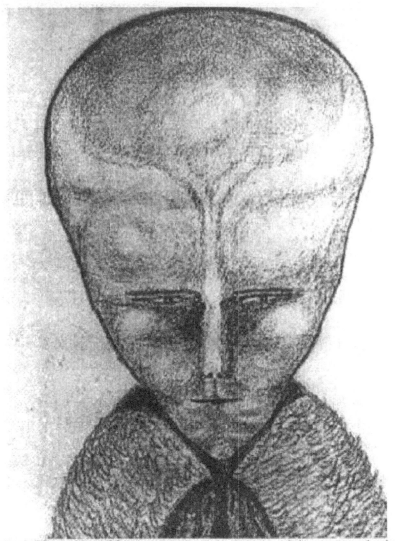

A striking resemblance appears between Aleister Crowley's materialized being known as "Lam" and the Greys encountered by many UFO witnesses and abductees.

The Navy Establishes Contact, But With Whom?

March, 1997 - The Times of London

DEFENSE CHIEF WARNS OF 'SATANIC UFOs'

by Ruth Gledhill, Religion Correspondent

A former head of the (British) Armed Forces has helped to form a pressure group to warn of the satanic nature of many unidentified flying objects.

Admiral of the Fleet Lord Hill-Norton, Chief of Defence Staff, 1971-73, is involved with UFO Concern out of worry that some UFO encounters are "definitely antithetical to orthodox Christian belief," according to today's Church Times.

The Rev Paul Inglesby, a sub-deacon in an Orthodox church, who is secretary of UFO Concern, said the truth about UFOs has been suppressed for many years. He had never seen a UFO himself but knew many who had. "It is what they do and the messages that come from them that are anti-Christian, or demonic." A memo about the new group had been sent to the editors of various UFO magazines, and letters of support had been received by, among others, a professor and a prisoner, he added.

Gordon Creighton, a Buddhist who edits Flying Saucer Review, said the group's founders were right to be concerned: "I do believe that the great bulk of these phenomena are what is called satanic."

Dr. David Clarke fully admits that he is often seen as a skeptic, though he would rather think of himself as a journalist and a historian who remains open minded that "some UFOs might have an exotic origin, most probably as UAPs – Unidentified Atmospheric Phenomena." Nonetheless, Clarke is the only researcher who followed up on Lord Hill-Norton's satanic revelations regarding the strangers in our midst. Adding to the package, he revealed that Hill-Norton had a cohort in a man of the cloth who also took the phenomenon exceedingly seriously and was also in Naval deployment during his career.

"*The UFO Concern Report*," Clarks explained, "was a 'restricted edition' aimed at alerting 'top people' to the dangers posed by UFOs and abductions. While Hill-Norton's memo was published in *Flying Saucer Review,* it got very little publicity in the mainstream UFO press. Some of the big names who initially supported it later distanced themselves because they didn't agree with the emphasis placed by the report's author, sub-deacon Paul Inglesby, on the spiritual dangers posed by UFOs.

"Inglesby was, before conversion to the Orthodox faith, an Anglican priest by the name of Rev. Eric Inglesby. It is largely through his and Gordon Creighton's influence that the demonic explanation of UFOs has been kept alive in Britain.

Rev Paul Inglesby of the U.K. organized a group to warn that aliens could be under Satan's control and he warned Her Majesty not to view the film Close Encounters of the Third Kind because of this.

"Paul Inglesby, formerly the Rev. Eric Inglesby, warned of the spiritual dangers of UFOs and wrote **UFOs and the Christian** (1978). Born in 1915, Inglesby is probably Britain's longest-serving UFO theorist, with contacts at the highest levels both in the church and in the British establishment. Much of what has been written on this subject in the UK emanates from his persistent and meticulous writings, even though most ufologists I've questioned have never heard of him.

"Inglesby is also unique in that his interest began a whole decade before the flying saucer era. In 1938, while serving with the Royal Navy under Lord Mountbatten, he contracted a tropical disease and was left dangerously ill for three months. During this time he underwent a 'devastating spiritual experience' during which he saw visions of a future atomic war and demonic forces controlling spaceships and nuclear weapons. While trapped in this timeless limbo, '...not only did I witness future events, in a mental telepathic sort of way, but throughout the whole of this time a battle was raging for possession of my soul.'

"Fortunately, Inglesby's prayers were answered and he was saved from the clutches of the demonic forces. Following his baptism of fire, he naturally remained on the lookout for evidence of evil influences. When the first reports of flying saucers appeared in British newspapers in 1947, Inglesby felt his visions were about to become reality. He found the extraterrestrial hypothesis, prevalent in the media and ufology, an unsatisfactory explanation for the phenomenon. Gradually, he came to believe the contacts and messages passed on by the UFO occupants were, at least partly, demonic in origin.

"Conversion to Christianity followed and in 1964 he was ordained as a priest in the Church of England. His conversion to the Orthodox Church came in 1980 following a meeting with Fr. Seraphim Rose at a monastery in California. Fr. Rose had written a treatise on UFOs as demonic signs which proved to be highly influential on Inglesby's developing theories. The monk advised him to take refuge in orthodox doctrine so that he would have spiritual protection in the campaign against flying saucery that was to occupy much of his life.

"Like other fundamentalists, Inglesby saw the decline of traditional religion and the arrival of New Age and UFO-based religious cults such as the Moonies as a sign that the End Times were imminent. Of course, this wasn't a new idea, or one exclusive to Christians. As Forteans are well aware, belief in the approaching apocalypse is a massively important theme throughout the history of ufology. It is particularly associated with UFO cults whose leaders have predicted world cataclysms in messages supposedly passed on by the space people. Fundamentalists, however, interpret these messages as being demonically inspired.

"Before the End Times can arrive, Satan must implement his evil plan for world domination. In order for it to succeed, large numbers of people – particularly those in high places – will be brainwashed or possessed by evil spirits in order to prepare them for the final battle on the side of the Antichrist. This idea of a creeping take-over alarmed those who believed UFOs were demonic in origin. Not for them the War of the Worlds invasion of aliens with machines and death rays. They feared a more deadly takeover of human souls and the horrifying idea of crossbreeding between demons and human beings to create hybrid creatures."

So much for Her Majesty's Navy personnel's absorption in UFOs. Meanwhile, back in the good old U.S. of A., the public has long been lead to believe that it is the responsibility of the United States Air Force to chase UFOs as they transverse the heavens and to analyze the massive amounts of data collected from the thousands of sighting reports gathered across the four corners of our nation.

Truth of the matter is that among the military services, the Navy seems to have more ties with UFOs – and of course USOs (Unidentified Submerged Objects) – than any other branch of the armed forces. And quite a bit of

The late Lord Hill-Norton UK's Minister of Defence saw the possible connection between UFOs and demonic forces which he warned about in a privately distributed report.

what they have gathered could be categorized as bizarre or truly "out of the ordinary."

I had the opportunity to meet Lord Hill-Norton, a Five Star Admiral referenced above, who headed Her Royal Majesty's fleet. He was introduced to me by my late friend Brinsley Le Poer Trench who, as the 7th Earl of Clancarty, chaired the House of

Lord's unofficial UFO group which I was invited to address. We spoke only briefly and at that point I didn't know of his demonic leanings toward the nature of UFOs. I did later see a privately issued publication called *The Concern Report* in which Hill-Norton attended to the matter of telling his fellow UFOlogical researchers that they should look more closely at a possible satanic intervention on Earth as related to the appearance of UFOs.

Case for the UFO and the Roswell Crash

We come now to the case of Dr. M.K. Jessup. The truth is Jessup's books on UFOs never really sold all that well.

Sure he had his followers....but they certainly were NOT his peers. Sure Jessup was a reputable astronomer who had gotten his MS degree at the Lamont-Hussey Observatory in 1926, but he also just happened to be a potboiler journalist. His books were mainly sought after by UFO fans and fanatics. There was no love lost between Jessup and the rest of the scientific community who probably would best describe him as a "trader." After all, he wrote about UFO bases on the moon and the *hoof prints of the devil on roof tops* (hmmm, very interesting!).

Jessup seemed convinced that there were elements of both good and evil to be found in the behavioral patterns of the occupants of these stellar craft. Apparently, he was of the opinion that UFOs had been with us for a long time, as he wrote in a book called **UFOs and the Bible,** keenly aware of the connection between the saucer mystery and archaeological evidence pointing to the fact that the space gods had mingled with ancient humankind.

Reprint Of A Rare Manuscript!

The Allende Letters And The VARO Edition of The Case For The UFOs

by Morris K. Jessup

A Navy think tank reprinted a classic book by astronomer Morris K. Jessup which contained the marginal notes of two interplanetary "gypsies" who discussed such topics as invisibility and teleportation.

What Dr. Jessup has become best known for is his connection with a special annotated edition of his *Case for the UFO* book, whereby a civilian contractor, on behalf of none other than the Office of Naval Research, had reproduced less than a dozen copies of this work complete with unorthodox annotations written by a bizarre duo who seemed to be "extraterrestrial gypsies" or interplanetary nomads. The notes contained references to time travel and the Philadelphia Experiment (now part of our lexicon), a project in which a huge warship had been made to vanish and its crew was thrown into another dimension. Several crewmembers were caught between this world and the next, having melted into the hull of the battleship in a horrific twisting of man and metal. The notes are very cryptic and the question as to why the ONR would want such arcane knowledge about magnetic fields, antigravity and cloaking techniques passed to them has long puzzled many in the UFO community, though it becomes perhaps a bit more obvious now that all the "facts" have been gathered into one place.

Eventually, the annotated version of Jessup's work found its way into the hands of Commander George Hoover, who had entered the Navy in 1944 to become a pilot before he moved to the Office of Naval Research to conduct a variety of early space-related programs side by side with Werner von Braun, resulting in the first American satellite. According to sources, Hoover, "in an official capacity," knew all about the UFO crash at Roswell, regarding both the recovery of the downed craft as well as the examination of its occupants. Obviously, from what can be gleaned from his sole interview on the subject, it is apparent that Hoover felt there was something askance about the visitors that put them in the "be-careful-how- you-deal-with-them category," as they possessed the unmistakable ability to cloud minds and manipulate humans.

UFO Iconoclast blogger Anthony Bragalin posted the following on Monday, October 11, 2010 under the title *Renowned U.S. Navy Commander Reveals Stunning Roswell Crash Secret:*

In 1995, George W. Hoover, Sr., left his testament for history with an associate of the History Channel. Some of Hoover's hints about Roswell that he had made to his own son were later corroborated in private, off-the-record conversations that Commander Hoover had with researcher William J. Birnes PhD, JD.

This included a visit by Birnes and others to Hoover's home in Pacific Palisades, CA. Birnes had sought out Hoover for information on a design issue for a technical "cockpit display project" that Birnes was working on at the time. The talk at some point turned to UFOs. In correspondence with this author, Birnes detailed his experience with Hoover to me and indicated that Hoover was lucid, articulate and serious.

Commander George Hoover had finally revealed what he really knew about Roswell. He explained the truth as he had learned it all those decades ago:

- UFOs are not the "biggest secret" – it is the entities behind them that was of most concern.

- Roswell was in fact a crash event of "visitors from somewhere else."

- The entities were "not so much interplanetary as much as they were literally also time travelers." They are extra-temporal.

- The visitors are clearly "from the future." There is reason to believe that they may even be "us" from a future Earth. These "future humans" have the ability to "manipulate reality around us."

- The government feared the intentions and abilities of the "visitors."

- These visitors are able to use the power of consciousness in extraordinary ways to morph reality.

- We human beings are far more powerful in potential than we ever dreamed that we are. We don't yet comprehend our extraordinary future capabilities.

- The visitors remain at essence though "corporeal" and "physical" – and secret attempts at reverse-engineering the visitor's crash material were made.

- Incredibly, Hoover admitted that he himself was engaged in such technology transfer as a Naval Intelligence Officer with Top Secret clearances.

Hoover appears to have commented only sparsely in his remarks to Birnes (just as Hoover did with his namesake son) but his insight still speaks volumes. We learn that the truth about UFOs is held in secret. Roswell really happened. The visitors manipulate time and matter, perhaps as future humans. The impact that can be made by fields of consciousness upon technology – and upon reality itself – is difficult to comprehend. And there have been efforts at replication of the crash debris by the U.S. Navy. When Birnes' interview with Hoover was relayed to his son Hoover Jr., the son replied that he was unaware that his father had said this, but neither did he discount it.

Commander Hoover never came out and called the Roswell crash victims demonic, but I guess the old adage still holds true – by their fruits shall you know them.

Sky Men A Demon-Like Breed

Educated at the U.S. Naval Academy with B.S. and M.A degrees, Commander Alvin Moore has been treated like a "kook" in several instances, even though his background was impeccable. He had frequently been vetted in front of Congress and other governmental bodies. He was a war hero serving in the U.S. Navy, and he later worked for the CIA. He also specialized in aeronautical engineering, serving as a patent engineer and attorney for the Werner von Braun team of space scientists in Huntsville, Alabama. In addition, Moore also worked as a U.S. Patent Office Examiner and held over 90 patents of his own. In 1952, when UFOs appeared over the nation's capitol and were shot at by our military, a chunk of one of the objects was blown into Moore's backyard in nearby Virginia. He put the piece of "wreckage" into a safe, but it "disappeared" under mysterious circumstances.

Serving as a nautical scientist with the Navy Oceanographic Office, Moore spent his early years reading the complete works of Charles Fort. Fort was a journalist who collected literally tons of oddball clippings and testaments about the Earth's least understood mysteries, which included the fall of objects from a clear sky, objects such as chunks of red meat, frogs, human body parts and huge chunks of ice.

Moore was sometimes ostracized by his peers for his conviction that UFOs were real and that they were occupied by a "demon-like breed" who have "kidnapped a multitude of Earth people and have long extracted blood from surface animals and men and committed mysterious murders." He even saw Jack the Ripper as somehow being part of this demonic conspiracy to capture the hearts and minds – and souls! – of humans.

In his highly footnoted work, *The Secret UFO Diary of CIA Operative Commander Alvin E. Moore* (Abelard Productions, 1997), the former Navy man stated openly that, "Much if not all of it (the phenomenon) is nefarious. . .a monstrous evil, but with occasional good," for the planet.

Moore professed the notion that there are invisible Sky Islands orbiting the Earth in several bands or chains around it – probably indicated by the jet streams, the bands of high tides, the zodiacal light and so forth. He believed that the occupants of these Sky Islands (i.e. Sky Men) have "caused legions of what we could call 'accidents,' but which are really NOT!" Furthermore, that the "Sky Men have been coming to Earth and exploiting it for many thousands of years." Moore believed that they had established homes in caverns on the Moon, on Mars, the Martian satellite Phoebus, and Jupiter, as well as the asteroids. He also declared that "probably some come from within hollows within the Earth, and possibly some from bases below certain regions of the oceans."

My motivation in pointing out the many well-referenced instances in which Naval personnel – officially or unofficially – have sought the secrets of the UFOs is to establish the credibility of the following incident, which appeared in the May, 1979 edition of the very-limited circulation *Second Look Magazine*. Though I remember reading the article when it first came out, details easily faded with time and it was only recently that the piece was "re-discovered" and posted on *The Presidents UFO Web Site* by Grant Cameron, who has visited all the presidential libraries in search of UFO-related documents. This highly controversial case consists of many fundamental elements which the believer in the supernatural aspects of UFOs might say essentially comes down to demonic possession and displays occult components which are not consistent with our view of physical reality, including the projection of voices into the minds of the participants.

Naval Commander Alvin E Moore spoke of mysterious Skymen who were kidnapping humans and committing even hideous murders around the planet.

The Day the Navy Established 'Contact'

Written by Jay Gourley

[This story is also told in another chapter in this book, although in a slightly different version. But, like all the really compelling stories of this kind, it never gets old. And one learns, when dealing with Ufology, that it sometimes takes telling a story two or three times in order to get it right. – TGB.]

From Second Look Magazine May 1979

On July 6, 1959, Robert Friend, an Air Force major and acting chief of the Aerial Phenomena Division (Project Blue Book) at Wright-Patterson AFB in Ohio, received a call from another part of the intelligence community requesting that he evaluate a 'discovery' by Navy Intelligence.

Three days later, Friend flew to Washington D.C. and met with two Navy commanders and several CIA intelligence officers. They began by asking Friend what he thought of UFOs.

"I soon learned why they were asking," Friend told SECOND LOOK. "They knew the Air Force often approached sightings with a jaundiced eye – expecting witnesses to be kooks. In this case, *they* were the witnesses."

These intelligence officers who had called him to Washington began to reveal what well may be the most dramatic UFO events in the annals of government UFO investigations.

According to Friend, this is what they told him:

During the preceding month, the two Navy officers had gone to South Berwick, Maine, at the request of a retired admiral, to meet a woman there who claimed to be in contact with extraterrestrials.

The officers met the woman and watched her enter a trance and become a "communications link." The woman sat mesmerized. Only her arm from the elbow down moved. It scribbled out meaningless circles interspersed with legible letters. They spoke questions to which answers appeared within the scribbling. The answers indicated they were coming from a kind of space patrol leader named "AFFA."

According to the officers, a number of unverifiable answers were offered to questions such as, "What is the population of Jupiter?" Among other things, AFFA said he and his men were part of an inter-solar-system police force investigating atomic tests on Earth.

But more interestingly, the Navy intelligence men posed questions incompatible with the woman's education or technical understanding – questions like "What is the length of the Uranus' day?" and "What is the distance between Jupiter and the sun at Jupiter's apogee?"

"Her" answers were correct, the two incredulous investigators later reported to Friend.

About 2 p.m. July 6, 1959, at a secret government office concealed on the top story of a garage at 5th and K St., N.W., Washington, D.C. one of the two commanders, just back from Maine, went into a trance during which he wrote messages which indicated they were from an individual named "AFFA."

AFFA's origin: the planet Uranus.

Another Navy intelligence and a civilian intelligence officer were present.

AFFA said he and his patrol team members were four extraterrestrials, officers in the OEEV, which meant Universal Association of Planets, assigned to EU or Euenza.

Euenza's meaning: Project Earth.

Among the more interesting interchanges later reported to Friend were the following:

Q. It's very interesting that we are talking with someone that we can see, but can we have proof of your existence?

A. What kind of proof do you want?

Q. Can we see you or your craft?

A. When do you want to see?

Q. Now.

A. Go to the window.

All the intelligence people went to the window, where they saw a UFO fly by (i.e., not stationary) a short distance away. As they later told Friend, it was saucer-shaped and brighter around the perimeter than in the center.

The confusion that followed ended the communication with AFFA.

The attempts to verify the target with Washington Center radar were unsuccessful. No unidentified targets were returning radar echoes from that part of the sky.

Within several hours, Friend was asked to come to Washington.

At 2 p.m., July 9, 1959, in the same secret Washington office, the Navy commanders, in the presence of the civilian intelligence officers, revealed the preceding events to the wide eyes of Maj. Friend.

Friend suggested attempting another contact.

A short time later, the Navy commander lapsed into a deep trance. "I saw it," Friend told SECOND LOOK.

"There was no doubt about that in my mind. I could see his pulse quicken. I could see his Adam's apple moving up and down rapidly. His handwriting was entirely different from his normal handwriting. The muscles in his torso did not appear to be strained, but the muscles in his arms were obviously stressed – as were the muscles around his neck – especially in his neck.

"I tried to ask some questions, but he did not respond to me. Others asked questions. He responded to only one man.

"I asked the one man that the Navy officer was responding to, to ask AFFA if he would arrange a flyby.

"The officer's arm jerkily wrote out, 'The time is not right.'

"That trance lasted 15 to 20 minutes. There was no tape recording. No one had come prepared to make contact," Friend explained.

"I was convinced that there was something there. It didn't make much difference whether they (the navy Commander and the woman in Maine) were in contact with people from outer space or with someone right here on Earth. There was something there that we should have found out more about."

Friend returned to Wright-Patterson AFB and prepared a memo to his commanding general. According to Friend, the general said that he would take charge of further evaluation personally.

Later Friend left the intelligence assignment and moved on to work on the staffs of various Air Force science advisors. He heard nothing more about the incredible communication with OEEV or its Earth project commander AFFA until after his retirement.

Friend is a credible source. He is now assistant director of engineering for Fairchild Stratos, a division of the Fairchild Industries, primary manufacturers of cryogenic releases for the space shuttle.

South Berwick, Maine, is not rich in retired Navy admirals. There was only one. Although Admiral H.B. Knowles is dead now, his wife still lives there – not far from Mrs. Guy (Frances) Swan, a woman who for more than 20 years has been in close communication with the U.S. intelligence community, and with the space captain AFFA of the OEEV patrol, at least according to Mrs. Swan and many of those who know her.

Mrs. Knowles considers Mrs. Swan absolutely credible. "She is a highly respected member of the community. I have never doubted that she was in regular communication with people from outer space," said Mrs. Knowles. "My husband was once asked the same question. He answered 'There's just no reason to believe everything that she is saying.'"

Mrs. Swan has been told to keep secret her involvement with U.S. intelligence. This she has done. She spoke with SECOND LOOK only because she mistook this reporter for an intelligence officer.

Mrs. Swann is neither well educated nor eloquent. She talks of "the good ones," spacemen patrolling the solar system to protect us from dangerous geological faults and of "the bad ones" who want to colonize this planet. She believes that her communication is a prelude to "the Second Coming of Jesus." She describes huge state-of-Maine sized satellites not too far past the orbit of the moon.

Mrs. Swan says that when the spacemen want to talk to her, they make a sound like the musical note "A." Though others in the room can hear this, only Mrs. Swan can communicate with the aliens.

Others should not try, she warns. She cites a recently-received letter from the Navy commander whose life in general and career in particular were greatly disrupted by his contact with these foreigners.

She no longer needs a pencil and paper to read the answers. "That was when I didn't have enough control over my own mind." Now she can sit quietly, remove all distractions, and hear and speak to them silently. She does this almost every day, although they are very busy and usually have very little time for the chats. She can contact them when she likes, but rarely does, waiting instead for them to contact her.

Lending further credibility to reports of these bizarre events is a document purportedly written by the civilian intelligence officer, who was with the Navy officer when they reported the events to Friend. According to the document, its author, as Friend presumed, was an officer of the Central Intelligence Agency.

If legitimate, the document substantiates everything said by Friend and most of what was reported to Friend by the Navy intelligence officers. It names the spacemen and their organization. It describes their purpose. It cites times and places of several meetings called to investigate the case – including the one at which the participants called upon the entranced Navy officer to produce the UFO, the UFO he did produce.

Author Robert Emenegger obtained, studied, and, according to him, verified the authenticity of the CIA document. Emenegger told SECOND LOOK he spoke with the CIA officer who wrote it. Although Emenegger has declined to identify the man, he told SECOND LOOK, "I am personally convinced that the document is valid – absolutely – and that the woman mentioned has been in contact with people from outer space."

Skepticism of the alleged CIA document's validity becomes much more difficult in light of information obtained from Col. William Coleman, former chief spokesman for the Air Force.

Coleman addresses the issue directly.

"The document is authentic, and even without the document substantiating him, Col. Friend's credibility is beyond reproach."

I have identified and located the CIA officer present at the secret CIA photo center July 6, 1959. His name is Arthur Lundahl, now retired.

Lundahl confirmed that he was the civilian intelligence officer present when the Navy commander went into the trance. He confirms many of the details supplied by Friend and substantiated by the purported CIA memo – with a number of notable exceptions.

Though Emenegger would not identify the author of the purported CIA memo, Emenegger says that the man was present at the July 6, 1959 event and that the man was the civilian who confirmed to Emenegger the authenticity of the memo. This description of the man means that it has to be Lundahl.

While Lundahl says that the navy officer did, in fact, report that he was in communication with AFFA and did instruct the group to look out the window for AFFA's craft, nothing was seen.

Lundahl says that there was no such memo to his knowledge. He further claims that when Friend arrived and met with them, Friend was told by those present that no UFO had been seen. And that the navy officer did not go into a second trance when Friend was present. This contradicts what both Friend and Emenegger told SECOND LOOK.

Lundahl swears that his statements are true:

"Never for a fleeting moment did I believe that this Navy officer was in communication with outer space, nor did I see a UFO. The demonstration was not done at our request. The man explained that Mrs. Swan had shown him something called 'Automatic writing,' and that if asked he would show me," Lundahl said.

"He probably chose me because I was a friend, and because I had done the photographic analysis work on the Tremonton (UFO) sighting.

"Though I believe in intelligent life other than ours, I felt nothing but sympathy and embarrassment on this occasion, for a man who was troubled, who was my friend, and who, if his superiors had learned of this, would undoubtedly have suffered in his career.

"There was one other person there. His name was Robert Nisham. He was a Navy photo analyst assigned to the CIA at the time. He and I have talked about this many times, and we agree that no UFO was seen. I swear I am telling the truth," said Lundahl.

If Lundahl is telling the truth, Nisham would have to be the other Navy commander, whose name was deleted from the CIA memo that Emenegger claims is authentic.

Whether this case is one of the most incredible UFO events in history, or the best-perpetrated UFO hoax in memory, will be explored in a future article. A search by the CIA and the Defense department for the document has begun through SECOND LOOK's request under the Freedom of Information Act. Emenegger has been asked to produce a copy of the document he purports is legitimate. And a search for Nisham, who retired from the intelligence community, is also underway.

Notes From Grant Cameron

From ThePresidentsUfoWebsite.com

Mrs. Swan confirmed to me, in writing, that she did in fact have an agreement with the Navy to "be still." Col. William Coleman confirmed to me, in writing, that "The (CIA) document looked authentic" and that the word of Col. Friend was "impeccable."

The secret office that is referred to in this article is NPIC, the National Photographic Interpretation Center. The construction for the lab began in 1954 in response to the building of the U-2 spy plane. NPIC, the most highly classified photo lab in the country, was the place where the U-2, SR-71, and spy satellite photos were analyzed.

Arthur Lundahl, referred to in the above article, was the man who discovered the missiles in Cuba, and the man who was taken into President John Kennedy's office the next morning to brief the President.

Lundahl had, according to Todd Zechel, the founder of Citizens Against UFO Secrecy (C.A.U.S.), the biggest UFO book collection he had ever seen. Zechel had a reliable CIA source that told him that Art Lundahl had acted as a briefer for three Presidents on the subject of UFOs.

It becomes apparent as Dr Pierre Guerin, senior researcher for the French National Council for Scientific Research, has stated, "UFO behavior is more akin to Magic than to Physics as we know it. And the modern UFOnauts and the demons of past days are probably related." People can of course make their own interpretation.

Salvador Freixedo:
The War Against the Gods

By Scott Corrales

He has challenged the might of the Catholic Church, been a witness to phantom animals up close, photographed the carcasses of freshly mutilated heads of cattle and climbed the heights of a mountain in search of alien contact until driven back by sonic booms. His books have examined every aspect of the UFO phenomenon and suggested frightening new theories. His personal archives contain Super-8 footage of a UFO seen during a christening in Spain and a polychromatic sliver of metal left behind by an alien vehicle. He has been present while alien visitors held a conversation with a contactee, after having "beamed into" the apartment.

Salvador Freixedo is certainly not an "armchair ufologist."

Respected for his ideas and erudition, the combative ex-Jesuit priest (he was granted an "ad divinis" suspension by the bishops

Salvador Freixedo's controversial views and opinions on the nature of UFOs and demons has the audience glued to their seats. According to Salvador, this world in which we live is what he calls "the human farm", a place where the visible and the invisible keep us in ignorance to continue to dominate our lives. This theory is respected in one of his books available in Spanish only.

He also founded the Mexican Institute for paranormal phenomenon studies and chaired the first International Congress organized by that institution.

of Puerto Rico on account of his controversial book Mi Iglesia Duerme in 1968) has investigated some of the most mind-bending cases on record in South America and Spain. The government of Ecuador discreetly solicited his advice concerning UFOs in the late 1970s, following a rash of aircraft disappearances over the Andes -- some of them within range of the airport traffic tower. On the other hand, he was accused by Mexican authorities of inciting a panic when he personally investigated a number of deaths that had occurred in San Luis Potosí (north of Mexico City) in which the blood had been extracted from the victims in almost vampiric fashion.

Round Trip to Hell in a Flying Saucer

There is no room for cowardice, intellectual or otherwise, in Freixedo's writings. He has openly stated his dissatisfaction with "official science," as he terms it, and its refusal to take an interest in paranormal and overtly supernatural phenomena which occur every day on our planet, and, what is even worse, suppressing the research efforts of other scientists who have manifested an interest in the phenomenon.

The translation of Visionaries, Mystics and Contactees (Illuminet Press, 1992) permits those unable to read him in the original Spanish to sink their teeth into the life work of a man who has been hailed by his peers as a source of information and inspiration.

Visionaries, Mystics and Contactees can be considered to be the first book in a "tetralogy" that explores in chilling detail--backed up by human legend and contactee lore--that Man is merely a creature of the gods, immensely powerful and non-corporeal entities who have masqueraded for centuries as the God. The worst offender among this gallery of entities is the biblical Yahweh, Freixedo tells us in Israel: Pueblo Contacto (Israel: the contactee nation). These gods (always with a small "g") avail themselves of humanity much in the same way that we make use of animals: we kill them without hesitation for their meat and hides, but we do so with little, if any, animosity. Earth is a farm of the gods, he writes, and they exploit us for two things--blood and the waves emitted by our brains when we are either in pain or suffering. He has said of these "gods" in a recent television appearance:

> ...the ones from within have always been here and have created humanity much in the same way it has bred animals. They have toyed with us since the beginning. [...] Some dwell in giantspaceships, others beneath the earth, some 100 to 1000 meters below the surface. Others are totally invisible as they move among us...

The last two books in this tetralogy, the monumental ! Defendámonos de los dioses! (Defying the deities) and La Granja Humana (The human farm) expand on this theory, providing case histories and commentary on a graphic, and often grisly, hypothesis.

Padre Freixedo has never backed away from controversy. In 1979, he squared off against Puerto Rican ufologist-contactee Orlando Rimacs in a lengthy and unprecedented radio debate in which he stated that the only truly human race was the black race. By popular demand, the debate was rebroadcast at a later date and was even carried over Spanish-language radio stations in New York City. In the 1950's, Cuban dictator Fulgencio Batista asked him to leave that country in the wake of having penned 40 casos de injusticia social: examen de conciencia para cristianos distraídos (40 cases of social unjustice--a soul-searching exam for forgetful Christians). Almost twenty years later, Mitos religiosos en las relaciones humanas, a book on human relationships emphasizing the myths created by Catholicism, landed him in jail in Venezuela.

This book is essential to understand the ideology of Freixedo. It explains his theories on the different levels of existence, and the fact that higher beings, but close to our own level of existence have tried to take advantage of us. "Entities" have taken various forms according to the period in which they appear. They have been very diverse but very obvious and have served many gimmicks and mystical tricks upon us.

Yet it was precisely in that country where Freixedo stumbled upon one of his most amazing cases: he made the acquaintance of a woman named Lula, a society hostess who had left her husband to marry a superhuman, if not outright supernatural, individual named Jorge. Upon the latter's untimely death, a medical exam revealed that the man had lived without lungs! Jorge's uncanny talents and his jokes of coming from "another world" were no longer a laughing matter. An autopsy was forbidden at the time, but the enigmatic personage was known to hundreds of witnesses. When Freixedo returned to Venezuela in later years to attend the exhumation of the body, he learned that Lula had disappeared off the face of the earth. The fascination that sex holds for non-humans he states thus: "...they are interested in three aspects of humanity: the generational, the genetic and the genital. I do not know the reason for this. What we have to do is conscientiously study the facts...there are many reasons why some entities are more interested than others in these matters. One group, the small ones, is becoming extinct. They have lost their reproductive ability, they claim, due to wars, atomic wars, which is why they are trying to stop them here. This has destroyed them genitally--they can no longer attempt male/female reproduction like we do

here. They are all clones, which is why they resemble each other...they say it is not exactly cloning, but a similar process."

While no stranger to the U.S. (he has taught and studied here), American audiences were first able to hear his message directly at the First World UFO Congress held in Phoenix AZ in May 1991. His presentation, entitled "Gods and Spacemen," was well received by the audience. More recently, he has appeared on the Spanish-language television shows like "The Cristina Show" as part of a panel of experts on the phenomenon.

The message of Visionaries, Mystics and Contactees remains a constant throughout his later works: Never turn over your mind to anything or anyone, not religions, politicians, cult leaders or anyone else. The brain, he explains, is the only means we have at our disposal to wrestle against the dominion of the gods. In an age when people are all to willing to surrender themselves to a cause, an ideology or a faith, Freixedo's words come as sound advice.

The Gods Do Exist!
The Researcher Himself Speaks

By Salvador Freixedo

A long time ago, I made the following distinction between the rational beings who are equal or superior to humans: humans, super humans, gods, GOD.

Superhumans are basically humans like ourselves, but trained to carry out a great mission, which is why they are endowed with outstanding qualities that enable them to perform such a deed. Some of them are fully prepared since birth, and others acquire these powers in a given moment of their lives, when they are chosen by one of the gods, whom we will discuss shortly.

The founders of great religions tend to be super humans. Anyone who wishes to see a superman in our times and witness the incredible powers they are often endowed with can go to India, where in a small town called Puttaparthi, near Bangalore and Hyderabad (the state capital), he or she can try to get as close as possible to one Sathya Sai Baba. I say "as close as possible" because it is not unusual that upon reaching Prasanthi Nilayam, the temple-place in which he dwells, there should be thousands--if not hundreds of thousands--of his devotees who will bar any physical proximity to the superman.

Zoroaster, Buddha, Mohammed, Moses, Confucius, Lao Tse etc. belonged to this order of beings.

And before we leave the subject of the superhumans altogether, we must make it perfectly clear that these exceptional human beings, no matter how great their powers, are but instruments that the gods make use of to carry out their wishes in human society and on our planet in general (which is not as entirely "ours" as we had imagined). These wishes, up to now, remain un-deciphered by the human brain, and will probably be utterly undecipherable to us until our intelligence takes a drastic evolutionary step forward.

Just as I have said, superhumans are fundamentally humans, either by their way of appearing in our world, their physical nature or their more or less normal way of dying, no different from that of other mortals. However, it is worthy of note that some of them, in the process of their manipulation by the gods, have deviated significantly from what is normal in most humans. This could be the case with Krishna, Virachocha, Quetzalcoatl and Christ himself. They give the impression of having partaken of the nature of the gods in some way, like some sort of hybrid between man and god, or else the gods prepared them for a specific mission on this planet.

Gods Disguised As Humans

On the other hand, gods are not humans. Some of them have the capacity to manifest themselves as such, and have in fact done so on countless occasions, even to live intimately among us when it suits their enigmatic purposes. As soon as their task is completed, however, or when they achieve their desire, they return to the plane of existence where they can function more naturally and conforming to their psychic and electromagnetic traits.

But the gods are not humans, and one of the few points in common we have with them is intelligence, although their knowledge and intelligence exceed our own by far.

There are many more differences among the gods than there are among men. These differences are of all kinds, and refer not only to their physical being in their natural state, but also in the way they manifest themselves; their greater or lesser ability to manipulate matter and enter our world; their level of mental, and therefore technical, evolution; and in a certain way, their degree of moral development, as some appear to take greater care about not interfering unduly in our world or not interfering at all. They are different in origin as well; some hailing from beyond our world, although I tend to believe that the ones who have meddled the most in human life and history are from our very own world. The reasons that prompt their manifestations among us, and the ends they seek upon doing so, vary as well.

These great differences among them are not the result--as among humans--of belonging to different races, nationalities, religions, cultures, social classes or languages. The differences among the gods is deeper, as humans, no matter how great their differences, are equal in their humanity. The gods do not belong to the same generic order of beings, and the differences among them could be perhaps as great as the differences between ourselves and an evolved mammal. It is also very possible that there is less difference between us and some of them than there is between their own ranks.

From the information we have received from them (and it is seldom entirely reliable), many of them ignore other gods that they have met during their forays into our level of existence, only realizing that they do not belong to the human world. If we are to believe what they have said, not only is there mutual mistrust among them, but on some occasions we have learned of open animosity between them and even pitched battles.

An example of this animosity appears in the rebellion that, according to Christian theology, Lucifer and many of his followers conducted against Yahweh. Those who believe explicitly in the classic teachings of the Church, and who believe unswervingly that that is the only and entire explanation of the origins of Man on Earth and his relationship with God, should be aware that all the great religions describe similar conflicts among their gods, or between a greater deity and lesser ones.

Nonbelievers who, on the other hand, regard these biblical stories as mythological and not worthy of attention should be advised that myths and legends are nothing more than history distorted by the passing of millennia. They should also know that these battles among gods appear in all of humanity's oldest books (which is to say the "sacred histories" of all religions) and continue to re-enact themselves today before our very eyes, as we shall see later on.

The controversial former Catholic Priest believes that UFO occupants are behind religious visions, miraclesand appear to formulate opinions of their liking.

Finally, we can say that these vast differences among the ranks of the gods translate into their widely divergent behavior upon our world and in their relationship with us, which vary greatly from one case to another and which, precisely on account of such variety, still have us wondering what it is they want.

While the physical being of the gods is different from our own, we can nonetheless say that the gods have some sort of body or physical presence. A small parenthesis becomes necessary at this point to explain that in the Cosmos, everything, even what we naively call "spiritual" is in a certain way "physical" (much in the same way that everything physical is in some way imbued with spirit). "Physis" is a Greek word meaning "nature," and in this sense we can state that everything natural, or belonging to the natural order, is "physical." The gods, then, do not belong to the "supernatural" order as it has been always been defined by theologians.

Bodies of the Gods

To understand the physical nature of the gods (and many other nonhuman creatures) we have no choice but to seek the help of atomic and subatomic physics. The "bodies" of the gods are electromagnetic and made up by waves. Those who find this wording suspicious should also know that the human body is composed of waves and nothing more than waves, because that is ultimately what matter is all about (This is the great wonder and secret of the entire Universe. This physical fact, beyond all sentimentality and all dogmatic and mystical concepts, brings us close to the unintelligible Entity that created the Cosmos).

The "matter" in the "bodies" of the gods, while basically similar to our own, is structured in a much more subtle form, much in the same way that the matter that forms the air is subtler than that which constitutes a bar of steel, although both are ultimately the same.

Shape Shifting

The superior gods, unlike us, have the ability to manipulate and control their own matter, adopting more or less elusive shapes and making them more or less accessible to being perceived by our senses, whenever they so choose.

Another thing in which many of them coincide with us is their place in the Universe, for while their level of existence (or "vibrational level," as the occultists have termed it for years) does not coincide with our own, our planet is nevertheless their planet, at least to many of them.

Habitation

Though Freixedo's ideas remain controversial, he is considered an icon among members of the Hispanic UFOlogical community. He is seen here with Benitas Raquejo. Freixedo believes that the aliens can make us see them pretty much as they wish – either frightening or friendly.

It is a little naive to ask where they live exactly. Their location obeys physical laws different to the ones that we know, because the ideas of time and space that humans hold are extremely crude. Many of them can live--and do so, in fact--here with us, and nonetheless manage to go undetected by our senses. Our senses capture only a small portion of the surrounding reality. With a physical nature similar to that of a stone, the air remains invisible to our eyes. Many sounds and many more smells go unnoticed by our senses, yet they are the normal environment in which animal senses function. The television waves that flood our homes are visible to us only through the use of a device. We should not be surprised, then, at the invisibility of the gods. The paranormal world provides an abundant casuistry with which to reinforce this thesis.

Aside from all this, the indisputable field of photography offers us cases in which a normally developed photo does not reveal the presence of objects that could only have been discovered when the negatives were "burnt" by the photographer's skilled hand.

We can conclude from what has been said earlier that the gods have no need of ground on which to stand or air to breathe and therefore have no need of being in any of the places of the world in which humans exist, with their matter and particular physical characteristics.

On the other hand, I believe that there is no choice but to admit that some or perhaps many of them originate from other parts of the Universe, with our planet being little more than a stopover or temporal residence, which would explain in part the lack of continuity in many of their activities on our world, and more concretely, in the great variation that can be witnessed in their interventions in human history.

By now, some reader must be wondering from where have we extracted the whimsical notion of the existence of such beings. Science says nothing at all about them, but then again, science says nothing about things like love and poetry, and in fact knows very little about either one. Even academic parapsychology itself, which is the branch of science that should be interested in the existence of these beings, says nothing about them and in fact rejects their existence whenever some bold parapsychologist makes a suggestion about their possible presence in some paranormal events.

In the Realm of Spirits

This is, sadly, the state of affairs, produced by the mental paralysis of many so-called scientists. So much for science and psychology with all their prejudices and myopia. "Amicus Plato, sed magis amica veritas." The truth of the matter is that, no matter how unlikely and disquieting it all seems, such beings exist and we have written accounts of them in all the writings that humanity preserves since Man began to keep a written record of what he thought and saw.

If mega-science says nothing officially about these beings (many high-ranking scientists have a lot to say, off the record and in private), religion, which is a very important aspect of human thought, says many things and has been doing so for centuries. When I say religion, I am referring to all religions, without the exclusion of Christianity.

UFO entities can take on many forms such as the imps in a tree that a priest tried to bless so that they would leave without causing trouble, to small elemental type beings that cross our path every day such as this one caught in a photo.

Most religions refer to these beings as "spirits" in general terms, although they may have an endless variety of names, depending on the religions and depending on the different "spirits." We must bear in mind that all religions are aware of the great differences that exist among these "spirits."

As nomenclature goes, the Greeks and the Romans hit closest to the mark and simply called them "gods." Although they realized that they were spirits that could assume corporeal form as it suited them, they also recognized an entire series of deities or lesser spirits that were beholden to these greater "gods."

No matter how strongly we believe that Christianity is far above all this polytheistic viewpoint, it accepts these sprits and in fact speaks of them constantly in the Bible and in all the teachings of the Christian doctrine throughout the centuries. Christianity calls them "angels" or "demons," and assigns them vast powers—some of them, in fact, are shown as being in rebellion against God in the sacred history—and significant distinctions are made among them. We must bear in mind the gradations among the different classes of "angels": archangels, angels, thrones, dominions, powers, principalities, cherubim, seraphim...all these names are proof that the Church has a well-defined and concrete idea of them. What is even more curious is that in the Bible itself, Yahweh himself is called an "angel."

Games of the Gods

The abundant and most eclectic mythologies of all peoples, which were presented to us in days of yore as the result of the almost childlike imagination of primitive cultures, have gradually gained credence in out times. We see in them no less than the recollection of events that took place many thousands of years ago, deformed by the passing centuries. Anthropologists have studied them and know them well, but focus upon them from a biased perspective in order to explain their own theories. Students of the new cosmic theology examine them from a completely different and more inclusive point of view, without falling into the trap of neither a priori theories concocted by anthropologists nor the hardened dogmas of any one of the religions that have imprisoned the minds of almost all the inhabitants of this planet.

Mythological Illuminations

Students of this new theology try to illuminate and corroborate these myths by comparing them with other facts we find in history and the myriad phenomena we encounter today.

What the study of these mythologies has yielded is that in the remote, and not so remote, days of antiquity (and we shall soon see that in our own times), beings that claimed heavenly origin manifested themselves before the startled inhabitants of this planet and claimed to be almighty "gods" or, more boldly, the Creator-God of the Universe. Primitive Earthlings, with a rudimentary knowledge of nature, were on the one hand amazed at the beauty they witnessed and terrified on the other, not questioning for a moment the fact that they stood before the rulers of the Universe, surrendering their minds without hesitation and placing themselves at their disposal unconditionally.

If this would have been the case with only one culture, we could ascribe it to a number of causes, but the truth of the matter is that the phenomenon of the manifestation of a "deity" has taken place in almost all the cultures of whom we have a written record. Collectively speaking, the phenomenon of divine manifestation and, individually, the phenomenon of "apparition" or "illumination" are events that have repeated themselves in all latitudes, all cultures and all ages throughout the centuries.

It is only fitting to discuss whether these beliefs common to all cultures are due to objective apparitions by these "celestial" beings or if they were simply a subjective creation due to the innate religiosity common to humans throughout the ages. Official science, with psychologists and psychiatrists at the forefront, will tell us that all these beliefs are unquestionably due to the latter, and that such objective apparitions never took place.

Contrary to their position we have religious fanatics (or simply ardent believers) who defend--with their lives, if necessary--that the objective reality of the divine manifestations and apparitions taught by their holy faith is unquestionable.

Who is in the right? As the reader knows very well, the truth is no one's patrimony and in this particular case it is exactly so. Science has the right to state that on countless occasions that which is portrayed as a "vision" is mere hallucination, the product of an unwell mind, and what is portrayed as a miracle-- meaning a proof of the immediate or almost immediate presence of God--is no more than the conscious or unconscious use of an unknown natural law by the miracle-worker.

This sums up the portion of the truth contained by official science, which is no mean amount. The religious contingent also has its share of the truth. Their error lies in distorting the facts and blowing them out of proportion, turning relative, local and temporal phenomena into absolute or universal truths. On many occasions, the event of the vision or apparition has occurred objectively, but it has not been exactly what the seers have thought it to be or more precisely, what they have been led to believe it was. This is where the deceitful activity of the gods comes into play. This deceitful activity not only takes place immediately and on the short term over the seers and their co-religionaries, but extends many years later, even unto scientists and human society in general, leading them to believe that such "visions" are purely subjective, "mythical" and utterly devoid of any reality.

As we can see, the gods play a double game: immediate witnesses are turned into raging fanatics (they have no choice after having seen and felt what they have seen and felt) and society in general--particularly the scientific community--who have not been immediate witnesses, experience a totally opposite effect, creating a special and uncanny mental resistance to accepting that such things can possibly be real, no matter how many times we see them repeated and documented to satiety in all the sacred and profane books of all cultures and all ages. Religions -- omnipresent throughout human history -- are the result of such "impossible" events.

Evil is all around regardless if it is the antichrist, the beast who is 666 or flying demons.
(Illustration by Carol Ann Rodriguez.)

Wizards of Odd and The Alien Mask of Evil

By Sean Casteel

In the modern UFO era, dating back to around 1947, when both Kenneth Arnold's famous sighting of flying saucers and the even more famous Roswell incident took place, many UFO researchers have looked past the veil of more recent times to place the phenomenon firmly in the context of history, dating it back to man's most ancient beginnings. UFOs and their alien occupants are nothing new, say these researchers and authors, and may represent simply a more technological guise for entities long regarded as evil spirits or demons.

John Lear

Shown here in the cockpit of a Lockheed Starfighter, John Lear, retired airline captain, with over 19000 hours of flight-time, has flown in over 100 different types of planes and holds almost every imaginable award in the test flight industry.

John Lear is the son of the inventor of the Lear Jet, William P. Lear. John Lear is also an experienced pilot with many thousands of hours of flight time as well as having an alleged background of CIA contacts gathered from flying missions he carried out for the agency.

According to Lear, the first contact between aliens and our government took place in 1964, and a formal treaty was negotiated around 1969-71. The treaty involved an exchange of superior alien technology in return for our government's cooperation in covering up alien "research" on this planet, which included the famous cattle mutilations and human abductions. Lear also says that the aliens and our government operate a joint research facility at the notorious Area 51 in Nevada. Lear helped to pioneer the Dark Side faction of the UFO community and, while he has his share of detractors, he has never been proven wrong for believing something evil is afoot that has long ago snared our government into helpless cooperation.

Containers of the Soul

Lear is quite forthrightly outspoken on the negative aspects of the UFO phenomenon. For instance, his take on the gray aliens is certainly on the sinister side of the table.

"The purpose of the grays," Lear said in an online UFO forum, "is to take care of the containers – us. We are containers of souls. When a soul is made, it lasts forever and ever. It never dies until it is beyond salvation. This is very rare. The future is already written and the date of your death is already determined. If you are in an accident or life-threatening situation, the grays secretly step in and save you."

A regular fixture on the Coast to Coast AM show, John Lear has come to some "strange" conclusions regarding the true nature of UFOs and their occupants.

Presumably to keep things on schedule so that one is there to meet one's moment of death at the correct predetermined time. Their interest in our souls, however, is a predatory one, driven by hunger. The grays suck the souls out whole, in order to feed on the energy of the misery the grays

A Strange Report From the Files of Karla Turner

A man in his late 40s came to us to explore several alien-related events in his life, and in the interview he told of a strange, although not apparently alien-oriented episode that had haunted him since childhood. When he was ten years old, his grandmother came to visit in his home, and since the house was small, she shared his bed on the first night of her visit.

During the night, the boy was awakened by a loud male voice. He couldn't understand what the voice was saying, but it sounded angry and was addressing the grandmother lying beside him.

The next morning, he asked his grandmother, "What was that voice in the bedroom last night?"

His grandmother, with tears in her eyes, pulled him tightly to her and said, "That was the devil." She said nothing more about the episode, but she did insist that her son take her back to her own home immediately. It was an unreasonable request, and her son tried to talk her out of it. But the grandmother was adamant, and finally her son agreed to take her home the following day.

The entire family made the trip of over a hundred miles back to the grandmother's farm, and within an hour of their arrival, the grandmother suffered a massive stroke and died. Ever since that event, the man had felt a heavy burden of guilt associated with his grandmother's death. Yet there was no conscious reason for him to have felt that way. The entire event was poignant and mystifying, but in all the alien encounters he had subsequently undergone, he had felt that the aliens were his friends and were helping him by expanding his psychic abilities.

A regression session was arranged, and in the course of the hypnosis, he was asked to look at that childhood experience. What he recalled was an abduction in which he and his grandmother were taken to a spacecraft in the company of reptilian aliens. He remembered the aliens telling his grandmother that they were interested in learning about her knowledge of medicinal herbs, and they offered to exchange medical information of their own.

They gave the boy and the grandmother a liquid to drink, explaining that it was beneficial and would make the grandmother feel young and attractive again. So both of them drank the liquid, and the man remembered seeing his grandmother indeed looking much younger. That was the extent of his recollection.

Both he and [Tulsa UFO researcher] Ms. Bartholic, who was conducting the regression, were puzzled by this, because there was nothing in the episode to account for the guilt he had felt about the grandmother's death. So Ms. Bartholic deepened the man's trance level and asked him to look at it again, with much clearer vision. And what he then recalled was much more disturbing.

The abduction, at first, followed his initial recollection. But when the liquid was drunk, he now remembered a very strong feeling of change in his body. And he saw that the grandmother didn't actually look younger. Instead, she was placed on a table and approached by one of the reptilian aliens who wanted to have intercourse with her. The liquid had acted as an aphrodisiac, yet the grandmother resisted and said that since her husband's death she would not have sex with anyone. The reptilian laughed and disappeared from the room momentarily. When he returned, he was accompanied by a man who looked exactly like the dead husband.

At this point, the grandmother agreed to have sex, but as the act was in progress, she suddenly realized that the image of her dead husband was a cruel illusion. It was actually the reptilian on top of her, and she cried out in great resistance for him to leave her alone. Once he was finished with her, he lifted up the little boy and placed him on top of the grandmother, forcing another sex act upon the both of them.

Then the grandmother was removed from the table and the little boy was victimized himself by the reptilian, forced to have anal and oral sex. The grandmother protested violently, pushing the reptilian away from her grandson and interposing her body between them. "By Jesus," she shouted, "you will not touch this boy!"

That must have been the wrong thing to say, because the reptilian became very angry and threatened her. "You will die for that!" he told her, and the two people were returned to the bedroom from which they'd been taken. The next morning, the grandmother told the little boy that the devil had been there the night before, and that was when she insisted upon being taken home. And, as it turned out, she did die immediately thereafter.

This, then, was the cause of the man's lifelong sense of guilt about her death. He had been forced to have sex with her, and her death had followed shortly after. But none of this story would have emerged if Ms. Bartholic had done as most investigators do and stopped the regression after uncovering the story about the exchange of medicinal knowledge.

There are other cases in our files that show a similar deception at work in the initial hypnotic recall. We cannot trust that first memory, it is clear, for like so much else in the abduction experience, there may well be further masking of events.

Before we allow ourselves to believe in the benevolence of the alien interaction, we should ask, do enlightened beings need to use the cover of night to perform good deeds? Do they need to paralyze us and render us helpless to resist? Do "angels" need to steal our fetuses? Do they need to manipulate our children's genitals and probe our rectums? Are fear, pain and deception consistent with high spiritual motives?

From UFO Universe, edited by Timothy Green Beckley
For additional material go to www.KarlaTurner.org

themselves cause, like a vampire's thirst for blood. Most likely the grays are doomed to suffer their hunger in eternity and can never get their fill of human torture.

The Government Is Their Ally

As if the nature of the grays wasn't bad enough, they're also working alongside our own government! This is one of Lear's major themes, that our government entered into an agreement with various alien life forms and was played for a sucker big time.

In his role as a researcher, Lear maintains a lively correspondence with many other researchers. The following case histories were reported to Lear by an investigator named Bill English, who claimed he got the information in 1977 when he was allowed to read a Top Secret document called PROJECT GRUDGE/BLUE BOOK REPORT NUMBER 13.

One of the reports was called "Darlington Farm Case," out of Ohio, and the incident took place in October 1953.

"A man, wife and 13-year-old son were sitting down at the dinner table. As they sat there, the lights in the farmhouse began to dim. Dogs and animals raised a ruckus outside. The 13-year-old boy got up from the dinner table to see what was going on. He called his mother and father to come look at the funny lights in the sky."

They saw a round ball of fire in the sky, and the boy began chasing it out into an open field. As the parents watched, the light came down from the sky and the boy began to scream for help. The father fetched his shotgun and returned to see that his son was being carried away by what looked like little men. The father fired several rounds at the light, but to no avail. They found one of their dogs with its head crushed, but no sign of the boy and no footprints left behind by the little men.

According to Lear the aliens are using the moon as a base in order to collect and store the souls of humans as indicated in this fascinating illustration courtesy of DavidIcke.Com.

The police were called but the official report read that the boy had run off and become lost in the forest. Within 48 hours, the Air Force determined that the family had experienced a true close encounter and forced the parents to relocate to a secret installation somewhere in the northwest part of the U.S. which had medical treatment facilities to deal with radiation poisoning and similar ailments.

Both the parents were in shock and required intensive psychotherapy.

The Demonic UFO Philosophy of the Late John A. Keel

Demonology is not just another crackpot-ology. It is the ancient and scholarly study of the monsters and demons who have seemingly coexisted with man throughout history. Thousands of books have been written on the subject, many of them authored by educated clergymen, scientists and scholars, and uncounted numbers of well-documented demonic events are readily available to every researcher. The manifestations and occurrences described in this imposing literature are similar, if not entirely identical, to the UFO phenomenon itself. Victims of demonomania (possession) suffer the very same medical and emotional symptoms as the UFO contactees. Demonomania is so common that it has spawned the minor medical and psychiatric study of demonopathy.

Throughout most of history, the manifestations of demonology and demonopathy have been viewed from a religious perspective and explained as the work of the Devil. The bizarre manipulations and ill effects described in the demonological literature are usually regarded as the result of a great unseen conflict between God and the Devil . In UFO lore, the same conflict has been observed, and the believers have explained it as a space war between the "Guardians" (good guys from outer space), who are protecting our planet, and some evil extraterrestrial race. The manifestations are the same, only the frame of reference is different.

The Devil and his demons can, according to the literature, manifest themselves in almost any form and can physically imitate anything from angels to horrifying monsters with glowing eyes. Strange objects and entities materialize and dematerialize in these stories, just as the UFOs and their splendid occupants appear and disappear, walk through walls, and perform other supernatural feats.

Did ancient man misinterpret UFO manifestations by placing them in a religious context? Apparently not. The literature indicates that the phenomenon carefully cultivated the religious frame of reference in early times, just as the modern manifestations have carefully supported the extraterrestrial frame of reference . Operation Trojan Horse is merely the same old game in a new, updated guise. The Devil's emissaries of yesteryear have been replaced by the mysterious "men-in-black."

The quasi-angels of Biblical times have become magnificent spacemen. The demons, devils and false angels were recognized as liars and plunderers by early man. These same impostors now appear as long-haired Venusians.

All of the major religions, and most of the minor ones, accept the God-Devil conflict, and their scriptures outline some possibly real episodes in which human beings have had some direct experience with this conflict. A large portion of all holy literature consists of material purportedly dictated to men by supernatural beings, and a good part of this seems more allegorical or metaphorical than real. The phenomenon may have passed along information about man's origin and purpose carefully disguised in terms and fictitious episodes that could be understood by the minds of the people during the period when the messages were transmitted.

Thus, the story of Adam and Eve might not be the actual truth but merely a great simplification of the truth.

In the Forgotten Books of Eden, an apocryphal book allegedly translated from ancient Egyptian in the nineteenth century, we are told that Satan and his hosts were fallen angels who populated the earth before Adam was brought into being, and Satan used lights, fire and water in his efforts to rid the planet of this troublesome creature. He even disguised himself as an angel from time to time and appeared as a beautiful young woman in his efforts to lead Adam to his doom. UFO-type lights were one of the Devil's devices described in the Forgotten Books of Eden.

Subtle variations on this same theme can be found in the Bible and in the numerous scriptures of the Oriental cultures. Religious man has always been so enthralled with the main (and probably allegorical) story line that the hidden point has been missed. That point is that the earth was occupied before man arrived or was created. The original occupants or forces were paraphysical and possessed the power of transmogrification. Man was the interloper, and the earth's original occupants or owners were not very happy over the intrusion. The inevitable conflict arose between physical man and the paraphysical owners of the planet. Man accepted the interpretation that this conflict raged between his creator and the Devil.

The religious viewpoint has always been that the Devil has been attacking man (trying to get rid of him) by foisting disasters, wars and sundry evils upon him.

There is historical and modern proof that this may be so.

A major, but little-explored, aspect of the UFO phenomenon is therefore theological and philosophical rather than purely scientific. The UFO problem can never be untangled by physicists and scientists unless they are men who have also been schooled in liberal arts, theology and philosophy. Unfortunately, most scientific disciplines are so demanding that their practitioners have little time or inclination to study complicated subjects outside their own immediate fields of interest.

Satan and his demons are part of the folklore of all races, no matter how isolated they have been from one another. The Indians of North America have many legends and stories about a devil-like entity who appeared as a man and was known as the trickster because he pulled off so many vile stunts. Tribes in Africa, South America and the remote Pacific islands have similar stories.

The above is a brief excerpt from John A. Keel's Operation Trojan Horse.

Run Like Hell

Another similar report indicates that the government is aware of incidents of human mutilation within their own ranks. An Air Force Sgt. named Jonathan P. Lovette was observed being taken captive aboard what appeared to be a UFO at the White Sands Missile Test Range in New Mexico. The incident took place in March of 1956 and was witnessed by Major William Cunningham. The two were out in a field downrange from the launch sites looking for debris from a missile test when Lovette went over the ridge of a small sand dune and was out of sight for a time.

Cunningham heard Sgt. Lovette scream in what he described as "terror or agony." The major ran over the crest of the dune and saw the sergeant being dragged into what appeared to him to be a silvery disc-like object that hovered in the air at a height of 15 to 20 feet. A long, snake-like object was wrapped around the sergeant's legs, dragging him into the disc, after which the disc rose quickly into the sky.

Search parties were sent out into the field. After telling his story, Major Cunningham was admitted to the White Sands Medical Dispensary for observation. After three days of searching, Sgt. Lovette's nude body was found approximately 10 miles downrange. His body had been mutilated; the tongue had been removed from the lower portion of his jaw. An incision had been made just under the tip of the chin that extended all the way back to his esophagus and larynx. He had been emasculated and his eyes had been removed. Also, his anus had been removed and there were comments in the report about the apparent surgical skill used in removing the various organs and tissues. When the body was found, there were a number of dead predatory birds in the area, apparently killed when they tried to feed on Lovette's body.

Lear groups cases like the disappearing 13-year-old farm boy and the mutilated Air Force Sergeant under the heading "The Horrible Truth."

"The best advice I can give you is," Lear said, "the next time you see a flying saucer and are awed by its obvious display of technology and gorgeous lights of pure color: RUN LIKE HELL!"

Jacques Vallee

French actor François Truffaut portrayed Dr. Vallee in Close Encounters of the Third Kind.

Jacques Vallee is a world famous researcher who is respected not only by UFO believers but also by those outside the field for his high quality scholarship and rigorous scientific dedication. Vallee was the model for the character of "Lacombe," from the Steven Spielberg movie "Close Encounters of the Third Kind." He received training as an astrophysicist and holds a Ph.D. in computer science from Northwestern University in Chicago. He is the author of some of the best books ever written on the subject of UFOs, including "Anatomy of a Phenomenon" (1966), "Challenge to Science" (1967) and "Passport to Magonia," (1970), the latter universally considered to be a classic. The book dealt with the relationship between UFO contact and the folktales of fairy lore and the Little People.

Vallee's research led him to concentrate on the sinister aspects of unexplained phenomena, which he expounded on in his 1979 book "Messengers of Deception." He would go on to write "Dimensions" (1988), "Confrontations" (1990) and "Revelations" (1991). His most recent book is called "Wonders In The Sky" (2009) and deals with ancient UFO sightings.

Daring to Face the Paranormal

In an interview conducted by Daniel Blair Stewart, and published online as "Strange Encounters: An Interview With Jacques Vallee," Vallee says that too many UFO researchers try to sweep the paranormal aspects of the phenomenon under the proverbial rug.

"That is due in part," Vallee said, "to the fact that witnesses tell you such things only after you have gained their trust. But very often they are a challenge to the beliefs or the worldview of the investigators. They may not be ready to hear it or they may not publish it because they think it would damage their credibility. And since they are in the business of giving credibility to the subject, they don't want to reveal the paranormal aspects of it. Every UFO sighting has some elements that are shocking to the 'rational' view, the nuts-and-bolts picture that these are simply spacecraft from outer space."

Vallee and Dr. J Allen Hynek - with Sir Eric Gairy of Granada in background -- make a serious presentation at the United Nations to promote a global study of UFOs.

In the last few decades, Vallee continued, "We've learned a lot of new things about this phenomenon that contradicts the idea that it is extraterrestrial. It is not a recent phenomenon. It is a phenomenon that has existed, as far as we can tell, throughout history in one form or another. So this certainly invalidates the idea that we're dealing with a civilization that has just discovered us and is coming here now. UFOs seem to have been a part of our environment for a very long time, perhaps as long as man has existed."

UFO Hostility

Vallee went on to recount a journey he had made to Brazil in which there seemed to be evidence of UFO hostility.

"Objects would literally zap people," he said, "with beams. In several cases, it seemed that it killed them. It certainly injured them. We couldn't really prove a direct cause-and-effect relationship in the cases of death, but there was a cause-and-effect relationship in the cases of the injuries. People were, in fact, injured by those beams.

"The phenomenon doesn't seem to care at all," Vallee continued, "whether it's perceived as good or bad. In fact, it may be beyond the level at which humans would define good and evil."

Whatever the phenomenon is, however, Vallee believes it extends to every culture, every race, every religion on Earth.

"I really have not found a single place that doesn't have a tradition about this phenomenon," he said.

Is There Evidence for Malevolence?

But the phenomenon does tally up more points on the sinister side in Vallee's view, in spite of those who believe we're dealing with something positive and benevolent.

"I can understand," Vallee said, "why the expectation has grown that this could be helpful and benevolent. It's a very complex, unexplained phenomenon and we always tend to project our own human fantasies into every such thing that comes along. It would be nice if somebody came down from the sky and told us how to stop wars and how to cure cancer. Unfortunately, the phenomenon itself, when you look at it objectively, doesn't seem to care about us at all. It seems to be benevolent in some cases and hostile or at least harmful in other cases.

"Notice that we could say the same about electricity. We couldn't live without electricity, but if you put your fingers in a socket it could kill you. That doesn't mean the utility company is hostile to you, it just means that there's a very powerful force out there and it doesn't care if it kills you or not. Electricity doesn't give a damn one way or the other, and I think that, to some extent, the UFO phenomenon is the same way. It does whatever it has to do according to a pattern we haven't detected. When people get in the way, they get zapped."

Vallee did concede that sometimes there is a long-term psychological change that manifests in witnesses to Close Encounters, a change that can be for the better or the worse.

"You occasionally meet people," he said, "who seem very enlightened, who have a very positive attitude toward life, who think they have psychic abilities, and when you ask them when they first became aware of this, they will trace it to a time when they saw a UFO. Some witnesses have actually described being healed as they were caught in the beam from a UFO.

"There are also numerous cases in which the reverse happens. People are confronted with a UFO and their whole life changes for the worse. When they tell their story, the local people don't believe them. They are ostracized, they get fired from their jobs, their wives leave them, they go through a tailspin, they sometimes end up as bums."

Vallee explained that the tailspin outcome happened to several American law enforcement people in the 1960s and 70s.

"The phenomenon tends to happen," he said, "away from towns, between say, one and four in the morning. Who is going to be away from a town between one and four in the morning but the highway patrol! So very often, in places like Nebraska,

North Dakota, Minnesota, there are cases of Close Encounters at night involving highway patrolmen. In numerous cases, their lives were destroyed or broken; they had to leave the force because people wouldn't respect them anymore. They were suspected of seeing things, maybe of drinking."

Elsewhere on the Internet, Vallee is quoted as saying in more blatant terms, "I believe there is a machinery of mass manipulation behind the UFO phenomenon. They are helping create a new belief system. They are designed to help change belief systems, and the technology we observe is only the incidental support for a worldwide enterprise of subliminal seduction. What we see here is not an alien invasion. It is a control system which acts on humans and uses humans. Human beings are under the control of a strange force that bends them in absurd ways, forcing them to play a role in a bizarre game of deception."

The "Oz" Factor

"I think UFOs are a special case," Vallee added, "that forces us to question what we call reality. In Close Encounter cases, there is a point at which the witness seems to enter a different reality. There is an English researcher named Jenny Randles who calls this 'the Oz factor.' There is a point where all of a sudden reality has split and the reality of the observer has been replaced by another reality. If we could measure that, if we could instrument the witness, we might be able to learn about what we call physical reality. But that also raises the question: how do we know that this reality is the real one? How would we prove that it's the real one? This reality is merely a human consensus."

The Oz factor has alternately been explained as the sudden heightening of the senses that happens to a UFO witness during the encounter experience. It is comparable to Dorothy, in the movie "The Wizard of Oz," moving from the black and white landscape of her native Kansas to the full color world of Oz. But again, as Vallee asks, how do we know which reality is real?

"One of the opportunities that the UFO phenomenon is giving us is to look at reality in a much larger context," Vallee said. "Whatever UFOs turn out to be, the opportunity is here. Simply by stretching our minds and forcing us to look at the universe in other ways."

John Keel

The late John Keel was one of the most revered of UFO and paranormal researchers. In 1975, he published "The Mothman Prophecies," an account of his 1966-67 investigation of sightings of the Mothman, a strange winged creature reported in and around Point Pleasant, West Virginia. The book was loosely adapted into a 2002 movie, starring Richard Gere and Alan Bates, who played two parts of Keel's personality in his search for the evil Mothman. Keel published several books with dealing with UFOs and the paranormal, to include the abominable snowman.

Keel's second book, "UFOs: Operation Trojan Horse" (1970) dealt with the fact that many UFO reports often paralleled certain ancient folklore as well as historical humanoid and religious encounters. Keel died in 2009 at Mount Sinai Hospital in Manhattan, a city he escaped to when he was still a teenager, having been raised upstate and looking to broaden his life's horizons.

Really A Demonologist

Keel told UFO researcher George Filer that Keel considered himself not a Ufologist but a demonologist instead.

"I do not feel that the aliens are from other planets," Keel said, "but I believe we are dealing with the Devil, fallen angels and his demons. These evil spirits have been with us as long as recorded history and use deception, trickery, stunts, etc., to make us think they are alien."

Keel went on to tell Filer that he felt fairies, mystery airships, phantom aircraft, mystery helicopters, creatures, poltergeists, balls of light, and UFOs are all a cover for the real phenomenon to hide their evil

John Keel bestows the prestigious Falling Frog Award on Timothy Green Beckley. This solemn ceremony took place at a meeting of the New York Fortean Society, sometime in the late '80s or early '90s.

operations. In "Our Haunted Planet" (1971), he explains that they are not visitors to Earth but are disdainful and hostile toward humans. They attempt to control us and influence our beliefs.

In the aforementioned "UFOs: Operation Trojan Horse," Keel lays out his beliefs based on his many years of investigation.

"The statistical data that I have extracted," he wrote, "indicate that flying saucers are not stable machines requiring fuel, maintenance and logistical support. They are, in all probability, transmogrifications of energy and do not exist in the same way this book exists. They are not permanent constructions of matter."

Meanwhile, the messages received by the contactees are nothing new.

"The endless messages from the space people would now fill a library," according to Keel, "and while the communicators claim to represent some other world, the contents of those messages are identical to the messages long received by mediums and psychics."

Keel also scoffs at the notion of believing in the benevolent alien entity "Ashtar."

"Thousands of mediums, psychics and UFO contactees," he wrote, "have been receiving mountains of messages from 'Ashtar' in recent years. Mr. Ashtar represents himself as a leader in the great intergalactic councils which hold regular meetings on Jupiter, Venus, Saturn and many planets unknown to us. But Ashtar is not a new arrival. Variations of this name, such as Ashtaroth, Ashar, Asharoth, etc., appear in demonological literature throughout history, both in the Orient and the Occident. Mr. Ashtar has been around a very long time, posing as assorted gods and demons and now, in the modern phase, as another glorious spaceman. The Bible warns us that during 'the last days' this planet will be overrun with wonders in the sky and false prophets and performers of miracles. Could anyone else have said it any better?"

Alien Side Effects

Are people made crazy by the UFO encounter experience? Keel doesn't think the truth is that simple.

"I do not believe any of these people are suffering directly from clinical insanity," he said. "Rather, the evidence seems to indicate that their minds are manipulated by an exterior influence and

Was, in fact, the appearance of the creature dubbed Mothman -- as made famous by John Keel -- just another variation of the demonic theme?

that sometimes their emotional structure is unable to retain its stability in the face of these experiences. So some of these people crack under the strain. Induced confabulation produces memories of experiences that are convincingly real, and a chain reaction of emotional responses creates irrational fanaticism.

"These people abandon their jobs," he continued, "and devote all their time and thought to spreading the gospel of the space people. Their family relationships disintegrate because all of their energies are channeled into one direction. They become martyrs to their cause, be it the eminent arrival of the Big Brothers or the Second Coming of Christ.

"What this all really means is that someone or something actually has the power to completely possess and control the human mind. Human beings can be manipulated through this power and used for both good and evil purposes. We have no way of knowing how many human beings throughout the world may have been processed in

Original paperback edition of Keel's Mothman Prophecy with its original art work by Sci Fi illustrator Frank Frazetta.

this manner, because they would have absolutely no memory of undergoing this experience, and so we have no way of determining who among us has strange and sinister 'programs' lying dormant in the dark corners of his mind.

"Suppose the plan is to process millions of people and then at some future date trigger all of those minds at one time? Would we suddenly have a world of saints? Or would we have a world of armed maniacs shooting at one another from bell towers?"

Karla Turner

Karla Turner was a highly respected abduction researcher, author, lecturer and teacher. She received her Ph.D. from the University of North Texas in Denton. She authored three books about the abduction phenomenon: "Into the Fringe," "Taken," and "Masquerade of Angels." In 1995, Turner contracted a very dangerous form of breast cancer immediately following an abduction experience. She passed away the next year at the age of 48. She was adamant in her belief that UFOs and alien abduction are evil and abhorrent, and her courageous stance on the subject continues to be of benefit to many abductees today.

What Kinds of Spirits Are Involved?

Dr. Karla Turner stands beside Radio Misterioso host and Excluded Middle author Greg Bishop.

"Before we allow ourselves to believe in the benevolence of alien interaction," Turner sternly cautioned, "we should ask, 'Do enlightened beings need to use the cover of night to perform good deeds? Do they need to paralyze us and render us helpless to resist? Do angels need to steal our fetuses? Do they need to manipulate our children's genitals and probe our rectums? Are fear, pain and deception consistent with high spiritual motives?'"

In an article written for the now defunct "UFO Universe" magazine, Turner laid out her arguments for calling alien abduction evil.

"Some researchers have pointed out patterns of events in the abduction experience, such as the physical examination, the taking of sperm and ova, and the later presentation of a hybrid baby to the abductee. Other patterns include the training of the abductee in some way and the delivery of a warning of some upcoming global disaster. Yes, these events are frequently reported, and it is tempting to think that the explanation for alien abduction may lie in these patterns.

"So the researchers announce that the problem is solved. The aliens are doing crossbreeding experiments, ufologists tell us. Never mind the overwhelming evidence against the viable commingling of different species. Or, we are told, the aliens are here to save us from destroying ourselves and our planet through violence, drug use, epidemic disease, pollution and resource depletion. Never mind that these problems have grown worse, not better, since the ETs began visiting us."

Turner next presents a long checklist of events and experiences typically suffered by abductees. We will present only a portion of it here.

- Aliens can alter our perception of our surroundings.

- Aliens can control what we think we see. They can appear to us in any number of guises and shapes.

- Aliens can take us – our consciousness – out of our physical bodies, disable our control of our bodies, install one of their own entities, and use our bodies as vehicles for their own activities before returning our consciousness to our bodies.

- Aliens can be present with us in an invisible state and can make themselves only partially visible.

- A surprising number of abductees suffer from serious illnesses they didn't have before their encounters. These have led to surgery, debilitation, and even death from causes the doctors can't identify.

- Some abductees experience a degeneration of their mental, social and spiritual well-being. Excessive behavior frequently erupts, such as drug abuse, alcoholism, overeating and promiscuity. Strange obsessions develop and cause the disruption of normal life and the destruction of personal relationships.

- Some abductees report being taken to underground facilities where they see grotesque hybrid creatures, nurseries of hybrid humanoid fetuses, and vats of colored liquid filled parts of human bodies.

- Abductees report seeing other humans in these facilities being drained of blood, being mutilated, flayed, and dismembered, and being stacked, lifeless, like cords of wood. Some abductees have been threatened that they, too, will end up in this condition if they don't cooperate with their alien captors.

- Aliens have forced their human abductees to have sexual intercourse with aliens and even with other abductees while groups of aliens observe these performances. In such encounters, the aliens have sometimes disguised themselves in order to gain the cooperation of the abductee, appearing in such forms as Jesus, the Pope, certain celebrities, and even the dead spouse of the abductee.

"It becomes clear," Turner writes, "from these details that the beings who are doing such things can't be seen as spiritually enlightened, with the best interests of the human race in mind. Something else is going on, something far more painful and frightening, in many, many abduction encounters."

Blaming the Victim

In the article, Turner goes on to blast certain UFO researchers for blaming the abductees themselves for their negative reactions to the experience, saying the abductee is not sufficiently spiritually or psychically advanced enough to perceive the encounter in more benevolent terms.

"Having worked with so many decent, honest, positively oriented abductees, however, I believe this theory is wrong," Turner writes. "It is worse than wrong – it is despicable, as despicable as blaming a rape victim for the violence committed against her. This attitude leaves many abductees feeling doubly violated, first by the aliens who took them and then by the UFO researchers to whom they turn for explanation and help."

There is an understandable need, she acknowledges, for humans to believe in the power of good.

"We need for the aliens to be a good force," she admits, "since we feel so helpless in their presence. And we need for some superior force to offer us a hope of salvation, both personally and globally, when we consider the sorry state of the world."

The aliens understand that we hope for them to be benevolent creatures, she reasons, and that they use that desire for goodness to manipulate us.

"What better way to gain our cooperation than to tell us that the things they are doing are for our own good? Looking at the actions, the results of alien interference such as on the list above, there is a great discrepancy between what we desire from them and what they are doing to us."

Abduction researcher Dr. Karla Turner. The late Dr Karla Turner saw a grand deception in regard to the aliens amongst us.

Practiced At the Art of Deception

Turner also details the consistent patterns of deception that make up a great deal of the abduction experience. People sometimes report that they were treated kindly by the aliens, and were told that they were "special" or "chosen" to perform some important task for the benefit of humanity. Given such a positive message, the abductees may ignore the fear and pain of their encounters and insist to themselves and others that a higher motive underlies the abduction experience. They may only recall, in some cases, a benevolent encounter and have no memory of any negative action.

But intensive research now shows that at the core of the human-alien interaction is a clear pattern of deception.

"We know, for instance, that 'screen memories' are often used to mask an alien abduction. Such accounts abound, in which a person sees a familiar yet out-of-place animal, like a deer or owl, a monkey or a rabbit, and then experiences a period of missing time. The person often awakens later to find a new, unexplained scar on his body.

"Uneasiness about the encounter will persist, however, and far different memories may start to surface in dreams or flashbacks, and then the person seeks help to explain the uneasiness. Quite often, hypnotic regression is used to uncover the events behind the 'screen memory,' and that is when a typical alien abduction surfaces. However, from several recent cases, it is apparent that these recovered memories may well be yet another screen, masking events that are much more reprehensible."

So, according to Turner, abductees can't trust their screen memories nor can they trust the recovered memories that may come later. It quickly becomes a wickedly complex hall of mirrors in which the truth perishes somewhere in the many reflected surfaces. If things like forcible sexual intercourse and all the other forms of victimization can be defended in moral terms, we are a long way from understanding how.

Whitley Strieber and Budd Hopkins Wrestling with the Forces of Good and Evil

By Sean Casteel

Is it possible that the aliens stay hidden behind a mask and that we never see their true form or character? — Still from Communion, the movie.

When I was still new to the freelance journalism game and doing my first interviews on the subject of UFOs and alien abduction, I often asked the question of my interviewees, "Are the aliens good or evil?" Looking back, I realize the question was quite naïve, because the UFO mystery never gives up its secrets so easily. The answer to my question has grown more complex with every passing year, and defining the phenomenon in black and white moral terms is no longer an option.

Whitley Strieber –
The Face Behind Communion

I began to realize this when I first interviewed abductee and author Whitley Strieber back in the late spring of 1989, around the time that his blockbuster first-person abduction account "Communion" was being made into a movie.

When I asked the question about malevolence versus benevolence, he answered, "I don't think it's time to close the question about what they are. I don't believe in dichotomies of black and white, good and evil. It isn't the way life works and it isn't the way this experience works. It can be a very rough experience; there's no doubt about that. It is very rarely a beautiful experience, in the sentimental sense of 'sweetness and light.' It can be devastating, which it has been for me at times, because of its sheer power and the tremendously difficult experience of facing an enigma that is so volatile."

Four years later, in 1993, I interviewed Strieber again, this time for "UFO Magazine." When I broached the same question as before, he replied a little differently. He spoke a little about what his life had been like since the previous interview.

"I went through three years," he recounted, "from the middle of 1989 to the middle of last year, when I was so deeply depressed that nothing, no drug that the psychiatrist tried on me, nothing would get me out of it. I was almost inert. Then I had a Visitor encounter which was as usual unspeakably terrifying. You know, encountering them in a slightly dreamlike state for three seconds or three minutes is bad enough. But when you are face-to-face with them alone and it's not a dream and you're wide awake and you're wearing your clothes and you see them the way they really look, you cannot imagine how terrible it is.

"I've come away from this experience convinced of one thing," Strieber added. "If there aren't demons out there, there might as well be, because these guys are indistinguishable from demons. Indistinguishable. To see them, to look into their eyes, is to be less. Forever. It hurts you, it

The film version of Whitley Strieber's Communion has been released worldwide attracting a great deal of attention including its eye popping cover and poster art.

takes from you, forever. Because then you know that it exists, and that makes you less. Then you have to try to build on the scar tissue."

Budd Hopkins – Various Shades of Gray

Budd Hopkins and Whitley Strieber go back a long way together. Hopkins is a major player in Strieber's "Communion," being the first to step in and help Strieber understand what has happening to him. Hopkins has written a series of books on the abduction phenomenon, all of which have set a standard for objective research into the alien mystery that knows few equals.

Again in 1989, when I asked Hopkins for his take on the good versus evil question, he responded with a question of his own.

"Is Exxon a malevolent company?" he asked. "Or a benign, helpful, wonderful company? First you start with the oil spill. There's no arguing with the oil spill. But the oil spill doesn't really let you know Exxon's intentions or its moral character, its nature. I try very hard to avoid a kind of final statement as to the nature of the UFO occupants."

Rather than envisioning a case of simple evil on the part of the aliens, there is more evidence in Hopkins' experience to support the notion that the aliens simply don't understand what they're putting abductees through.

Sean Casteel (left) and Budd Hopkins at a 1996 meeting of the Mutual UFO Network in Ventura County, California. Hopkins says he refuses to draw any final conclusions as to whether the aliens are demonic.

"What you have to do," Hopkins said, "is pick this up by the human end of it. The aliens simply do not understand human emotions. They do not understand what they're putting us through on a psychological or traumatic level. They seem to be able to manipulate us physically and to wipe out our memory and have some sort of operative skill that way. But that doesn't necessarily give anybody an understanding of the entire situation. In my research, I strive to maintain this kind of pragmatic objectivity. Often I have to force down a lot of hopes and a lot of fears, too. Who the hell wouldn't want it to be different than it is? But what you get is what you get."

In that same interview, Hopkins approached the question from another angle. He told me that it was unfair to call the aliens either demons or gods because we don't make that same judgment with people.

"For example," he said, "if someone is rude to you or says something stupid or hurts your feelings, you might say, 'Well, he's usually very nice to me, and I don't know what happened.' But you don't say, 'Now I realize that he's a demon.' Just as when someone is nice to you and buys you a present or takes you out to dinner, you might say, 'Well, it was so good of him,' whatever. But you don't say, 'Now I realize that he's a god.'"

The upshot being that we should be at least as fair in moral terms with the aliens as we are with our own kind. Whether that comparison would have meaning to someone who's literally had a close encounter with something evil is another question altogether. And the answer to that question is still as morally complex as it was before.

Extreme Warning To Potential UFO Contactees

By Brad Steiger

Well-intentioned and earnest men and women often write to us asking how they might establish contact with alien intelligences from other worlds, beings from the Fairy Realm, entities from other dimensions, or angels from the higher planes. We always advise extreme caution to these folks, who truly may not be aware of what they are asking.

To seek to make contact with any form of multidimensional intelligence--whether elf, guardian angel, spirit guide, or space entity--without first undergoing an extensive program of study, self-examination, and disciplined training can be very risky. To open your psyche to these energies before you have achieved a high degree of spiritual balance is to run the risk of setting destructive forces loose on you and your household or inviting a parasitic, disruptive intelligence into your soul.

To demonstrate our point, we present herewith the experience of a group of very able, highly intelligent young men who thought that they could successfully interact with the UFO mystery and become masters of the universe.

They Thought Their Intellect Could Control the Alien Intelligences

Bill Fogarty saw a UFO in the early 1970s when he was a twenty-year-old college junior at the University of Indiana at South Bend. One night a short time later, he mentioned his sighting to the members of an informal group that got together one evening a week to discuss politics, philosophy, and art. The discussion became freewheeling as members argued the pros and cons of the reality of flying saucers and the possibility of extraterrestrial life-forms.

That night on his way home, Fogarty sighted another UFO. He was reluctant to mention this second sighting, thinking that his friends would hardly find it credible, given the topic of the evening's lively discussion. The next day, however, he was astonished to learn that four other members of the group claimed to have witnessed a low UFO over-flight that night as they drove hack to their respective apartments.

In his written report to us, Fogarty emphasized that he and his friends were all physically fit, nondrinkers, and non-dopers. Two of them were Vietnam War combat veterans. Each of the five prided himself on maintaining a cool, analytical approach to all aspects of life, and all were especially skeptical of anything that smacked of the occult or the bizarre.

And yet each of them swore that he had seen what was unmistakably an object in the night sky that he could not identify as a conventional aircraft, an ordinary celestial manifestation, a weather balloon, a bird, or anything else that could have been flying above them.

Four nights later, two of the five saw another UFO.

Then, on the next evening, Fogarty and the other two saw a brightly glowing object overhead as they returned around one o'clock from a movie.

"We decided to form a splinter group in order to focus on the UFO phenomenon," Fogarty said. "We were well aware that the main group of culture vultures would mock us for our flying saucer experiences, so we headed for an all-night pancake house to compare notes and thoughts on our subjective responses while undergoing the experience of encountering what certainly appeared to us to be unknown phenomena."

Brad Steiger

It was not long before the five of them had a group sighting of a UFO. From that evening on, they instituted nightly sky watches.

"We all witnessed UFOs cavorting in the midnight sky," Fogarty said. "On one occasion I stood within ten feet of two nocturnal lights hovering silently in midair. Later, we heard rappings in the dark, hollow voices, heavy breathing, and the crushing footsteps of unseen entities. Strangely enough we were all able to maintain our cool toward the phenomena occurring around us. Maybe we had been chosen for some kind of special interaction with higher beings. Perhaps, secretly, we were beginning to view ourselves as masters of two worlds."

After all, Fogarty pointed out, they were all dean's list students, all athletic young men, normally balanced emotionally, mentally, sexually. "I guess we felt that modem

Renaissance men such as ourselves should be able to deal rationally with such phenomena and stay completely in control of the situation."

But then, suddenly, the manifestations became more aggressive and hostile. Just when they thought they were capable of exercising control over the invisible forces emanating from the UFO, the apprentice wizards found that not only were they far from being the equals of the unseen visitors, they were also in danger of losing control over themselves.

One night invisible energies swept through the home of one group member, pounding on the walls, yanking furiously at the bedposts, striking the startled young man in the face, terrorizing his entire family. Some of the group were followed by automobiles that seemed a bizarre mixture of styles and models.

Within the next few months, the number of harrowing incidents directed against the students increased and expanded to include strange, dark-clad, nocturnal visitors in the apartments of several of them.

Radio and television sets switched on by themselves.

Doors opened and closed--although when they were tested, they were found locked.

One member of the group made the extraordinary claim that he had been teleported one night from his bedroom to the middle of a forest on the outskirts of the city. "As preposterous as all this might sound," Fogarty stated, "I'm sure that most of us accepted all of these experiences as true, since we had all undergone some incredible encounters. We had all lost our sense of perspective."

Fogarty admitted that he had begun sleeping with a light on and a .38 special under his pillow. Another of the five invested heavily in weapons and began running with a group that offered sacrifices to Odin. A third was "born again" into fundamentalist Christianity. The remaining two dropped out of college a month before they would have graduated with honors.

By the time that he made his report to us, Bill Fogarty had had several years to consider the big question of what it all had meant, the bold quest of five bright young men to tackle the UFO mystery and to seek to become one with its energy.

"I think the five of us believed that we had entered a kind of game, a contest, a challenge, a testing experience," he said. "The trouble was, we just didn't know all the rules.

"Modern society doesn't prepare its youth to play those kinds of games. Modern society doesn't tell its kids that there is another reality around them. Our educators have ignored the individual mystical experience and the other dimensions that can open up to those who enter altered states of consciousness--whether it be through drugs or through accidentally stumbling into the twilight zones."

Bill Fogarty recalled that at first he had the feeling that they were dealing with some kind of energy emanating from outer space, from some alien world, but he now believes that they somehow activated some energy that is a part of this planet. "I think we might have triggered some kind of archetypal pattern with our minds. Maybe that's what magicians have tried to do since Cro-Magnon days--interact with and control the energy with their minds."

But how had such intelligent, resourceful young men lost control of their experiment? Why had they ended up paranoid, frightened, or converted to widely disparate philosophies?

Bill Fogarty's answer was honest and direct: "Because we weren't magicians obviously. We had no idea just how deadly serious the game could become. It really is a game for wizards, not for some smart-ass college students who believe that their brilliant intellects and the theories in their physics books can provide an answer for everything."

Mark Allowed His Body to Become an Alien's "Reference Point" on Earth

A much worse scenario than that experienced by Bill Fogarty and his friends was that of a young man named Mark, who believed that he had made contact with an extraterrestrial being. After a period of increasingly dramatic interaction, this entity agreed to grant Mark certain concessions in return for allowing it to use his body.

The being did not give itself a name, saying only that it was a multidimensional being whose substance was to any energy. While its essence permeated the entire universe, it could, by effort of will, concentrate its force and be at any point in the cosmos for the purpose of making contact with beings still bound to the physical plane. Its reason for making the contact with Mark was to enable it to have a point of reference on Earth.

The entity had originally represented itself to Mark as neutral in the affairs of humans. But, tragically, by the time Mark realized the entity's true nature, he was forced to remain committed to the contract that he had made.

According to Mark's friend Bob: "The being at last identified itself to Mark as 'Asmitor,' and his description of it was very similar to those H. P. Lovecraft uses in his stories of the Elder Gods and the Old Ones. The entity was infinite in its expanse, a tenuous network of energy that stretched throughout the universe, but which had consciousness and the ability to concentrate itself at any one point on this level of reality, but only when expressly invited--or, in Mark's case, unknowingly invited. Mark had opened the door to the entity by his use of psychedelics without proper protective preparation."

Mark learned that there were two types of entities, essentially equal in power and scope, perpetually at war over the ownership of the physical universe. Mark was led to believe that Asmitor and his forces would win the next great battle and that he would be rewarded by receiving some of the spoils of war.

Such beings as Asmitor needed human points of reference on the earth plane of reality because the more points they had, the better they would be able to fight against the opposing force, which was also working to gain its own points of reference on the planet. "Apparently, these entities were not able to perceive our level of existence directly," Bob concluded, "but only indirectly through the minds of their servitors."

Mark became disenchanted when most of the powers that Asmitor promised him failed to materialize. He was unable to levitate objects; he had no demonstrable powers of telepathy; the curses he levied upon his enemies seemed to have no effect. But the deceitful Asmitor was now so completely in control of his body that Mark felt the only way to achieve freedom from the entity was to destroy himself by committing suicide.

Although the name "Asmitor" had meant nothing to Bob when Mark had first identified it, after his friend's death Bob chanced across it in a medieval text on magic:

"It was--I believe--in the works of Agrippa (1486-1535), a German soldier, physician, and an adept in alchemy, astrology, and magic. I am convinced that Mark had never read this book; and I am also convinced that he did not simply make up this name. In my opinion, my discovery of the name was a piece of corroborating evidence to indicate that rather than a case of insanity, Mark's case was one of true demonic possession."

Bob has become a very serious student of magic and mysticism, and he stated firmly that he has come to believe in entities from other planes of existence. Although he personally refers to these beings as the "Secret Chiefs," he concedes that they might just as easily be called angels, masters, guides, UFO beings, or even gods, who operate from another plane of being to influence humankind's development and to direct it in ways that are not always comprehensible to the people being subtly manipulated: "The overall goal of these beings may be incomprehensible to us--or from a human and very limited point of view, may seem to be evil. Human value judgments really don't apply on these levels ... We must accept that [the Secret Chiefs] are a natural development of the universe and that they exist with as much validity as we do."

Bob reminded us of the line in C. S. Lewis' "The Screwtape Letters," in which a demon declares that once humankind has produced the true materialist magician—an individual who will worship what he calls "Forces" without acknowledging the existence of consciousness behind those Forces—the demons may then consider that they have won the eternal battle between good and evil.

"Too many modern materialistic scientists fit this description," Bob observed.

The Devil's Horn: A Minister Confronts Satan's ET Principalities

By Sean Casteel

Minister, researcher and author Tom Horn says he came to his calling as a minister at a young age and served as a pastor for almost 25 years. His interest in demonology began during that period for personal reasons, including an incident that happened to his sister when he was still a child that will be expounded upon as we go on. That incident, which today would be called an "alien abduction," has remained lodged uncomfortably in his memory to the present time.

As an adult, Horn, as is typical in the aftermath of an abduction, felt he had no one he could talk to about the experience, that the subject was fringe and taboo at best.

"If you pressed the question," he said, "there was only ever one answer, and that was that it was demonic activity, which I came to believe that a very large part of it is. But it still wasn't really helpful to me at the time to just have pat answers because having the experience in my

One of the most articulate spokespersons for the darker side of UFOs. Dr Horn has written numerous books explaining his position on the paranormal and has a very active website www.raidersnewsnetwork.com/

family made the whole question so much deeper, so much more personal, because I wanted to be able to help my sister, and ultimately her daughter and her daughter's daughter. So it became a generational thing."

The problem of his sister's abduction was always in the back of Horn's mind, and he felt nothing that he was taught in seminary, the pat answers and the proof texts, had prepared him to deal with the supernatural on a personal level. Thus began his quest for answers.

Life's Biggest Questions

"There are hidden or unseen intelligences all around us," Horn said. "And sometimes, for reasons we may not possibly be able to understand, this reality tries to reach through from this other dimension and touch us or interact with us. It's something that intersects with our humanity on so many different levels, including spiritually.

"I would think that most people," he continued, "to some degree, at some level, have an interest in knowing the answers, right? To life's biggest questions, like is there a beyond? And if there is a beyond, is there life after death? Are we the only thing there? Are there other realities there? Is the Bible true? Are there angels? Is there a God? Are there demons? These really form the crux of some of the biggest unanswered questions for the humanist, if you will, in life."

Horn said his interest in demonology sprang from that same average inquisitiveness, but that his curiosity was not unhealthy in the sense that he didn't set out to conjure contact with spirits or something like that, preferring instead a theological, philosophical approach.

Confronting the Supernatural In Person

During his years as a pastor, Horn was present at an incident he felt could only be called "supernatural." It involved a possessed boy who was the son of another pastor.

"Out of rebellion against his dad," Horn said, "he tried to find the most demonic music he could and to do anything and everything he could. He became, in the very classic sense, possessed by demons."

In a scene right out of the movies, with 40 or 50 of the congregants of Horn's church there as witnesses, the possessed boy charged toward Horn.

"I was the pastor," he explained, "so I was the target. This kid ran toward me and leaped and I don't know what happened. He hit something, and he hit it instantly and very hard. We couldn't see anything there, but it was just like there was a giant pane of unbreakable glass or something because he hit it and abruptly fell straight down to the ground.

"And I'll tell you, the impact of that moment was so powerful that I watched as, like a wave, all 40-some people that were standing there fell to their knees and raised their hands and started worshipping God. I mean, instantly."

One could not have concocted such a moment, Horn said, and for everyone present it was their first brush with something that couldn't be explained by the laws of physics as people understand them.

"But at that moment," he continued, "they knew that there is a God in heaven and at his right hand is a man by the name of Jesus and that every power on Earth is subject to his authority. That was the one and only time I've ever seen anything that legitimately to me could not be explained other than to describe it as a supernatural event. Well, then, that, of course, raised my interest beyond the theoretical."

Horn would later work for three and a half years with a group that dealt in exorcism but declines to talk about that period because of privacy issues for the people involved.

What Is A Demon?

Just how does Horn define the word "demon" after all these years of study? In his book "Forbidden Gates" (2010) he lays out several possibilities for what a demon is.

"I describe these different theories," he said. "Demons as spirits of a pre-Adamic race. Demons as otherworldly beings, ET. Demons as offspring of angels and women. Demons as the spirits of dead, evil people. Demons as fallen angels. That happens to be the one that's the most popular in classic Christianity. But in the book, I describe theory number six, which is several of the above. And frankly, for me and my worldview, that's probably the most legitimate. It's probably unwise to try to define the kingdom of the demonic world.

"What constitutes, as in Ephesians 6:12, 'principalities and powers, rulers of darkness, evil spiritual forces in high places,' it's a mistake to classify all of that as being one single thing, like fallen angels. It's possible that that is exactly what it is, but it's also possible that we're talking about a variety of spiritual influences that during the fall of Lucifer were impacted in different ways."

Satan's Hold On the Government

However one defines demons, the fact is they exert a definite influence on the governments of the world.

"When you see the machinations," Horn said, "that are going on sometimes, let's say, in Washington, DC, and you can't quite figure out where in the world these guys are coming from, why don't they represent us better, whatever, it could be that whispering in their ear is this evil influence that comes from the cosmos."

Horn justified this belief by referring to the New Testament.

"The Bible," he said, "in several places refers to Satan as the 'god of this world.' In fact, you notice when Jesus came, Satan takes him up to a high mountain and shows him all the kingdoms of the Earth. And he says, 'If you will bow down and worship me, I will give you these.' And Jesus doesn't dispute that it's within Satan's authority to do that. We are still in a situation where the Devil is the god of this world.

"And so it is from that dominion," Horn continued, "that his influence seeks to reach through into the mind of politicians and the government, because if he can lead a government to become selfish, to no longer serve the needs of the people, then they become Luciferian, they become like Lucifer, who was raised up, saying, 'I will be like God, and I will do all these things.'"

This same devilish influence is also directed at the churches and local governments and seeks to undermine the country's social philosophy as a whole. But Horn believes these multiple evils can still be overcome by fervent prayer on the part of "prayer warriors."

"Fervent prayer by the righteous," he said, "would be the battering rams that could push through that demonic oppression."

Are ET Grays Simply Demons?

The above question was posed to Horn, and he gave a surprisingly open-ended response.

"I think the question might be a little more complicated," he replied. "Meaning, for instance, that there's a theory that suggests that alien activity, including abduction by these grays, might actually be something that's outside the sin or moral or malevolent question and therefore outside the question, is it a demon?"

Horn went on to explain that he was shown an archetype by a friend named Dr. Michael Heiser, and it's an explanation Horn has come to call "Heiser's Lion."

"What Heiser was saying," Horn began, "was that ET possibly is something that is intelligent, was created by God, but is not something that we really know anything about. It's similar to like an unknown animal."

Horn had written to Heiser asking a hypothetical question that went like this: If ET behaves in a fallen manner, does that indicate that he is demonic? That he is sinful?

Heiser replied that one would only use words like sin if the entity doing the action was morally culpable, which ET might not be. If a dog or a lion – thus Horn's reason for calling the theory "Heiser's Lion" – attacks a person, we would not say that the dog or the lion sinned. What we might say is that the dog or lion did what it did as a general, even if it is awful, byproduct of the fall of all humanity and nature. So we don't assign moral culpability to creatures.

"If you're a missionary," Horn went on, "and you go to Africa and you walk out in the middle of a field and a lion runs up and eats you, we would say that was horrible. We would say that was the result of the fall of man. We'd say all those things. But what we would not do is ascribe immorality or malevolence to the lion. We would say the lion simply does what lions do. In this current world condition, they are predators."

Heiser's point was that it was overly simplistic to say that ET either was or was not demonic.

"It could be that we're talking about something," Horn said, "that is outside that paradigm. God didn't bother to explain who or what these creatures are. Now is Heiser right about that? I have no idea. I can tell you that, as a pastor, that there is a great deal about the whole ET phenomenon that to me is demonic in the very classical, Biblical and historical sense. But to answer your question, I would offer that just as a theory."

Demons and Their Use of UFOs

"Then I would add, and this is more along the lines of my own thinking," he continued, "that there's no doubt that demons in the Biblical sense could be producing UFO phenomena, alien abduction phenomena. And doing it for their own reasons. In theology, there's a term called 'transmogrification,' where spirits can take form. They can move things around, like poltergeist activity. Well, the only way they would be able to do that is if they have some capacity for manipulating energy, manipulating matter.

"And that being true, maybe demons produce the phenomenon that is known as, for instance, unidentified flying objects, that they do that by manipulating energy. There is a whole list of reasons around why they might do that, including for the purposes of deceiving mankind."

In fact, demons may be the driving force behind what is called in Ufology the "Disclosure Movement."

"I do believe there is a point coming at which there is going to be an official disclosure," Horn said. "If the demons are involved with any of that activity, what might be their purpose?"

One of the obvious purposes would be to confuse the field of human origins and to draw Christians and other believers away from their faith in God as the creator.

"This ageless question, where did we come from? If people believe that Ufonauts are advanced extraterrestrials scurrying about in spaceships, and that those creatures perhaps even visited Earth in ancient days, the ancient astronauts theory, that they tinkered with hominid DNA, apes or whatever, and uplifted them to our current status and created homo sapiens, then that would obliterate portions of the Judeo-Christian doctrine concerning the age of the Earth and Biblical creation. In other words, people would be led to believe that we're nothing more than an alien zoology program. So that's one of the areas in which this could be a problem."

A Great End Time Deception

"Secondly," Horn went on, "it might also have something to do with eschatological issues, End Time issues, a great deception, in other words. It says in the New Testament that the appearance of the antichrist is going to be accompanied by quote, 'fearful sights and great signs from heaven,' end quote. You have the book of Second Thessalonians even saying that when the antichrist is revealed he's going to be accompanied by 'lying wonders.'

Often obsessing with the occult can open a doorway to another realm where good or bad entities can enter
(Photo by Tonya Mathews)

"What are these lying wonders? Some people believe they might be like a UFO armada, something that could be used to introduce the Man of Sin, the antichrist. Wouldn't the world react to the sudden arrival of an intergalactic wise man with an armada of ships with paralyzing awe and wonder? So maybe this deception could be a part of how the demonic world would use it, to paralyze humanity, to stop all the social structures as we know them. I mean, who's going to be going to the bank and drawing out some money and going to Walmart shopping for a Christmas present if all of a sudden you've got a mile-wide UFO hovering over the White House? It would literally stop all of the economies of the world."

The intergalactic wise man could suddenly step forward, according to Horn, and declare himself to have all the answers humanity needs. Meanwhile, the world would be on its knees, reeling from the shock of economic chaos and the shaking of the Earth to its very core. The state of collapse would lead people to quickly warm up to the antichrist as a genuine messiah, which would be a crucial element in a great deception. We, the general populace, are even now being prepared for disclosure and/or a great appearance of ships in our skies, a program of "warming up to the idea" or being conditioned to accept it once it comes.

Some UFOs Are Righteous

Horn does acknowledge that he's in agreement with another Christian scholar of prophecy and UFOs, Gary Stearman, of the satellite television program "Prophecy In The News," who believes that God also employs what we would call UFOs as a kind of "celestial transportation vehicle."

"I like that," Horn said, "and it's probably valid. Because the Bible does discuss things like God riding on a cloud and his angels using chariots, such as the Old

Testament story of Elisha and his servant. In fact, the term 'chariot' in the Old Testament Hebrew is the 'merkavim,' and this is a flying vehicle. Sometimes it's visible to our eyes, sometimes it's not. Even the Lord himself is moved about with the merkavim."

Horn next made reference to the familiar first chapter of Ezekiel, in which the Lord appears to the prophet on what can only be seen as one of these flying chariots. But Horn went into more detail on a Biblical story that is less well known.

"Have you ever looked at First Chronicles 28:18?" he asked. "Anybody who's studying in this field ought to read this verse, because it's a little bit mind-blowing in that it's describing how the priests are instructed to build a golden model of the chariot of the cherubim that 'spread out their wings.' Now the reason why that is so extraordinary is – and by the way, wouldn't you want to find that golden replica of the chariot of the cherubim that spread out their wings? The whole term 'that spread out their wings' is an Old Testament-era phrase. It is in the Hebrew Old Testament.

"But in many cultures, you see the winged flying geniuses, you see winged discs. This is an ancient terminology that was used whenever you wanted to typify something that had the power of flight, it had the power to move through the air. Gary Stearman pointed out that when you look at this description of the priest being told to build a golden model after the pattern of the chariot of the cherubim that spread out their wings, that that pattern seemed to be wheel-shaped or circular, a flying wheel. That is consistent within the Old Testament. Daniel the prophet uses descriptive language associated with God in Daniel 7:9, where he talks about how God's 'wheels are as a burning fire that go back and forth from his throne.' Those seem to be the chariots of the angels, the circular-shaped merkavim."

The idea of celestial craft, even celestial wars, fought by angelic beings, is a universal story, and cultures around the world have documented such events, from the Sumerians to the Egyptians to the Greeks.

"The ancient Chinese told of a primeval war involving flying carts," Horn said, "and there's a Sanskrit text that actually documents dogfights by angels in their flying machines. So this is a very widespread story. It is a mistake for people to perceive that angels or demons lack physical or scientific ability and that they are not at some level using these merkavim, that they're using an advanced form of science as transportation devices, just like Gary Stearman says."

Setting the Stage For A Mystery

The conversation returned to the story of Horn's sister's abduction. It began with Horn's father, who was working as a police officer in the Arizona desert region.

"He hunted all over the desert," Horn said. "He knew the desert like the back of his hand. He knew all the Indians and all the reservations, and they liked him. He could go on their land and do anything he wanted to do."

Horn's father was hunting for mule deer on the northeastern ridge of an Arizona mountain range when he came around a corner and saw three very large, perfectly spherical craters in the earth.

"These things are maybe like 20 feet across and they're 8 or 10 feet deep," Horn said. "They're so precise that they look like an enormous white hot ball had simply been pushed down into the rock, white hot to the point where it could just literally melt the rock. He'd never seen anything like this."

Water had collected in the spherical holes, and local deer attempted to drink there. Some of them slipped into the holes and drowned.

"One of them was still alive," Horn continued, "and was swimming around in a circle while my dad was there. So dad took pictures of these holes, and, as a police officer, when he got back, he called the Army Corps of Engineers and talked to them about it. He couldn't figure out where these holes had come from. How were the made? What are they? What would be the purpose behind them? They had appeared so quickly that even the local Indians weren't even aware they were there."

A story about the holes, complete with a photo of Horn's father holding his hunting rifle, appeared in "The Phoenix Gazette," the largest newspaper in the Arizona. The Army Corps of Engineers finally dynamited the holes full of rock in order to prevent further local wildlife from sliding into them and dying.

Many years later, in 1975, the famous Travis Walton abduction case took place in the same approximate location.

"Travis Walton claims that he stepped out of a pickup," Horn said, "to look at a glowing object. According to his report, while his logger buddies waited nearby, he approached this UFO and was jolted by a blast of inexplicable energy. His companions all take off, leaving him there. He claims he was taken onboard an alien spacecraft and subjected to a whole variety of physical examinations. His story throughout time has been considered to be perhaps the best-documented case of abduction in history."

Touched By A Demon?

The connection between the mysterious holes and the Travis Walton abduction is an important one to Horn because of something that happened a few weeks after Horn's father made the bizarre discovery.

"My aunt, who lived just a few doors down from us, showed up one day petrified, claiming that she had seen a large, disc-shaped object hovering over our home. I can still to this day remember that a few days later I was lying in bed – I was really young – and all of a sudden I hear my sister screaming in a way you never want to hear a person scream. We all ran to her room, but my dad made me and my brother go back to our rooms. I did not know for many years what had happened that night. But it happened."

Horn's sister related her experience to him when he was an adult and a pastor and beginning to struggle with many unanswered questions.

"She said, 'I woke up and there were these three small bubble-headed gray beings. They were standing at the edge of my bed, by my feet. They were talking in a language I couldn't understand.'"

She had closed her eyes and started screaming, and by the time she opened her eyes, the family was gathered around her and the three small grays were gone.

Dr. Tom Horn's sister had a recent brush with what Tom believes may be a gray or a demon. This unexplainable image -- see figure over her head to the right -- appeared while she was on webcam chatting with friends on the computer.

"There was nothing there," Horn said. "But her case had all the earmarks of the classic alien abduction phenomenon. The story gets very interesting and complicated because years later she married a guy who was a nuclear physicist who worked for General Atomic and later at Los Alamos. She told him, finally, after they'd been married for a while. She told him about her experience as a child and how those experiences had been repeated at different times throughout her life."

The sister's husband acknowledged that he knew the phenomenon was real but instructed her not to talk about it. Shortly after this conversation, the husband vanished without a trace and neither the sister nor anyone else ever saw him again.

Horn says the legal complications that followed are well-documented. After two years, the husband's employers at Los Alamos finally admitted he had been killed there, but would not say how. Horn's sister was also not able to obtain a death certificate and was therefore unable to draw on her husband's Social Security. Horn's sister's daughter was a federal employee in the Social Security division and she managed to step in and get the death benefit payments for her mother even without a formal death certificate.

"As far as I know," Horn said, "that's never happened before. So you have to wonder, somebody at some level, what are they trying to hide? To cover up?"

Another incident took place more recently. Horn's sister was at home using her computer, which was equipped with a Skype-type camera.

"She's chatting with her friends when all of sudden in the camera there appears something behind her that looks very much like some kind of reptilian or gray alien. It's only in one frame. Well, she freaked completely out. Then she sent me the picture."

Horn forwarded the picture to expert photo analyst Stan Deyo, who reported back that whatever the image was, it had not been faked and appeared to be something genuinely three-dimensional.

"So very strange," Horn said. "If you understand the whole story, here on the one hand you have a very traditional, old-fashioned, conservative Christian, conservative theology, conservative in every sense of the word. So why would a guy like me even be interested in talking about this crazy stuff like aliens and alien abduction and UFOs? Partly because that history is there."

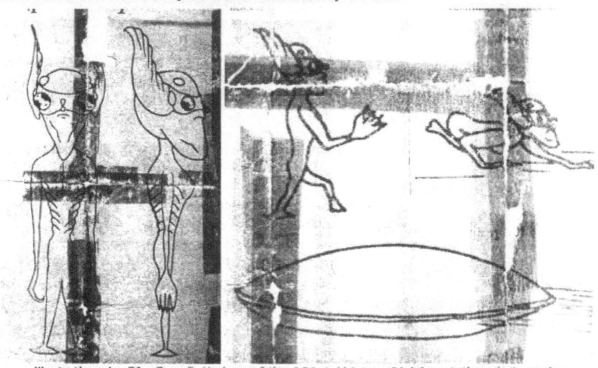

Illustrations by Pfc. Gary F. Hodson of the 101st Airborne Division stationed at nearby Fort Campbell, who was sent to interview the witnesses of the Hopkinsville incidents

Visual evidence of the resemblemce of demons and aliens.

The Kelly–Hopkinsville encounter, also known as the Hopkinsville Goblins Case, and to a lesser extent the Kelly Green Men Case, is the name given to a series of presumably connected incidents of alleged close encounters with supposed extraterrestrial beings. The incidents occurred in the fall of 1955, the most famous and well-publicized of which centered around a rural farmhouse at the time belonging to the Sutton family, which was located between the hamlet of Kelly and the small city of Hopkinsville, both in Christian County, Kentucky, United States. It is from these main incidents that the entire case takes its name.

Witnesses included not just the two families present at the farmhouse but also numerous other civilians, although only members of the two families -not any policeman or member of the military personnel- ever alleged to have actually seen the creatures themselves. All other people were only witnesses to lights in the sky and sounds.

However the events at Hopkinsville in Kentucky, 1955, are regarded as one of the most significant, well-known and well-documented cases in the history of UFO incidents, and a favorite for study in ufology, as witnesses there included policemen and state troopers, and were taken seriously enough as to be officially investigated by the United States Air Force.

There was also another encounter with allegedly the same creatures in another part of the United States along the Ohio River a week prior to the incidents in Kentucky, which itself had numerous witnesses. An incident in the United Kingdom occurred some two decades later also with allegedly the same creatures, amongst other alleged sightings of the creatures elsewhere.

From Wikipedia.com

Exorcising Hitler's Demons

"Follow Hitler! He will dance, but it is I who has called the tune! I have initiated him into the Secret Doctrine, opened his centers of vision, and given him the means to communicate with the power. Do not mourn for me: I shall have influenced history more than any other German
                                    Dietrich Eckart, from his deathbed, December, 1923

History shows him to have been a beast – a demon incarnate!

When Hitler first emerged as a political figure from a bleak European landscape after World War I there was no way humankind could know what terror he would shortly unleash upon the world.

My estimation of the situation is that many – but not all – of the of disc-shaped devices parading across the sky in the late 1940s and 1950s were in fact constructed by Nazi engineers and scientists – INCLUDING WERNER VON BRAUN – brought here unlawfully from Germany under the auspices of the highly classified Project Paperclip. I said this as far back as 1962 but no one listened. They were more hell-bent on promoting the mistaken concept that flying

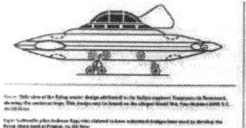

The earliest non-fiction assertion of Nazi flying saucers appears to have been an article which appeared in the Italian newspaper Il Giornale d'Italia in early 1950. Written by Professor Giuseppe Belluzzo, an Italian scientist and a former Italian Minister of National Economy under the Mussolini regime, it claimed that "types of flying discs were designed and studied in Germany and Italy as early as 1942". Belluzzo also expressed the opinion that "some great power is launching discs to study them".

saucers HAD to be craft from outer space. As thoughts of the crash at Roswell danced in their heads like sugar plum fairies, no other theory was acceptable under threat of being ostracized from the fledgling UFO community. Chances are the craft that crashed outside this little New Mexican desert town was piloted by those who made the swastika their good luck symbol, the "alien" craft having been constructed by means of channeled information bought to this world through mediums associated with a German Secret Society organized circa 1919.

All one has to do is study the history of the UFO movement in America to realize that while the government discredited almost everything to do with the subject, they did push hard to make it known that if you were going to believe in flying saucers you had to believe that they were interplanetary in origin and piloted either by bug-eyed aliens or long haired Venusians, the latter no doubt done with a wink and a chortle behind our backs, realizing that the blonde "Venusians" represented the Aryan race which Hitler hoped would facilitate his conquering the world. Such groups as the National Investigations Committee on Aerial Phenomenon (NICAP) were top heavy with official brass – including CIA informants – who, though officially they were reluctant to acknowledge UFO reality, were essentially willing to offer more than just quasi-support to an organization who proclaimed flying saucers were from outer space! Among those consulted was an elderly German rocketry expert named Professor Herman Oberth, who kept close company with Werner Von Braun and spouted his belief in the extraterrestrial theory that has never been proven beyond a shadow of a doubt. Talk about a fox in the hen house offering up a heaping serving of disinformation and misdirection to throw us off the track and conceal the fact that his brother Nazis were involved in the UFO mystery more than anyone could realize at the time.

Abducted by Aliens author Chuck Weiss has researched the Nazi occult "conspiracy" extensively and observes that, as a young man, "Hitler came under the influence of Germany's darkest occultists, members of the Thule Society and its inner circle of Black Magicians called 'The Luminous Lodge,' although amongst themselves these Magicians referred to their order as the 'Vril Society.'"

This, says Weiss, was the beginning of the twentieth century's "great struggle between the Light and the Dark, when Adolph Hitler rose to absolute power in Germany and almost succeeded in his attempt to dominate the world. What only a few people understood at the time, and what was never publicly acknowledged, was the fact that the Nazi hierarchy, including Hitler himself, was deeply involved in the practice of Black Magick." In fact, Hitler himself claimed to have met the "superman" and stated that he was evil beyond belief!

Did this "superman" originate on another world or did he pop in from another dimension?

Unequivocally so!

The Beautiful Mediums of the VRIL

Maria   Traute   Sigrun   Gudrun   Heike

Einige der wichtigsten "Vril-Damen" zwischen 1922 und 1945

The female Vril members were all beautiful and captivating and grew their hair long as they claimed it was sort of an antenna that allowed them make contact more easily with their interdimensional "masters."

Round Trip to Hell in a Flying Saucer

Das Schnellste von allem was fliegt, ist der Gedanke.

Rig-Veda

Though she used several names Maria Orsic was without a doubt the most powerful of the female Vril mediums.

They were utterly fetching.

Almost beautiful beyond belief.

A true Aryan's dream.

Even the top-ranking officer of the SS, Rudolf Hess, was smitten,

so much so that he listened enraptured as the young mediums formed a séance circle and began to channel communications from an unknown race far removed from the bunkers of Berlin.

Artist and historical architect Jim Nichols of Tucson has examined the role of UFOs and ETs in the formation and development of Nazi Germany, noting: "The medium Maria Orsic was leader of the Vrilerinnen, the beautiful young ladies of the Vril Gesellschaft. Characteristically they all wore their hair in long horsetails, contrary to the popular short bobbed fashion of their day, claiming their long hair acted as cosmic antennas that helped facilitate their contact with extraterrestrials beings from beyond."

And furthermore, says Nichols, "According to the legend of the German Vril Society, a fateful meeting was held in 1919 at an old hunting lodge near Berchtesgaden, where Maria Orsic presented, to a small group assembled from the Thule, Vril and Black Sun Societies, telepathic messages she claimed to have received from an extraterrestrial civilization existing in the distant Aldebaran solar system, sixty-eight light years away, in the Constellation of Taurus. One set of Maria's channeled transmissions was found to be in a secret German Templar script unknown to her." When translated these transmissions held the key to constructing a circular flying craft capable of traveling around the world at great speed as well as exiting the Earth's uppermost atmospheric levels.

The Vril Society as stated was an occult "Luminous Lodge" that was a sort of inner circle for the Thule society that was in close contact with an English-based group called the Hermetic Order of the Golden Dawn, a magical cabal that had great influence on western occultism throughout the 18th and 19th centuries. The members of the Golden Dawn were Rosicrucians and Masons and it is said they conjured up many an obstinate spirit. The Vril ladies claimed their group was formed as a meditation and mystical society meant to awaken the Vril force or "prana," as many would come to call this invisible mystical cosmic force today. Any of the ancillary benefits such as contacting extraterrestrials would come as a bonus . . . a bonus that Hitler and his henchmen became fascinated with as it offered up a potential power comparable – perhaps surpassing – anything being developed by the Allies.

The Vril mediums were perplexed by the content of the messages from off world. One of their order, a psychic known as Sigrun (named after one of the nine daughters of Wotan of Norse mythology), joined the gallery and began to decipher the images being channeled via automatic writing. It is generally thought that the transmissions were strikingly similar to ancient Sumerian.

The History of Nazi Flying Discs

Sources that describe the Nazi flying disc program are sketchy and frequently contradictory. The following narrative has been posted on various sites on the worldwide web and seems as coherent as one could hope to find on the subject of Hitler's flying discs at this point. Some of it may be based on reality; other parts may be pure fantasy. All one knows is that its inherent evil may still be present upon the Earth, hidden in Nazi-governed bases underground and in remote areas. The Nazi allegiance to dark forces can still be felt.

In 1922, Thule and Vril constructed Germany's first flight disc, the JFM (Jenseitsflugmaschine) or "Other World Flight Machine," in Munich, for channeled flight testing that lasted two years. The project was led by W.O. Schumann of the Technical University of Munich. The project was halted in 1924 and the machine dismantled and shipped to Messerschmitt's Augsburg facility, where it was stored for future research. Professor Schumann developed a levitation unit from the research, which was called the Schumann-Munich or SM-Levitator.

Schriever's "Flying Top"

Various types of craft were built by the Germans during WWII. Some of them were adapted from channeled messages received through the Vril Society's mediums.

Members of the Vril Society are said to have included Adolf Hitler, Alfred Rosenberg, Heinrich Himmler, Hermann Goering, and Hitler's personal physician, Dr. Theodor Morell. These were original members of the Thule Society, which supposedly joined Vril in 1919. The NSDAP (Nazi Party) was created by Thule in 1920, one year later. Dr. Krohn, who helped to create the Nazi flag, was also a Thulist.

With Hitler in power in 1933, both Thule and Vril Gesellschafts allegedly received official state backing for continued disc development programs aimed at both spaceflight and possibly a war machine.

The new RFZ (Rundflugzeug), or "Round Aircraft," series began in 1937, after Vril bought the fallow land surrounding the Arado-Brandenburg aircraft facility. RFZ discs 1, 2, 3, 4, and 6 were tested there under Vril supervision while Thule was helped by special SS technical branch unit E-IV, which was tasked with developing alternative energies. Thule worked on a separate disc at a secret location in NW Germany referred to as Hauneburg from 1935 on. As such their product was known as the H-GerÃ¤t (Hauneburg Device) but this was shortened to Haunebu in 1939 once the disc's Triebwerk (engine) was perfected. Haunebu I was briefly designated as RFZ-5 when Thule moved from Hauneburg to Arado-Brandenburg.

The Thule Triebwerk was a revolutionary EMG (electro-magnetic-gravitic) engine also known as a Tachyonator 7. It used a modified Hans Coler Magnetstromapparat (a gravitic free-energy battery) turned into a converter that was coupled to a Van De Graaf band generator and a Marconi dynamo (spinning tank of heated mercury). Once activated, the Triebwerk produced strong rotating EMG fields that affected gravity. The rotating fields also turned the dynamo, creating a reduction of mass at incredible RPMs.

Vril also developed its own Triebwerk by 1941 with the RFZ-7, which was re-designated Vril-1 JÃ¤ger (Hunter).

After 1941, Hitler forbade secret societies, so both Thule and Vril were documented under the SS E-IV unit. Vril also became secretly known as Die Kette – "The Chain" – which refers to the mental links between their members. Vril had strong contacts with Canaris of the Abwehr, the Ahnenerbe (SS occult bureau), and worked with the engineers at Arado.

Both the Thule and Vril discs were built from 1939-1945. Thule produced the Haunebu I-III series of large discs while the Vril series were more concerned with resuming channeled flight. By 1944, construction of a Vril 7 Geist (Spirit) channeled flight disc was achieved, as well as a huge 139 meter long cylindrical mothership called the Andromeda-GerÃ¤t (Andromeda Device).

A special unit named Sonderbureau (Special Bureau) 13 was created by the Luftwaffe to "officially" investigate strange aerial phenomena over the Reich but "unofficially" was created to cover-up these reports of flight discs and flying cigars. In September 1944 a ME-262 jet pilot caught sight of one of the Andromeda craft and reported it. Sonderbureau 13 immediately tried to feign ignorance of such a device.

The Vril magic eye is a mythical Nazi espionage and reconnaissance device supposed to have been developed in 1945. The story is that Rolf Engel of Vril Gesellschaft Ing developed a miniature Electro-Magnetic-Gravitic engine and installed it in a lightly-armored melon-shaped body about a foot in diameter. The body had a reception antenna, a small television camera, a weapon, and a telescopic arm that held another miniature camera and a microphone.

By virtue of its design and connection to Vril, the Magic Eye was to have had the ability to appear and disappear at will. Such a device would have been suitable for a wide range of military duties that included aerial recon, submarine protection, and especially espionage. While the main body of the probe remained invisible, the telescopic sensor arm could lower its other camera and microphone into our dimension for spying.

There are those who maintain that craft constructed by Nazi scientists still roam the "unfriendly skies" having been sanctioned by U.S. who allowed German scientists and engineers into the country under the top secret Project Paperclip program.

By early 1945, the story goes, Rolf Engel had performed lab tests with the power plant for this device and work was well underway on miniaturizing television equipment. The HS-293D missile had television guidance and composite aircraft were being developed at this time. The Argus AS-292 target drone had been converted to a remotely piloted vehicle equipped with cameras. These went unnoticed by the Allies and none were shot down. The difficulty would have been in the inter-dimensional travel and invisibility features.

There is no evidence that a functional prototype was ever made. The claim of an ability to travel in some inter-dimensional mode is similar to Vril claims of channeled flight with the Jenseitsflugmaschine (Other World Flight Machine) and the Vril Flugscheiben (Flight Discs).

Meanwhile, as the Allies advanced further into the Reich, Vril planned to evacuate its technology to bases outside of Europe, especially to a secret Antarctic base – Base 211, while their own personal plan was to evacuate their mediums to the stars by channeled flight of the Andromeda. They left in March 1945 and were never found again.

VRIL Today

Today the self-proclaimed government-in-exile of Sealand under Johannes W.F. Seiger promotes Vril free energy and also has started linking to Vril disc aircraft and history. This gives some weight to allegations that the Seiger group is in contact with Neo-Nazis, especially the self-proclaimed Reichsregierung.

Nazi UFOs and JFK

By Kenn Thomas

A salient thing about New Orleans district attorney's prosecution of his case on the JFK assassination is his identification of the grassy knoll shooter as Fred Lee Crisman. Crisman is also famously known as one of the witnesses to the Maury Island UFO incident in 1947.

Round Trip to Hell in a Flying Saucer

Much of Crisman's life prior to this public record comes in the form of rumor and secondary speculation. During World War II, for instance, he supposedly belonged to the Office of Strategic Service (OSS), a forerunner of the CIA, which according to UFO lore had a hand in transferring flying saucer technology from the Nazis after the war; and so, if there was anything to the connection, this may have been the origin of Crisman's involvement with Maury Island. More importantly, Crisman's OSS associates

Numerous flying disc were believed to have been constructed by the German's though it is hard to determine exactly which ever left the drawing boards. Art © Jim Nichols

may have included Clay Shaw, the New Orleans socialite that Jim Garrison actually prosecuted, a "toe-hold" to Garrison on the larger conspiracy.

Shaw also belonged to the board of directors of Permindex, a group described variously as a shadowy, transnational corporate presence and "a CIA front company." Other members of its board included an OSS major named Louis Bloomfield and Ferenc Nagy, the premier of Hungary overthrown by communists in 1947. Shaw's military service apparently did develop around his CIA/OSS involvement dating back to the late 1940s. According to one writer, Shaw "had been in business with former Nazis and European fascists involved in several CIA-sponsored covert operations throughout Europe."

Those covert activities included Paperclip, a spoils-of-war operation that successfully transplanted top Nazi aerospace scientists into the American space program, along with scientific equipment and files on the Nazi rocket program rumored to include its occult and extraterrestrial origins. Werner Von Braun and Walter Dornberger were among the top Nazi rocket scientists so incorporated. They directed a team of 118 former Nazis stationed at Redstone Arsenal in Huntsville, Alabama, and

The Third Tramp is thought by some to be Fred Crisman, a controversial figure whose roots go back to the days of World War II and the Kenneth Arnold sighting in 1947.

became architects of the successful U.S. space program which ultimately landed men on the moon.

While many regarded these geniuses at rocketry as having been exploited by the Nazi state, their enthusiasm for Hitler's cause and their role in developing weapons of mass destruction ultimately stained the history of U.S. successes in space. Von Braun had been a major in Hitler's SS and not only developed the V-2 rocket, which terrorized and killed thousands in the UK during World War II, but did it through the use of slave labor at the Nazi Nordhausen, Dora and Mittelwork concentration camps, where slaves were starved and exterminated by the hundreds.

In 1945 Von Braun and the other Paperclip Nazis abandoned their rocket research facility at Peenemunde and surrendered to First Lieutenant Charles L. Stewart near the Austrian border. Among the other U.S. soldiers possibly connected to the event: Major Clay Shaw, who served as an aide to the deputy chief of European operations General Charles O. Thrasher.

Occult Nazi UFOs

The German Luftwaffe excelled in aerospace weaponry. It created the V-2 rocket missile, responsible for the devastating blitz of Paris, London, and Antwerp during World War II. In 1939, they flew the first jet plane. They were also unsurpassed in the theoretical physics behind atomic bombs, creating the first nuclear fission reaction in Berlin in 1938. While these facts are now well-documented, theorists also suggest that the Nazis worked on technological advances beyond rocket missiles, jets, and atomic power: that, in fact, they had produced and flown a flying saucer.

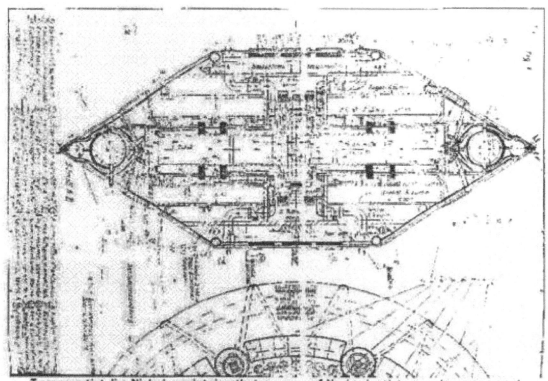

Tucson artist Jim Nichols maintains that a group of Nazi scientists may have escaped Germany during the end of WWII and have established a base at the Pole.
www.jimnicholsufoart.com/

Round Trip to Hell in a Flying Saucer

A witness account of an event in an airport hangar near Prague in February 1945 reported "a disk some 5 to 6 meters in diameter. Its body is relatively large at the center. Underneath, it has four tall, thin legs. Color: aluminum. Height: almost as tall as a man. Thickness: some 30 to 40 centimeters, with a rim of external rods, perhaps square orifices." The report of this sighting first appeared in the German flight magazine Flugzeug in February 1989. "Along with my friends," the reporter continued, "I saw the device emerge from the hangar. It was then that we heard the roar of the engines, we saw the external side of the disk begin to rotate, and the vehicle began moving slowly and in a straight line toward the southern end of the field. It then rose almost one meter into the air. After moving around some 300 meters at that altitude, it stopped again. Its landing was rather rough."

Such a craft may have emerged from the work of Dr. Richard Miethe, a German scientist who, after World War II, joined the A. V. Roe Company in Canada and designed the disk-shaped, but largely earth-bound, Avrocar hovercraft (film footage of which is often used to depict UFOs.) Miethe and two other scientists, Klaus Habermohl and Rudolf Schreiver, reportedly worked on a secret Nazi UFO project known variously as Haunebu or Flugdiskus. According to some versions of the UFO story, however, the saucer at Prague reached an altitude in excess of 7.5 miles [12 kilometers) and a speed of 1200 mph [1930 kmph) in less than 3 minutes. That would be a fairly incredible feat, of course, and one certainly not reproducible by the Avrocar or even the craft in the Flugdiskus report.

During the 1950s, a number of detailed technical sketches and blueprints began to circulate, along with stories about the work of Miethe, Habermohl, and Schreiver, that suggested technological designs even farther advanced than Nazi aerospace weapons. The stories included an Austrian forester, Viktor Schauberger, whose arcane research provided for the propulsion capacity of the craft, and which may have involved energized water or tonal harmonics.

Schauberger frequently resurfaces in UFO literature as the true designer of the disc that was launched from Prague, having, as early as 1938, taken ideas regarding the turbine power of water and applied them to flying saucer design. The Flugdiskus team developed the earliest scale-model versions of the craft in 1942. Shortly afterward, Nazi command conscripted Schauberger into a UFO development project at the Mauthausen concentration camp. After the War, Schauberger continued his research work on experimental energy under American auspices and died in Chicago in 1958. Schauberger has been the subject of several biographies and interest in his ideas about the energetic properties of water still get discussed among people interested in the alternative energy.

Critics maintain that many of the stories of German UFOs stem from modern-day Nazi sympathizers trying to add an exotic appeal to the ideology of fascism. In the mid-1970s, Ernst Zundel, a former Canadian, published a book about the German flying saucers that referred to Viktor Schauberger and the flying disk of Prague, and included the proposition that Nazi saucers still flew out of a base in the Antarctic. In 1985, Zundel was convicted in a Canadian court for "publishing false news" and claiming that the Holocaust against the Jews had not happened. The Supreme Court of Canada struck down the law against "publishing false news," however, after Zundel appealed his conviction in 1992.

Other conspiracy researchers maintain more exotic theories about Nazi UFO propulsion. They trace the origins of Nazism to an occult lodge in 1920s Germany known as the Thule Society, which indulged in black magic to summon other-worldly spirits. The idea that occult forces could power flying saucers re-emerged among 1950s UFO contactees in America, such as George Adamski and George Hunt Williamson, who have been charged by various scholars with having neo-fascist sympathies and of being members of the CIA.

In the late 1940s, the United States began to bring captured German rocket scientists into the space program and its tangle of defense contractors, and this is Fred Crisman's point of contact with the JFK assassination as a contract killer in the employ of Boeing.

Former Nazis such as Werner Von Braun and Walter Dornberger helped create America's Apollo space program, which landed a man on the moon on July 20, 1969. Von Braun recounts, in his memoirs, an argument with JFK about what propulsion system should be used for the moon lander. As a rocket scientist, Von Braun says, he argued for rockets; what JFK had in mind, and whether it connected to occult Nazi UFO technology, is lost to history.

Artist Carol Ann Rodriguez depicts Hitler surrounded by demonic forces which he no doubt has conjured up using occult forces.

The Real Plan Nine From Outer Space

By Timothy Green Beckley

Everyone was a bit incredulous when John Keel recounted in his best selling *Mothman Prophecies* the incredible story of a Red Cross bloodmobile that came very close to being "sucked up" by an unidentified craft that had been following it very closely down an isolated stretch of Route Two along the Ohio River on the West Virginia side.

"Witness Beau Shertzer, accompanied by a young nurse," as Keel tells it, "had been out all day collecting human blood and now they were heading back to Huntington, West Virginia, with a van filled with fresh blood. The road was dark and cold and there was very little traffic. As they moved along a particularly deserted stretch, there was a flash in the woods on a nearby hill and a large white glow appeared. It rose slowly into the air and flew straight of their vehicle."

The couple neared panic mode with the nurse exclaiming, "My God. What is that?"

Her 21-year-old male companion pushed the pedal to the metal and headed into the darkness, not anxious to look back.

Keel says, "The object effortlessly swooped over the van and stayed with it. Shertzer rolled down his window and looked up. He was horrified to see some kind of arm of extension being lowered from the luminous thing cruising only a few feet above the Red Cross vehicle."

The nurse concurred that the object was "trying to get us!"

Moments later, they watched in fright as "another arm reached down on her side. It looked as if the flying object was trying to wrap a pincers-like device around the vehicle." Keel continued his horrific narrative, noting further that the driver "poured on the horses, as the object kept pace with them easily."

The visual imagery of this episode would have made a chilling scene in the motion picture version of *Mothman Prophecies*, but alas it was not to be included.

Keel concludes his account by saying that the bloodmobile and its passengers were saved from an almost certain alien space napping upon the sudden approach of an oncoming vehicle, its headlines blazing. "As the other car neared, the object retracted the arms and hastily flew off. Both young people rushed to the (nearest) police station in a state of hysteria," notes the late paranormal researcher and close friend of the author. "The incident was mentioned briefly on a radio newscast that night but was not picked up by the newspapers."

Keel did a bit of checking to make sure no other bloodmobile had been carried off. His theory is that UFOs and their occupants have long had a lust for blood.

Such a connection is easily borne out by an examination of the material presented in the next few pages by a number of astute authorities who have not discounted that there is a dark and ominous side to the UFO mystery.

More Than Just Your Average 'Love Bite'

It was originally titled *Grave Robbers From Outer Space* and it has a reputation as being the worst science fiction film ever made. Everyone has heard of Hollywood's most outrageous low-budget producer of all time. Johnny Depp portrayed the cross-dressing Ed Wood in a recent Tim Burton film. *Grave Robbers* is better known as *Plan 9 From Outer Space*, and I personally loved the film and its producer so much that I subtitled one of my Mr. Creepo horror film productions *The Curse Of Ed Wood* (Chemical Burn, 2010).

Some say Plan Nine From Outer Space is one of the worst movies ever made, but Bela Lugosi did make an appearance in the film shortly before his death.

The film features a few shots of the very strung out master of the macabre, the late Bela Lugosi, a few days before his death, and the creepily attractive Vampira, both as ghouls with close ties to invading flying saucers (some seen dangling on wire as they "float" shabbily on the silver screen or on your long ago tossed out black and white TV). The plot of the film is focused on extraterrestrial beings who are seeking to stop humans from creating a doomsday weapon that would destroy the universe. In the course of doing so, the aliens implement "Plan 9," a scheme to resurrect Earth's dead as what modern audiences would consider zombies (called "ghouls" in the film itself, but appearing much like vampires) to get the planet's attention, causing chaos.

As a sidebar that is not common knowledge – when Ed Wood ran out of sources to finance his ramshackle epic, the only funding that came his way was offered by a local Baptist Church who would only cough up the needed capital with the understanding that the aliens had to be made to look demonic. Even back in the

1950s, there were those who were convinced that ET was more a fallen angel than a benevolent space traveler.

But do aliens actually bear a resemblance to ghouls or vampires in their various forms?

There is evidence that they are interested in more than just your average "love bite."

March 16, 1971, West Akron, Ohio.

Madeline Teagle of Cuyahoga Falls, Ohio, was herself an experiencer. But she was also a credible researcher in her own right who collected and documented some very weird and unholy accounts that can easily be tied in with the blood theme of this chapter. The following is excerpted from Brent Raynes' *Alternative Perceptions* online magazine:

Mrs. Dollie Hansen and her youngsters, accompanied by her neighbors, happened to be talking outside when they observed directly to the south a huge golden ball, with sort of rays or flames seemingly shooting out from it, making it appear like a small sun or ball of fire. At that time, they estimated it to be about the size of a nickel. As they watched, it began to get smaller, turned a brilliant bright red, then a deep dark red dot about the size of a pea, then poof! It was totally gone. No noise was noticed, and no other unusual physical sensations noted either. There was a heavy cloud cover, with scattered rain showers at the time.

Prior to this, Mrs. Hansen had complained of being extremely fatigued, wanting to sleep all the time, and only three nights before she had called relating an incident in which she could not explain a small neat pinhole with a small bruise directly over her left wrist veins, and a sort of imprint on her left thumb. Her hand was not sore or tender. However, after this experience, she found herself getting rather dizzy, and unable to walk with coordination. She fell, loosening the cartilage on her knee. When she went to the hospital for X-rays of the knee, they also took X-rays of her hand because by this time a large lump had developed on her wrist area, just above the bruise and pinhole. The results: on her wrist, either the formation of a new bone ridge or floating cartilage from an old wound. The lump is not now present and she has not had any reoccurrence of her physical difficulties.

Shortly before the above experience, on Sunday the 14th and Saturday the 13th, we had two others calls very similar and in the same general area. One had come from the Copley Road section, concerning a young lady who, while talking to her sister-in-law in the kitchen, suddenly felt a sharp pain on her right hand, third finger. She looked down and saw two small dots like bruises had appeared (they were not there moments before, according to both her and her sister-in-law) directly in line with each other. Later, when we saw them, they had taken on the appearance of a small blister with a scab forming atop of it. Suddenly her sister-in-law exclaimed "Look at your knuckle," and looking down they both saw small perfect teeth marks on it, red and angry looking! Later this girl complained of feeling extremely tired, was pale, drawn and exhausted.

On the following day, Sunday, March 14th, another report came in from the Ellet section, in which a woman had awakened in the middle of the night to find her arm hurting terribly. She got up, turned on the light, and saw on her left arm, about at the elbow, on the inside, eight small pinhole marks, in a circle. She was chilled to the bone. Not an outer chill, but an inner one, from the bone out, and she said she heard a voice say (in her head) "Alien forces are here. We will post a sentry before you that this will not happen again." And then she says she saw, or dreamed or imagined, she does not know which, a bubble, with two large, oversize tomato worm things wriggling inside of it. They had sucking protrusions on their mouth portions and she felt this was what had bitten her arm. She said she had never been so frightened in her whole life.

We have no explanation for these incidents, but they have been occurring with far too much regularity in the same general areas to ignore. All reports have the same general information: bites, marks, or bruises, extreme tiredness, inability to concentrate, difficulty in keeping their balance. We do not have reports such as this from other areas of the locality. Also these reports seem to follow a specific geographic line, along which we have in years past had some rather extraordinary sightings.

Satan's Need For Blood

So why all this bloody interest among the aliens or ultradimensional beings who are plundering Earth?

David Icke has delved into the matter, trying to discern just who we are contending with. He sees shape-shifting extraterrestrials identified as the Reptilians consuming live human flesh and drinking blood. The Reptilians have been here since close to the "very beginning" and have melted into our society very easily since they are able to shape-shift from slithering serpentines into humanoid form. Icke claims that many of the planet's elite, such as Queens, Kings, and Presidents are all able to morph into hideous demonic beings to cannibalize and hold human sacrifices and blood rituals.

One of Icke's disciples, Arizona Wilder, whom he interviews on a video called *Mother Goddess*, claims to have been a mind-controlled slave of this Satan-worshipping group whom some might identify as the Illuminati.

Maintains Arizona Wilder in a piece titled *Reptilian Blood Legacy*:

The closer the Earth's field is vibrationally to the lower fourth dimension, the more power the reptilians have over this world, and its inhabitants. Satanism ...from the Brotherhood's point of view, is to control the Earth's magnetic field; to worship and connect with their reptile masters; to drink the life force of their sacrificed victims; and to provide energy for the reptilians, who appear to feed off human emotion, especially fear.

Satanic rituals generally take place at night because that is when the magnetic field is most stable. During the day, the electrically charged particles of the solar wind cause turbulence in the field and make inter-dimensional connection more difficult. It is most stable during total eclipses and this is when native peoples held their most important ceremonies to contact and manifest other-dimensional entities. Some world politicians are addicted to blood taken from a victim at the moment of sacrifice because of the adrenaline which is produced at that time. I am told this addiction is quite common among Satanists, and researchers into the reptilian question suggest that this is the substance the reptiles also want. It all fits.

They have therefore capitalized on every Druidic and Magical date to try to get as much use out of the effect of the lunar cycle on female menstrual blood. They call this aspect of the menstrual blood Starfire, and indeed, one of the people in the UK Arizona Wilder 'fingers' as a Shape Shifter is called Lawrence Gardiner and has written an article about 'Starfire and menstrual blood' in "Nexus" magazine. He is also behind the 'Order of the Dragon,' an attempt to assemble and register the pure bloodstock of the UK in London Reptiles.

In the ceremony they would have sacrifices and during the bloodletting, especially if there were infants involved, these beings would change into a reptilian form. And the interesting thing about it is that there would be this yellow-green slime residue after the ceremonies. It would be on my body and on the altars and on the flooring. I have also since found it on my children as well, which is disturbing to me.

It is obvious that for various reasons (including the goals set down in the secret Iron Mountain government report), the government (including cooperating agencies like NASA) decided to use an alien abduction theme rather than a Satanic Ritual Abuse theme to their mind-control programming. The major difference in the programming methodology is that the blood rituals of the

The Masons were frequently accused of performing blood letting for the benefit of the horned Satan.

SRA are no longer used. The reason why blood rituals are no longer needed is that the high-tech harmonic machines (which implant thoughts) and other high-tech methods eliminate the need for the blood traumas. The victims of alien abductions are taken at random, whereas the Illuminati victims are abducted more frequently around ritual dates. The person who believes in UFOs and aliens is going to receive the same type of treatment as those who believe in Satanic Ritual Abuse. The legal system and society at large are conditioned to treat them as nuts. This protects their abusers.

Satanism and Luciferianism and other similar cults are blood cults that require blood to be sacrificed to pull in certain demons. For instance, blood may be taken from both the tongue and the genital area and mixed in a certain ceremony to invoke a particular demon. Demons are not bought with gold or silver, they are bought with blood. Some spirits are invoked by placing alcoholic enemas into the child. These children get totally intoxicated with alcohol, some to the point that they even die from the ceremony. This is all done to bring in particular demons. The Spirit Choronzon and Typhon are critical spirits to place into a person for the Mind-Control to work.

The specific bloodlines of the Illuminati hybrid families have been preserved through inter-marrying over the ages. Instead of trying to keep alien and DNA contamination out of their bloodlines, they work to keep pure human DNA from entering into their bloodlines. Those in these families are born with a specific alien DNA that can be activated through ritual and blood drinking to allow for the alien possession of their bodies. The aliens can literally possess their bodies. This possession allows these humans to shape-shift and be controlled by the aliens themselves. These bloodlines are not controlled by the Grey aliens but the lizard type known as the Reptilians. Many people such as Arizona Wilder, Cathy O'Brien, and Bryce Taylor have seen people from these bloodline families such as George Bush Sr., Dick Cheney, Al Gore, Queen Elizabeth, and others shape-shift into Reptilians. It is not "humans" that run our governments.

The Blood Legacy

By Andrew Hennessey

Born 1957AD in Edinburgh, Scotland, Andrew Hennessey was trained as an industrial biologist and worked in several labs, including the Institute of Terrestrial Ecology, Central Microbiology Lab, National Museum of Antiquities, East of Scotland College of Agriculture, and the British Geological Survey.

In 1984 Andrew formed his theatre group called the Solan Company, putting together various original Grail-quest projects in many styles with a veritable army of talented helpers.

As an amateur scientist he has also developed a Grand Unifying Theory and new scientific advances, e.g. artificial general intelligence, a new model for gravity, cosmology and particle physics, a new kind of game theory and a new kind of systems theory. These advanced ideas could technically progress the human race beyond its cul de sac of paradoxes.

As a result of an attempted alien abduction in 1980, he trained as a medium at Albany Street Spiritualist Church in Edinburgh, 1982/3. He has had ongoing interaction with both good and bad non-humans, through the nineties and into the millennium. He wrote of those in his book on HiddenMysteries.com called *The Turning of the Tide – Alien Intrusion in Scotland*. He complains there of outrageous reality-engineering.

He has various photographs and scientific analysis to back up the alien truth behind his encounters. He also claims to have been contacted by a powerful civilization not from around here and had his photo taken with an Imperial Princess who wished to introduce him to her Mother.

He would contend that there is an incredible ancient, alien and geopolitical reality behind the scenes in Scotland involving the Annunaki and the Greys.

Of greatest importance in his life, however, was his recently becoming Catholic to become connected to the Angels and Saints who have protected him from a dark campaign of spiritual warfare.

In his book *The Turning of the Tide – Alien Intrusion in Scotland*, Andrew makes a number of shocking points. . .

1. There are non-humans amongst Humanity and there have been for some considerable time.
2. The planet's surface is, historically, some kind of artificial learning zone for Humans.
3. Good and Evil beings vie either for our eternal salvation or to acquire our soul for their dark purposes.
4. Big changes and big plans for Mankind are unfolding now.
5. Wherever we came from to be human here, we take with us our glorious baggage when we leave.

Today's most popular shows such as HBO's True Blood utilize blood drinking concepts.

"The black magic rituals we know as Satanism are the modern expression of the rituals and human sacrifice in ancient Babylon and the Brotherhood- infiltrated societies of the Sumerian, Phoenician, Hittite, Egyptian, Canaanite and Akkadian peoples, among many others across the world. It has been a seamless procession through history of the same rituals to the same deities and this remains of fundamental importance to the initiates of the Brotherhood today.

My use of the term Satanism has nothing to do with the Christian version of Satan. I use it only to describe a system of ritual sacrifice and torture which, staggering as it may seem to most people, is commonplace all over the world today. Satanism is just another name for the worship of a highly destructive, negative force which has been given endless names over the centuries. Nimrod, Baal, Moloch or Molech, Set, the Devil, Lucifer – there is no end to them.

Satanism perverts everything positive in the same way that the Nazis took a positive symbol, the swastika, and turned it around to symbolize the negative. This is why the Satanists invert the pentagram and why they use black to symbolize the darkness, hence their Black Mass. But they also reverse the symbolism of white and that is a powerfully negative color to them.

The Satanic networks, under the names of their various deities, were created by the Babylonian Brotherhood to serve their needs. We have seen that the accounts of the Watchers and their offspring, the Nefilim, include references to their blood drinking activities. The Brotherhood knows that blood contains the life-force energy.

Drinking menstrual blood has always been a feature of the reptilian bloodlines because they need blood to live in this dimension. It was known as the Star Fire, the female lunar essence. The female menstrual cycle is governed by the cycles of the Moon and the blood contains that energy. Its ingredients are supposed to ensure a long life. In India it was called soma and in Greece it was ambrosia. This was said to be the nectar of the gods and it was the reptilian gods who are genetic blood drinkers. The 'holy grail' chalice or cup is also symbolic of the womb and drinking menstrual blood, as well as being a symbol of the reptilian 'royal' bloodline itself.

Menstrual blood was provided for the Elite of the reptilian 'royal' line by virgin priestesses and this is the origin of the term 'Scarlet Woman' or, to the Greeks, 'Sacred Woman.' The Greek word for this, Hierodulai, was eventually translated into English as harlot and into German as 'hores,' the origin of 'whore.' The word 'ritual' derives from this practice (ritu = redness) and so do the words 'rite' and 'red.' Menstrual blood is one reason why the color red is so important to Satanists and it is another reason for the constant use of the color gold by the 'royal' bloodlines. Gold is called the metal of the gods, but to the Anunnaki of the Sumerian Tablets, menstrual blood was the 'gold of the gods.'

The reptilians and their crossbreeds drink blood because they are drinking the person's life-force and because they need it to exist in this dimension. They will often shape-shift into reptilians when drinking human blood and eating human flesh, I am told by those who have seen this happen. Blood drinking is in their genes and an Elite high priestess or 'Mother Goddess' in the hierarchy, who performed rituals for the Brotherhood at the highest level, told me that without human blood the reptilians cannot survive in this dimension. Her name is Arizona Wilder, formerly Jennifer Ann Green. Interestingly, she said that the reptilians had been pursuing the Aryan peoples around the universe, because the blood of the white race was particularly important to them for some reason and the blond-haired, blue-eyed genetic stream was the one they wanted more than any other. They had followed the white race to Mars, she said, and then came to Earth with them. It is far from impossible that the reptilian arrival on this planet in great numbers was far more recent than even many researchers imagine. An interbreeding program only a few thousand years ago between the reptilian Anunnaki and white Martian bloodlines, already interbred with the reptilians on Mars, would have produced a very high reptilian genetic content. This is vital for the reasons I have explained earlier. They appear to need a particular ratio of reptilian genes before they can shape-shift in the way that they do. But when the interbreeding happened is far less important than the fact that it did happen.

Satanism is based on the manipulation of energy and consciousness. These deeply sick rituals create an energy field, a vibrational frequency, which connects the consciousness of the participants to the reptilians and other consciousnesses of the lower fourth dimension. This is the dimensional field, also known as the lower astral to many people, which resonates to the frequency of low-vibrational emotions like fear, guilt, hate and so on. When a ritual focuses these emotions, as Satanism does, a powerful connection is made with the lower fourth dimension, the reptilians.

These are some of the 'demons' which these rituals have been designed to summon since this whole sad story began thousands of years ago. This is when so much possession takes place and the reptilians take over the initiate's physical body. The leading Satanists are full-blood reptilians cloaked in human form.

These rituals invariably take place on vortex points and so the terror, horror, and hatred created by them enters the global energy grid and affects the Earth's magnetic field. Thought forms of that scale of malevolence hold down the vibrational frequency and affect human thought and emotion. Go to a place where Satanic rituals take place and feel the malevolence and fear in the atmosphere. What we call 'atmosphere' is the vibrational field and how it has been affected by human thought forms. Thus we talk about a happy, light or loving atmosphere, or a dark or foreboding one.

Blood sacrifices were part of the Aztec rituals to appease the gods.

The closer the Earth's field is vibrationally to the lower fourth dimension, the more power the reptilians have over this world and its inhabitants. Satanism is not just a sickness and a perversion, although it is that also. Its main reason for existence, from the Brotherhood's point of view, is to control the Earth's magnetic field; to worship and connect with their reptile masters; to drink the life-force of their sacrificed victims; and to provide energy for the reptilians who appear to feed off human emotion, especially fear. These sacrifices are, literally, sacrifices to the 'gods,' the reptilians, and they have been happening for thousands of years. The mass sacrifice of people by the Aztecs in Central America, and so many others, was to provide food for the physical reptilians and crossbreeds who eat the bodies and drink the blood, and energy nourishment for the non-physical reptilians of the lower fourth dimension.

Phil Schneider, a builder of US underground bases, told the writer and researcher, Alex Christopher, that when children reached the point where they could not work anymore in the slave conditions underground, they were consumed by the reptilians. They prefer young children because they are not contaminated like adults. Hard to accept, isn't it? I'm sure your mind is screaming 'nonsense' at you because who wants to face a truth like this? But unless we do, how is it ever going to be stopped?

To reiterate, Satanic rituals generally take place at night because that is when the magnetic field is most stable. During the day, the electrically charged particles of the solar wind cause turbulence in the field and make inter-dimensional connection more difficult. It is most stable during total eclipses, and this is when native peoples held their most important ceremonies to contact and manifest other-dimensional entities. The tribal shamans know this. Satanic rituals and human sacrifice, especially of children, are performed on a vast scale and involve some of the most famous politicians, business people, media owners and entertainers on the planet.

Of course they do. It would be amazing if they did not, given the background. These rituals and human sacrifice have always been the foundation of the Brotherhood 'religion' since ancient times. And the Brotherhood manipulates its Satanic initiates and 'go-fers' into positions of political, economic, business, military, medical and media power, and into influential positions in the world of entertainment.

Therefore the ratio of Satanists and child sacrifices at the top of these professions and institutions is staggeringly high compared with the general population. Apparently, according to former Satanists I have met and read about, some world politicians are addicted to blood taken from a victim at the moment of sacrifice because of the adrenaline which is produced at that time. I am told this addiction is quite common among Satanists, and researchers into the reptilian question suggest that this is the substance the reptiles also want. It all fits."

Go to http://www.atsdeck.com/ for more information.

As we continue, master researchers Tim Swartz and Adam Gorightly will provide us with more shattering information that serves to warn us of the blood-letting and ritualistic caprices of the aliens – a literal all-consuming trap for those who get caught in their tightening web.

The Invasion of the Psychic Space Age Vampires

By Adam Gorightly

Stories of alien entities engaged in sexual soirées with human abductees have been recounted from the beginning of the UFO phenomenon, and perhaps since time immemorial. This theme of alien/human sexual high jinks has been a mainstay in sci-fi literature going back to Edgar Rice Burroughs' John Carter of Mars, who – after reigning victorious over the red planet's many strange creatures – won the affections of Martian princess, Deja Thoris. Illustrations of scantily-clad Earth gals being abducted by bug-eyed aliens were featured time and again in the pulps of the 40s and 50s, further imprinting this titillating theme of sex and saucers on the mind at large.

In the early 20th century, Aleister Crowley used hallucinogenic drugs in combination with sex magick and "Enochian calls" to invoke otherworldly entities. These Enochian calls were presumably derived from the Book of Enoch, which relates the story of wicked angels who abducted and mated with human women. The Old Testament says "The sons of God came in unto the daughters of man." This intercourse and interaction resulted in a hybrid race, the Nephilim. These biblical tales could be interpreted as an alien invasion that came to Earth to practice genetic manipulation.

Controversial producer Ed Wood incorporated the very creepy -- but stylish --Vampira in his low budget classic Plan Nine From Outer Space.

The offspring of this mating, as noted, was the Nephilim, who, in turn, went on to further commingle with the Earth gals, and – as recorded in Genesis – taught their earthling lovers "sorcery, incantation, and the dividing of roots and trees." UFO Researcher Guy Malone equates the "dividing of roots" to the use of shamanic drugs.

Parallels can be drawn between the Nephilim and the changelings of fairy lore. As Jacque Vallee noted in Passport to Magonia, these sexually charged stories were sanitized from later fairy tales, although such un-sanitized tales were prevalent in Scottish lore, which spoke of beautiful creatures of an aerial order who frequently took the form of succubi in seducing young men. This is what Vallee suggests may be going on in the case of many current day abductees: a continuation of a tradition of encounters with incubi and succubi that in modern times has taken the form of ET encounters.

Modern day encounters feature aliens abducting men and women from their beds, often during sleep, or semi-sleep states or trances, taking them aboard futuristic craft where they are probed and violated, semen samples taken and ovum's extracted, and of course the ever-present anal probe.

One of the kinkier episodes in UFO lore was the 1957 Antonio Villas-Boas case. Villas-Boas, a 23-year-old Brazilian farmer, was allegedly taken aboard a UFO, then slipped an aphrodisiac mickey and "forced" to have hardcore sex with an attractive, red-haired, pointy-breasted feminoid who made odd animal-like grunting noises during their "close encounter."

Apparently, Brazilians have had a number of sexual encounters with alien sex fiends. In 1979, 25-year-old Antonio Ferreira witnessed a saucer land, followed by the appearance of some robots that abducted Ferreira and took him aboard their craft. There Ferreira encountered a repulsive female alien with bad breath and icy cold skin, as well as red pubic hair, a feature noted in the Villas-Boas case. Wanting nothing to do with this skuzzy alien broad, Ferreira resisted. In response, the robots tore Ferreira's clothes off and gave him an injection, causing him to succumb. Then the rascally robots covered Ferreira in an amber colored oil (emotion lotion, perhaps?) followed by the alien dame jumping his Brazilian bones.

Perhaps the most well known abductee is Whitley Strieber. Many aspects of Strieber's recounted experiences appear clearly sexual in nature, one of which featured a wrinkled old alien grey gal who instructed him to make it "harder." When Strieber realized it was his you-know-what she was encouraging him to stiffen, he became understandably disturbed, although upon later reflection the incident left Strieber somewhat confused and, admittedly, aroused. Another common feature of the alien abduction experience is the probing of earthling rectums with electronic probes, such as described in Communion:

"...The next thing I knew I was being shown an enormous and extremely ugly object, gray and scaly, with a sort of network of wires on the end. It was at least a foot long, narrow, and triangular in structure. They inserted this thing into my rectum. It seemed to swarm into me as if it had a life of its own. Apparently its purpose was to take samples, possibly of fecal matter, but at the time I had the impression that I was being raped, and for the first time I felt anger..."

Later in the saga, Strieber recounted having semen drawn from his johnson – with some sort of vacuum device – alluding once again to the sexual nature of his "communion."

Anal probes, insemination, pokes and scratches, and other intrusive behavior are commonly attributed to these otherworldly visitors. Some have even suggested, like Streiber, they are a form of rape.

According to the International UFO Reporter, a young Australian, Peter Khoury, was in bed early one morning in 1992 when two "unusual looking naked women" appeared from out of nowhere. One -- a tall blond – tried to force Khoury to put his face on her breast, but he resisted and decided to bite off a piece of her nipple, although this strange woman apparently felt no pain. Shortly afterward, both women vanished.

Afterwards, Khoury discovered two humanoid looking hairs wrapped painfully around his penis. He saved one of these hairs in an envelope, and years later gave it to a group of Australian scientists to analyze. The result, apparently, indicated that these women were hybrids of some sort, with DNA close to that of humans.

Probably the one person on this planet most responsible for the advance of alien/human sexual relations is Pamela Stonebrooke, a talented jazz singer also known as The Intergalactic Diva. Stonebrooke has claimed numerous sexual bump and grinds with a group a fun loving alien reptilians who she believes are preparing her for an apocalyptic planetary upheaval. I bet they tell that to all the Earth gals.

So what's attracting these apparent otherworldly beings? One theory suggests that women's menstrual cycles are at the root of many of these strange encounters. Fortean researchers have long noted that Bigfoot, various monsters, apparitions, ghosts and UFO sightings often happen near lover's lanes, or during women's menstrual periods.

Some ancient cultures suspected that women's menstrual cycles open a gateway into the void, through which forces can be invoked, a theory Carlos Castaneda entertained in The Second Ring of Power. It has been noted by certain researchers that – in addition to the uncanny ability to locate women experiencing their menstrual periods – Bigfoot and other reported Fortean beasts tend to appear when the moon is full. Of course, menstruation itself is believed to have a basic concurrence with moon cycles. According to occultist Kenneth Grant, the human menstrual flow is the vehicle of the lunar vibration. Grant seems convinced that this peculiar force gives rise to an entity known to the ancient Egyptians as the Ape of Thoth, a beast which loomed large in Aleister Crowley's magical practices. Maybe Bigfoot and the Ape of Thoth are more closely related than has been previously suspected. Also, some of the stranger Bigfoot sightings have coincided with the appearance of UFOs. This lends credence to the theory that Bigfoot is more paranormal in nature, rather than an actual flesh and bones beast.

Dr. Wilhelm Reich theorized that a mysterious life force, Orgone – closely connected with human sexuality – could be gathered in containers which he invented called Orgone Accumulators, devices that are used to promote optimal health and well being. In The Rebirth of Pan, author Jim Brandon speculated that the energy collected in Orgone Accumulators was akin. to automobiles containing erotically inclined couples parked in lover's lanes engaged in carnal couplings. What this suggested to Brandon is that the power behind these manifestations – UFOs and other paranormal materializations – may not be entirely under control, but are acting chaotically, like a moth to light, in response to whatever is gathered in metal boxes, such as sexual energy. In essence, UFOs, aliens – or whatever "they" are – feed off this sexual human energy like psychic vampires.

The Cloudbuster – another Reich invention which resembled a large Gatling gun like contraption – could theoretically pull rain out of the clouds. Additionally, Reich discovered that his Cloudbuster could drain energy from lights in the sky, dimming them from view. In essence, the Cloudbuster was also an Orgone Accumulator of sorts, sucking Orgone from the atmosphere. While experimenting with the Cloudbuster, Reich encountered what he perceived as UFOs and came to believe that they were coming to Earth to suck up Orgone and exhaust a waste product he dubbed Deadly Orgone Energy (DOR). DOR, Reich contended, was causing adverse environmental effects on the planet.

At some point, Reich decided to aim the Cloudbuster on a contingent of UFOs he observed over his Rangeley, Virginia, research facility, which caused said UFOs to turn tail and retreat. This led Reich to triumphantly proclaim that, "Tonight, for the first time in the history of man, the war waged for ages by living beings from outer space upon this Earth . . . was reciprocated."

The Mysterious Mutilators

By Tim R. Swartz

Researchers of the UFO phenomenon have openly speculated over the years that if UFOs do represent extraterrestrial visitors, why do they operate in such secrecy? Alleged UFO contactees say that the aliens are friendly and are here to help mankind. However, evidence that extraterrestrials have a sinister, hidden agenda when dealing with Earth's inhabitants tells a different story. The most obvious example of nefarious UFO activity has to be the mutilation of cattle. The evidence is mostly anecdotal that UFOs are involved with cattle mutilations, but the unusual circumstances surrounding this mystery seem to point to UFOs, or at least UFO-like activity.

If the thought of alien creatures from another planet that are here to maim and mutilate us wasn't bad enough, there is the even more frightening possibility that these vicious attacks are being done by spiritual beings who are not only after our flesh and blood, but who are also after our immortal souls.

Blood Is The Life

Over the years, strange attacks on animals and humans have been recorded and attributed to predators, other humans and even vampires. What makes these incidents similar is the general lack of blood found on the bodies. Primitive man believed that blood was sacred, the source of life in all creatures. When you lost your blood, you lost your life. So it made sense that the life force must be contained in blood. The Old Testament is a good example of ancient beliefs regarding blood. Leviticus 17:14 states, that "the life of every living creature is its blood." The verse goes on to say that it is forbidden for anyone to eat blood because it is the source of all life.

Because of these early beliefs, man has always had a superstitious horror when dealing with unusual attacks that involve the loss of blood. Throughout history, there have been numerous reports of strange attacks and mutilations that seem to go beyond normal animal predators. In 1874, near Cavan, Ireland, for several months something killed as many as thirty sheep a night, biting their throats and draining the blood. In 1905, at Great Badminton, Avon, sheep were again the target for attacks. A police sergeant in Gloucestershire was quoted in the London Daily Mail, "I have seen two of the carcasses myself and can say definitely that it is impossible for it to be the work of a dog. Dogs are not vampires, and do not suck the blood of a sheep, and leave the flesh almost untouched." In a single night in March of 1906, near the town of Guildford, Great Britain, fifty-one sheep were killed when their blood was drained from bite wounds to the throats. Local residents formed posses to hunt down whatever was killing their livestock, but nothing was ever caught, and the killings remain a mystery. Events of this kind have probably occurred regularly throughout history. The cases that have received media attention are those involving a large number of deaths, but there are probably hundreds of smaller attacks that have gone unnoticed over the years.

Are Chupacabras Demons From Hell?

These strange livestock attacks are eerily similar to the recent attacks by the so-called Chupacabras, which means "goat sucker." Confining itself chiefly to the southern hemisphere, the Chupacabras has been blamed for numerous attacks on small animals. The animals have had their throats bitten and their blood sucked out by the creature that reportedly stands on two legs, has large black or red eyes and is about four feet tall. Unlike past killings, the Chupacabras has been seen by shocked eyewitnesses whose descriptions seem to describe an animal that superficially resembles the "Grays" of flying saucer lore. As in past cases, attempts to track down the Chupacabras have met with failure. If history is any indication, the Chupacabras will never be caught, and the strange events will remain a mystery. It is as if the mystery mutilators appear out of thin air, do their damage, and then, just as quickly, disappear again.

The mutilation of cattle seems to involve a different set of circumstances than past vampire-like attacks on livestock. While cattle mutilations almost always involve the complete draining of blood, physical mutilation of the flesh is so apparent that seasoned ranchers are shocked by the unusual nature of the deaths. No one really knows when the first unusual cattle mutilations began. Records show that in the middle of 1963, a series of livestock attacks occurred in Haskell County, Texas. In a typical case, an Angus bull was found with its throat slashed and a saucer-sized wound in its stomach. The attacks were attributed to a wild beast of some sort, a "vanishing varmint." As the attacks continued through the Haskell County area, the unknown attacker assumed mythic proportions and a new name was created, "The Haskell Rascal." Whatever was responsible for the mutilations was never caught, and the attacks slowly stopped. Throughout the following decade, though, there would be similar reports of attacks on livestock. The most prominent of these infrequent reports was the mutilation death of a horse named Lady, in 1967. Area residents of southern Colorado reported UFO activity the night before Lady was found dead, and the consensus was that the unknown craft were somehow responsible.

In 1973, the modern cattle mutilation wave can be said to have begun in earnest. It is interesting to note that a huge UFO flap was occurring across the country in 1973, with many sightings taking place in the same areas that cattle mutilations were happening. In November of 1974, rumors began to connect the sighting of UFOs with mutilated cows that were being found in large numbers in various Minnesota counties. Dozens of UFOs were reported in Minnesota and dozens of cattle were found dead and mutilated. Although the sightings and mutilations were never correlated, many felt that the number of sightings was added proof that the UFOs were somehow involved.

In 1975, an unprecedented onslaught of strange deaths spread across the western two-thirds of the United States. Mutilation reports peaked in that year, accompanied by accounts of UFOs and unidentified helicopters. By 1979, numerous livestock mutilations were also being reported in Canada, primarily in Alberta and Saskatchewan. In 1980, there was an increase in activity in the United States. Mutilations have been reported less frequently since that year, though this may be due in part to an increased reluctance to report mutilations on the part of ranchers and farmers. In the 1990s, the mutilations continued. In the United States, over ten thousand animals have reportedly died under unusual circumstances.

Satanic Drinkers of Blood

Because of the strange nature of the killings, wild stories and rumors have surfaced over the years in an attempt to explain what is really going on. Chief among these are stories that aliens are harvesting cattle at night for their evil purposes. The extraterrestrials' preoccupation with cattle is apparently due to the fact that the ET's absorb nutrients through the skin. The blood that they acquire from the cattle is mixed with hydrogen peroxide, which kills the foreign bacteria in the mixture, and is "painted" on their skin, allowing absorption of the required nutrients. Supposedly human blood is preferred by the aliens, but cattle blood can be altered to serve the same purpose.

While it may seem far-fetched that animal blood could be used in place of human blood, recent scientific discoveries seem to confirm that animal blood can be altered for human transfusions, according to The Observer, a respected weekly paper in Great Britain. The scientists who helped engineer the first cloned sheep are reportedly close to generating human blood plasma from animals. PPL Therapeutics, the Scottish firm that helped Edinburgh's Roslin Institute clone a sheep, is developing the means to replace the plasma genes of sheep and cows with the human equivalent. PPL told the paper it plans to raise herds of the animals and manufacture plasma from the proteins extracted from the animals. The Observer quoted Dr. Ron James, the firm's managing director, as saying, "Only 5 percent of Britain's population regularly gives blood. Genetically modified animals could produce 10,000 times more plasma a year than a human donor."

Heavy metal albums today abound with such themes as blood letting rituals.

In 1991, DNX Corp., a Princeton-based biotechnology firm, announced that it had developed genetically engineered, transgenic pigs that produce large quantities of recombinant human hemoglobin. When commercialized, DNX's blood substitute could provide a cost-effective, virtually unlimited alternative to the human blood supply that is entirely free from the threat of contamination by infectious agents that cause diseases such as AIDS and hepatitis. In addition, DNX's recombinant hemoglobin-based transfusion product will be universally compatible with all blood types, eliminating the need for blood typing and cross matching, and will have improved shelf-life and storage characteristics. DNX's announcement was made to the 1991 World Congress on Cell and Tissue Culture in Anaheim, Calif., by John Logan, vice president of research at DNX. Perhaps the wild stories are not so far-fetched after all.

The Nightmare of Human Mutilation

If the stories are true, some would ask why aren't the aliens catching and mutilating humans instead of animals? The truth could be that human mutilations and deaths are occurring on a regular basis, but that the stories are too horrible to contemplate. If murderous, UFO-related human mutilations have taken place, they have either gone unrecognized for what they really are, or have been adeptly covered up by official intervention. Thousands of people worldwide disappear every year, never to be seen again. A majority of these disappearances can be attributed to homicides or other more common situations.

However, some disappearances are so unusual and unexplained that more disturbing scenarios must be examined. In 1956, at the White Sands Missile Test Range, an Air Force major reported that he had witnessed a disk-shaped flying object kidnap Sgt. Jonathan P. Louette. Louette had been missing for three days when his mutilated body was found in the desert near the test range. Louette's genitals had been removed and his rectum cored out with surgical precision. Like many cattle mutilations, Louette's eyes had been removed and all of his blood was missing. The Air Force filed a report stating that Sgt. Louette had died of exposure after being lost in the desert.

A human sacrifice in Stanley Kubrick's Eyes Wide Shut certainly opened some eyes.

The late Leonard H. Stringfield, a former Air Force intelligence officer, wrote in his self-published book, UFO Crash/Retrievals, Status Report No. 6, about the testimony given by a "high ranking Army officer" whom Stringfield says he has known for several years and who is allegedly a "straight shooter." The officer claimed that while he was in Cambodia during the Vietnam War, his Special Operations group was involved in a fire fight with aliens, whom the soldiers came across sorting human body parts and sealing them into large bins. Subsequently the unit was held for several days and interrogated under hypnosis. The officer claimed that he and his men were given cover memories which only began to surface years later. The implications here are staggering. If this story is true, then the possibility exists that military and government officials are aware of the aliens' interests in the physiological makeup of the human body.

In 1989, the mysterious death of a man a decade earlier came to the attention of the MUFON State Director of Idaho, Don Mason. According to the report, in 1979, two hunters in the Bliss and Jerome area of Idaho stumbled across the almost nude body of a man that had been hideously mutilated. The body's sexual organs had been removed, its lips were sliced off, and the blood had been drained. Although the body was found in very rugged country, its bare feet were not marked, and no other tracks, animal or human, were evident. After the police were notified, an intensive search was mounted and the man's possessions were recovered miles from where the body was found. No one knows how the body ended up where it was found, or even more importantly, what happened to him. It should be noted that this area over the years has had many unexplained UFO reports and cattle mutilations.

In Westchester County, New York, in 1988, several morgues were broken into late at night. Fresh human bodies had undergone mutilations involving partial removal of the face and total removal of the eyes, stomach, thyroid gland and genitals. An assistant medical examiner, who had broken the silence concerning the case, stated that checks were immediately run on the employees who were on duty at the morgues. No links connecting morgue employees with the crimes were found. While there is no evidence that UFOs were responsible for the bizarre incidents, once again we see human bodies being mutilated in the same ways that cattle and other animals are being mutilated.

Another interesting case that has received little publicity in the United States is the Brazilian Guarapiranga Reservoir case. Brazilian ufologist Encarnacion Zapata Garcia and Dr. Rubens Goes uncovered a series of sensational photographs obtained from police files. The photos are of a dead man whose injuries are similar to the wounds of countless UFO-related animal mutilation cases. The body had been found near Guarapiranga Reservoir on September 29, 1988. The name of the man has been withheld from the media and UFO investigators at the request of his relatives. After studying the photos, Encarnacion Garcia was impressed with how similar the wounds of the body were to those found on the carcasses of so many mutilated animals. The initial police report noted that the body, although extremely mutilated, showed no signs of struggle or the application of bondage of any kind.

The body appeared to be in good condition. Rigor mortis had not set in and it was estimated that the victim had been killed approximately 48 to 72 hours previously. There were no signs of animal predation or decay which might be expected. Strangely, there was no odor to the body. Bleeding from the wounds had been minimal. In fact, it was noted that there was a general lack of blood found in the body or on the ground around the body. Police photos show that the flesh and lips had been removed from around the mouth, as is common in cattle and other animal mutilations. An autopsy report stated that "the eyes and ears were also removed and the mouth cavity was emptied." Removal of these body parts, including the tongue as here, is common enough in animal mutilation cases.

The "surgery" appeared to have been done by someone familiar with surgical procedures. The lack of profuse bleeding suggested the use of a laser-like instrument producing heat, thus immediately cauterizing the edge of the wounds. The autopsy report states that, "The axillary regions on both sides showed soft spots where organs had been removed. Incisions were made on the face, internal thorax, abdomen, legs, arms, and chest. Shoulders and arms have perforations of 1 to 1.5 inches in diameter where tissue and muscles were extracted. The edges of the perforations were uniform and so was their size. The chest had shrunk due to the removal of internal organs." The autopsy report continues, "You also find the removal of the belly button leaving a 1.5 inch hole in the abdomen and a depressed abdominal cavity showing the removal of the intestines." The report also noted the victim's scrotum had been removed, and that the anal orifice had been extracted with a large incision about 3 to 6 inches in diameter.

It is significant that the police and medical examiners were convinced the holes found in the head, arms, stomach, anus and legs were not produced by bullet wounds. What is most disturbing about the anal incision and the extraction of anal and digestive tract tissue is that it is a carbon copy of the surgery seen in so many UFO-related animal mutilation cases. While no evidence linking the Guarapiranga Reservoir mutilation case with UFOs has been found, Brazilian ufologists and police have hinted that there may be at least a dozen or more cases similar to this one. In fact, Brazil has had past incidents where UFOs have reportedly attacked people and possibly taken blood from them. The July 12, 1977, edition of the JORNAL DA BAHIA reported that, "A fantastic story of a flying object emitting a strong light and sucking blood from people circulated from mouth to mouth among the population of the counties of Braganca, Vizeu and Augusto Correa in Para', where many people fear leaving their homes during the night so they won't get caught by the vampire-like light from the strange object which, according to information, already has caused the death of two men. No one knows how the story started, but the truth is that it reached Bele'm and grabbed headlines in the local newspapers."

Months later, on October 8, the newspaper O LIBERAL launched the first in a series of reports, about the Chupa-Chupa (suck-suck) phenomenon. "Sucking animal attacks men and women in the village of Vigia: A strange phenomenon has been occurring for several weeks in the village of Vigia, more exactly in the Vila Santo Antonio do Imbituba about 7 kilometers from highway PA-140, with the appearance of an object which focuses a white light over people, immobilizing them for around an hour, and sucks the breasts of the women, leaving them bleeding. The object, known by the locals as "Bicho Voador" (Flying Animal), or "Bicho Sugador" (Sucking

Animal), has the shape of a rounded ship and attacks people in isolation. One of the victims, among many in the area, was Mrs. Rosita Ferreira, married, 46 years old, resident of Ramal do Triunfo, who a few days ago was sucked by the light on the left breast and passed out. Increasingly it looked like she was dealing with a nightmare, feeling as if there were some claws trying to hold her. She was attacked around 3:30 in the morning. Another victim was the lady known as 'Chiquita,' who was also sucked by the strange object with her breast becoming bloody, but without leaving any marks."

Compared to reports of mysterious animal attacks and mutilations, reports involving humans are somewhat rare. The probable reason is that many such incidents involving people are not recognized for what they are. The possibility is that a massive cover-up by officials worldwide exists to hide the fact that something is preying on humans. If we consider that extraterrestrials are visiting Earth, the likely reason for such visitations is scientific exploration. Consider that, with billions of galaxies and the likelihood that there are multitudes of different kinds of life scattered across the universe, the Earth is just another source of specimens for extraterrestrial scientists to gather and study.

Another possible scenario postulates that mankind is caught in the middle of a great, universal battle between the forces of good and evil. Religious scholars for centuries have warned that our souls are in jeopardy from demonic forces that will stop at nothing to gain ultimate control over us. The Bible calls Lucifer the deceiver, and declares that he will appear as "an angel of light" to fool us into believing his lies. Could it be that the attacks and mutilations that have been blamed on extraterrestrials are actually the work of Satanic creatures who have disguised themselves as beings from other worlds?

So as you try to sleep tonight, wondering what that noise was in your closet, or what strange thing is moving in the shadows just beyond the headstones in the cemetery, remember that we are not that far removed from our distant ancestors whose blood and flesh nourished unseen horrors and demonic nightmares. For even safely behind our locks and security cameras, we still cannot hide from the monsters.

Adam Gorightly

Exposing the Sinister Secrets and Rituals of the Dreaded Men In Black

By Dr. Allen H. Greenfield

Editors Note: They threaten and harass UFO witnesses. They command UFO contactees to stop telling of their experiences. They have the ability to materialize, levitate, read minds, listen in to telephone conversations, and in general know what you are doing day or night. Sometimes they knock at your door. Or they can appear in your home in the middle of a mist. You can encounter them on the street. If it were two centuries ago it's possible they would try to run you over in their black carriages or today in a dark ominous looking Cadillac.

Dr. Allen H. Greenfield is a chief scribe on the occult-UFO connection as well as a sought after guest on many shows such as UFO Hunters and The Paracast. He is pictured with ace MIB hunter Tim Beckley.

They look sinister all dressed in black. Sometimes they are immaculately dressed. Other times they are rumpled and slovenly. They don't have a great command over the language they are speaking; they look odd in general; have no sense of humor; and always appear out of place. They have been encountered throughout history. Dressed in black cloaks. Black turtlenecks. Hats pulled down over their often imprecise faces. Sunglasses black out the blank stare in their eyes.

Occult scribe and adapt Bishop Allen H. Greenfield has followed their activities closely. He recognizes their connection to the paranormal forces and the Dark Side of UFOlogy. He sees their secret messages clearly as he uses a series of arcane ciphers, as detailed in his e-book *Secret Rituals of the Men In Black*, which we abridge below.

The Stuff Of Dreams

In 1980 I ran into the dead end wall that many UFOlogists have encountered in their research.

The evidence I had accumulated suggested to me that the UFO mystery was something closely akin to an infinite series of nested boxes, and that illusion after illusion after illusion produced much speculation but little useful information. My old friend Gene Duplantier had once described UFOlogy as "like a long walk down an endless tube," and many of the best, most thoughtful students of the subject, on realizing this, simply gave up.

Publisher Timothy Beckley is believed to have photographed a true MIB in front of the Jersey City apartment of Jack and Mary Robinson during a particularly strange UFO wave on the East Coast circa 1966-67.

Ten years were to pass before another break came my way in the form of the Ultra-terrestrial Cipher that provided the breakthrough that explains, for me, not only the UFOs, but many Masonic passwords, ancient legends and occult secrets.

I stumbled upon the cipher; I did not invent it, owe no allegiance to it, make no claims for it other than that it "fits" easily the subject matter I have applied it to in this and my previous work, "Secret Cipher of the UFOnauts." I regard it as experimental, but consider it a working solution to some of the most profound enigmas thoughtful people have dwelt upon over the last several centuries.

Two things to take note of: First, in discussing various Masonic degrees, words and "secrets," I have been at some pain to avoid violation of the ritual privacy of these societies. The Degrees I have discussed are, essentially, archaic (that is, no longer working) Degrees from the York and Memphis systems. The York materials are available at virtually every bookstore in Duncan's Ritual of Freemasonry.

The Memphis materials exist in manuscript form, but are not held under copyright and have recently been published in modern editions based in John Yarker's work. I have avoided quoting or referring to any ritual not routinely in current public distribution or available at bookstores. In passing, I will say that to read about a ritual is not to perform it. Such rituals are "Mystery Plays" and are fully understandable only in the doing, not merely in the telling.

Second, there is a sense in which the Oannes Mythos, the Mystery Plays and Rituals presented here, the very Ultraterrestrial Visitors themselves, inherently overlap with the stuff of dreams.

They represent a Reality more profound than our own, and as such cannot be taken verbatim or too literally. In this volume I have pulled out the stops and taken a plunge beyond the Reality Barrier. What I have found is the core of the Ultraterrestrial Secret, too numinous to be other than ineffable.

When there are no words to literally describe what one knows, one speaks in the language of mythos.

So have I done.

"To puzzle out an imaginary meaning for this 'nonsense' sets one thinking of the Mysteries; one enters into deep contemplation of holy things and God Himself leads the soul to real illumination."

A. Crowley, "An Interlude," Book Four

Ashtar - Angels, Demons or Men In Black?

EARLIER ciphers were presented to initiates in a ritual context. This ritual context has, from at least the times of the Egyptian and Babylonian Priesthood, formed the bridge between human initiates and their Ultraterrestrial sponsors, sometimes associated with the double star system of Sirius, even in ancient times.

Thus, we find the 'modern' Egyptian Masonic Rite of Memphis conferring a secret Degree called ADEPT OF SIRIUS, the name of which, decoded using the eleven-fold cipher encrypted in The Book of the Law, means SECRET CHIEFS and, also, SECRET MASTER.

Fortified with the 1904 Cipher, we can take, for example, the case of Trevor James Constable, author (as "Trevor James") of the seminal 1950s work "They Live in the Sky," and an active experimenter today with Reichian Energies.

John A. Keel long ago noticed that UFO contact incidents seemed to step out of time in the usual sense. Without the UFOnaut Cipher, however, the predictive aspect of this non-linear factor can be lost.

In April, 1965, a piece of parchment was found wrapped around a glass vial containing some silver sand. This was the site of Arthur Bryant's encounter with "Yam-ski" the newly made "ascended master" who emerged from a UFO the day after contactee George Adamski's death half a world away. The parchment contained the Greek words Adelphos Adelpho ("brother to brother").

Two years later, in December of 1967, student Tom Monteleone encountered a UFO being in Adelphi, Maryland. The name of the town should alert us to a probable 'coded' relationship to the earlier case. Monteleone was told by the entity he met that it was named VADIG. Later, he met Vadig in Washington, D.C. (where Adamski had died and was buried) in 'civilian clothes' several times.

On each occasion VADIG, as if for emphasis, closed his conversation with the phrase, "I'll see you in time."

Keeping in mind that one of Adamski's main contacts had been Firkon, and that this name had been adopted by an Adamski and Williamson follower who disappeared without a trace, along with his partner 'Ramu' we are not surprised to find that VADIG = 61 = RAMU, but also, LODGE. The value again shows up in the recent ZARKON case.

As we have seen, the strange words and names that show up in Masonic Lodge settings are similar in form and purpose to those which show up in contact cases. They show up in modern cases of Angelic Visitation, which, in a sense, resemble the visitations of the Men in Black. The Hebrew word for "angel" literally means "messenger" and the names of these messengers are often equivalent to the names of Ultraterrestrial Messengers. They also show up in demonology.

Sinister and demonic the UFO Silencers warn UFO witnesses to keep their mouth's shut regarding their encounters with the unknown.

The original "etheric" and "astral" contacts took place in the '50s, and are a lot like the Richard Shaver "hidden worlds" material. It is of interest that an old acquaintance from both the lore of classical occultism and the legends of modern Ufology, known as "Ashtar" shows up in these contacts as well.

"Ashtar" is, in traditional occult circles, a demon of considerable power. In UFO lore, he is usually a "positive force" or is so identified by percipients. A variant name that shows up in UFO contact cases is ASHTAR SHERAN. Constable also was in communication with one ANDOLO. Interestingly, ASHTAR tells Constable which beings are "etheric" and "good" and which are "astral" and "satanic".

He tells Constable that one of the bad guys, so to speak, is ERANUS, who he identifies as Satan himself.

These contacts are somewhat puzzling, because they contain, when viewed in light of the Secret Cipher of the UFOnauts, aspects of deception on the part of certain Ultraterrestrial parties, and we note the pattern of even a bizarre humor entering the picture.

- ASHTAR SHERAN = 108 = FINGERS, while SHERAN by itself = 61 = TOES.
- ASHTAR = 47 = ATLANS (one of Shaver's Ancient Races) and AEON.

- ANDOLO = 37 = AGE.
- ERANUS, on the other hand, yields 74 = SOLAR DISC and TERRA.
- ASHTAR (47) also yields DISC.
- Both ASHTAR (47 or 4+7=11) and ERANUS (74 or 7+4=11; note the 47/74 reversal) both reduce to the 'code key number,' eleven.

I should emphasize again that a reduction to eleven is usually only possible in significant cases, eleven being the "cycle key" to the UFOnaut cipher, as explained elsewhere.

- ERANUS = 74 = RIDDLE. It makes an anagram for SUN ERA = 74 = SOLAR DISC!
- SUN ERA = 74 = SOLAR DISC brings to mind Aleister Crowley's anthropological observations on "Satan".

He informs us that, "The Devil does not exist. It is a false name invented by the Black Brothers to imply a Unity in their ignorant muddle of dispersions...'The Devil' is, historically, the God of any people that one personally dislikes... This 'Devil' is called Satan or Shaitan, and regarded with horror by people who are ignorant of his formula, and, imagining themselves to be evil, accuse Nature herself of their own phantasmal crime."Satan is Saturn, Set, Abrasax, Adad, Adonis, Attis, Adam, Adonai, etc."The most serious charge against him is only that he is the Sun in the South. The Ancient Initiates, dwelling as they did in land whose blood was the water of the Nile or the Euphrates, connected the South with life-withering heat, and cursed the quarter when the solar darts were deadliest...

"But to us, aware of the astronomical facts, this antagonism to the South is a silly superstition which the accidents of their local conditions suggested to our animistic ancestors."

Ashtar, on the other hand, is more suspect. He is frequently mentioned in the UFO literature.Early contactee George Van Tassel mentions him in 1952 as, "Ashtar, commandant of station Schare" and a very powerful ruler. Van Tassel's Giant Rock conventions became the fountainhead of the entire contemporary New Age movement. Van Tassel's trance channel group, in fact, included advanced students of Parmahansa Yogananda's Yogic Philosophy.UFOlogist Bryant Reeves told his wife Helen that Van Tassel, "reminds me of a veritable modern 'John the Baptist' crying in the wilderness, 'Prepare ye for a new cosmic age.'"The occult literature has always considered ASHTAR, or Astaroth, a fallen angel, that is, a malevolent demon.The Lemegeton (the Lesser Key of Solomon, or Book of Evil Spirits) tells us that Ashtar,

"...discourses willingly on the Fall but pretends that he himself was exempt from their lapse." This sounds suspiciously like what ASHTAR was doing with Trevor Constable, and other contactees, particularly in America.Interestingly also, The True Key of Solomon (Grimorium Verum, dated 1517 and allegedly translated from an earlier Hebrew source) tells us that ASHTAR migrated to America, presumably around the time of Columbus.So, when ASHTAR SHERAN (= "FINGERS & TOES") tells us to watch out for the "Satanic" ERANUS (= SUN ERA or SOLAR DISC), watch out for

Ashtar. Constable, be it noted, has come to have a more wary view of his early communications experiences, for which he has our admiration.

The More Angelic side is represented here too.METATRON, the classical angelic being said to be the ascended Patriarch Enoch and the "original man in black" who wrestled all night with Jacob in The Book of Genesis and gave him the name "Israel" has the value of 128 in NAEQ6, that of SPACE SHIP, TWO FOLD NAME (Enoch-Metatron; Jacob-Israel) and NEW AGE KEY.TIME Magazine for December 27, 1993 features a cover story on "The New Age of Angels". It offers a remarkably uncritical account of the New Age Angel Fad, which seems to have replaced dolphins, crystals, unicorns and fairies, all so trendy in the '80s.

Some of the accounts resemble the encounters with Men in Black in UFO lore or the 'black man' of medieval demonology, the major difference, as one expects from the New Age perspective, being that these visitors are taken to be benevolent in nature,

In the summer of 1977, Ann and Gary Cannady were visited at a time of extreme stress in their lives. Ann had been diagnosed as having advanced uterine cancer, and was three days away from major surgery. Gary's first wife had died of the same disease, and Ann's diagnosis had been confirmed by repeated tests. The door bell rang, and Gary answered.

Standing on the step was a large man, a good inch taller than her 6-ft. 5-in. husband."He was the blackest black I've ever seen," Ann says, "and his eyes were a deep, deep azure blue."The stranger introduced himself simply as Thomas. And then he told her that her cancer was gone.

They invited the mysterious stranger inside, where he re-affirmed that she was healed. Ann asked, point blank, who he was, to which the stranger replied, 'I am Thomas. I am sent by God.' He then proceeded to perform a sort of laying-on-of-hands healing. Ann felt a burst of light and heat go through her body, and passed out. Subsequent testing showed no trace of the cancer, and there has been no recurrence.

The obsidian angel quoted Isaiah 53:5 to the couple, a text concerned with healing through sacrifice. THOMAS = 62 = ORDER and SACRED and AIWASS & LAM in NAEQ6, thus identifying the commonplace name with the current of the present Aeon.But, lest the omen be misunderstood, on the next page TIME gives another modern angelic account, a being seen by Melissa Deal Forth with her dying husband Chris Deal, comforting him and seemingly communicating to him a profound sense of peace. When her husband was discovered missing from his hospital bed only days before his death, she found him in the hospital chapel "with a man she had never seen before."

He was tall, dressed rather like Chris usually did, in a flannel shirt, new Levis and lace-up work-boots that appeared as if they, too, had just been taken off the shelf.The clothing of such visitors in UFO lore also often appears to be taken "directly off the shelf.""There was no real age to him," Melissa says. "No wrinkles. Just this perfectly smooth and pale, white, white skin and icy blue eyes. I mean I've never seen that color blue on any human before."Students of MIB cases will recognize the basic fabric of all the visitation cases here.

Enoch and Mutan Mion

" By using a collection of different 'glasses,' or crystals, and special 'shew-stones,' Kelly was able to communicate with extraterrestrial intelligences. Dee directed the ceremonies, observed the proceedings, and carefully wrote down the results. It was in this way that the entire magical system, which is called Enochian, originated."

Gerald J. Schueler

The cipher brought to light (or, in a sense, "hidden in plain sight") in 1904 by Aiwass, the præterhuman contact associated with Aleister Crowley, was not the first magical cipher or system developed in the English-speaking world.

In 1581, Dr. John Dee and Edward Talbott, who took the last name "Kelly" as they began their work together, conducted a long series of Magical Workings which produced intense and detailed communication with Ultraterrestrial Intelligences of a high order. A language, cosmology (scheme of the universe) and a (now lost) set of practical instructions emerged, which foreshadowed the New Aeon Cipher, just as the Enochian "language" echoed earlier Rosicrucian models.

Three hundred years later the Hermetic Order of the Golden Dawn, organized by High Grade Freemasons associated with John Yarker and Kenneth Mackenzie, and utilizing their esoteric approach to the Mysteries, took up the Enochian work as part of their late-Victorian "magical revival."

The English magick of the culturally rich Elizabethan Era was to an extent perfected in the equally fertile Victorian Age. What developed was a reconstituted and perfected version of Dee and Kelly's partially lost practical system of instruction for contacting Ultraterrestrial Entities, and for "astral" travel (sometimes physical travel) to other celestial spheres (or "planets") called "Aethyrs" or "Aires" of the Universe.

When Aleister Crowley, still rather fresh from the dictation of The Book of The Law, took up the exploration of the Enochian Aethyrs in 1909, he did so not far from the home of Max Theon, then himself taking the dictation of The Cosmic Philosophy associated with the Hermetic Brotherhood of Light he had once headed.

These unique ethereal communications ended for Theon shortly thereafter with the untimely death of his wife, the gifted trance medium Alma Ware.Crowley worked in these sessions with his disciple Victor Neuburg. Having done some preliminary workings during his active period in the Hermetic Order of the Golden Dawn in 1900, Crowley produced a truly remarkable document of Communication with Higher Intelligences – that is, Ultraterrestrial Contacts – and Travel to Other Realms.Published as "The Vision And The Voice" in his famous journal, "The Equinox," it ranks as world-class mystical literature, with methodical notes on the ceremonial methods used which could be reproduced by any dedicated experimenter – though, it is true, not without some risk.

The implication here should not be underestimated; in fact, there is good reason to believe that the 13th Enochian Aethyr, called "ZIM," transports the scryer directly to the Sirius planetary system, where one can meet the Oannes, or NOMMO, as the Dogon ("people of the fish god Dagon") call him, under the name NEMO.

This scientific methodology approaching mystical phenomena was in keeping with Crowley's philosophy of "Scientific Illuminism" – described uniquely as "the aim of religion, the method of science."

The "Enochian Universe" consists of Thirty "Aethyrs" or "Worlds," each quite unique and inhabited by quite different entities.

Through a Ritual Opening of the Portal of the Adepti and the recitation of certain Enochian "Keys" or "Calls," any specific Aethyr can be reached, and the contactee can interact with the inhabitants and function within the rarified environment.

In 1991-92, the present writer organized and conducted a series of 30 experiments with this very system, one each week over a thirty week period. This was preceded by two instructional Intensives devoted to educating prospective participants on the Enochian System of Contacting the Ultraterrestrials at various levels.

I took upon myself the Induction, but deliberately selected a number of relative novices for my "seers" or contactees.In this way, any results would be relatively untainted by preexisting knowledge of what to "expect." Due precautions were taken, but every one of the twenty or so participants (some of whom came and went as the long and challenging series of workings ran their incredible course) were told that this was, truly, Risky Business.

The results were quite spectacular, by anyone's account. Conducted under the auspices of a Major Lodge of one of the Great Magical Orders of Antiquity, in the fashionable Temple located in a historic and elegant building mostly tenanted by a number of holistic health practitioners and environmental groups, every single amateur contactee was successfully propelled by us into the targeted "Aethyr" or specific Ultraterrestrial Sphere I invoked, met with and had communication with the Entities or Forces of that realm, and returned.

In the process, eerie physical effects were frequently, almost routinely produced. On one occasion, at the critical moment of closure, electrical power failed not only in the building but for a block in either direction from the Temple. Casual participants and hardened veterans alike sometimes saw Entities physically appear within the Temple during sessions, although all doors and windows were locked from the inside and monitored by my assistants and myself.Some effects were "picked up" by tenants in the building who were totally unaware of the Ceremonies, and sensitives several miles distant spontaneously and accurately sometimes "picked up on" peak events.

Uncannily, a recap at the conclusion of each session revealed a startling degree of correlation with the experiences recorded by Crowley for the same Aethyr in 1909.

Although my amateur contactees ("scryers" or "seers") were not particularly learned regarding such matters (they did not, in fact, even know one another very well for the most part), the parallel was so close at times that I resorted to switching scryers at the last minute for a particular session in case someone was "boning up" on a particular Aethyr. It made no difference in the result.

Sometimes two contactees "co-scryed" the same Aethyr, interacting with one another rather like astronauts on the lunar surface or in space, as well as with the denizens of the Aire being traveled to. I had maintained substantial control throughout, acting as a kind of guardian. On one memorable occasion, the contactee being in some difficulty, I took a (quite physical) consecrated magical tool (a sword, as it happens), and handed it "up" to the scryer, who was quite able to perceive, grasp and use it to unravel her predicament with it.This was clearly a direct interaction between one plane or dimension of existence and another on an intentional basis. But, unlike in many UFO abduction episodes, my scryer and I were calling the shots.

I realized that what we were utilizing here was something in the way of an ages-old "ritual technology" for producing human-alien contact. The ancient Priestesses of Delphi used such a technique, and the modern RA Material produced by the Kentucky-based contactee Lightlines group, centered around Carla Rueckert and the late Don Elkins, had been doing much the same thing when they would take perfectly ordinary people and, applying their own metatechnology, produce communication with the same group of Entities, even though they were careful to isolate one contactee from another.

I did not, then, "need" a talented medium like Mark Probert or Richard Shaver to produce meaningful results. Nor did I approach these Entities with undue reverence. In fact, assisted by an Ordained Exorcist, I routinely ended each session with a full scale Formal Exorcism.

Again, and this is very important, unlike the Adamski-type contacts, the place and time of contact was under our control, not Theirs. (This is aside from the question of whether classical contacts were in some sense "guided" by a "secret magician" – in the case of Adamski, perhaps George Hunt Williamson.)This was human over alien, not the other way around.

Dee and Kelly had not been so lucky, back in Elizabethan England. Dr. Dee started out as a distinguished scholar in a world peopled by Bacon, Shakespeare, and the savants who gave us the King James translation of the Bible. Dee's library was eventually looted by a mob and partially destroyed.

Kelly, for his part, contacted the Forces of the Seventh Enochian Aethyr, encountering an entity that sent him running forever from scrying, taking with him the pitiful remnant of Dee's once-considerable fortune...and Dee's wife. He disappeared into oblivion. A somewhat similar occurrence ended the famous "The

Babalon Working" of John W. Parsons and L. Ron Hubbard in the 1940s. Parsons claimed, after opening a Star Gate, that "BABALON is now incarnate on the earth in the form of a mortal woman." Hubbard went on to develop the influential Church of Scientology.

What Kelly encountered in the Seventh Aethyr – known as "DEO" – was a female entity associated with Venus and the Tarot Card called "The Star." This Arcanum, of unknown antiquity, usually depicts a nude woman next to a body of water with a blazing star overhead. This, originally, referred to Sirius, which is similarly depicted in bas reliefs from the ancient Sumerian-Babylonian civilization, and the semi-aquatic nature of the Visitors "from" the Sirius system called "Oannes".

The Star Gate "Scrying Table" of Dee and Kelly served as a portal to other universes. Modern experiments reproduce these results.

In whatever event, the Lady, spectacularly erotic and "beyond good and evil" (that is, beyond Duality) in a way totally unpalatable even to a rogue like Kelly in the time of Elizabeth I or King James, told him, "I am Understanding, and science dwelleth in me; and the heavens oppress me. They come and desire me with infinite appetite; for none that are earthly have embraced me, for I am shadowed with the Circle of Stars, and covered with the morning clouds."

Phrases such as "the heavens oppress me" in this instance, or "I come from a country much weaker than your own" in the INDRID COLD close encounter case, are generally made by entities from worlds which have been conquered by the Gray Aliens, unlike the Earth. Kelly ran, in terror and without understanding. Crowley, scrying the same Aethyr on December 7, 1909 in the Algerian Desert, described her as, "...the Daughter of the King. This is the Virgin of Eternity. This is she that the Holy One hath wrestled from the Giant Time, and the prize of them that have overcome Space." Even Crowley could almost not bear the intensity of the contact.

All of this closely parallels an episode in the short novel published by Ray Palmer in Amazing Stories in March, 1945. "I Remember Lemuria" launched the late Richard Shaver's remarkable career as a mystic seer in the totally inappropriate context of a science fiction pulp magazine.

Shaver's protagonist was Mutan Mion, an antediluvian hero of Inner Earth in the last thrashings of any kind of real civilization. Mutan Mion goes to visit the highest ranking NORTAN he can reach, the Nortans being the most ancient of space faring races who live in Deep Space away from the detrimental radiation of all Stars, in a state of virtual endless growth and near immortality. As Mion relates it: "We were drawn as by a powerful magnet toward a huge figure which was an intense concentration of all vitally stimulating qualities that make beauty the sought-for thing that it is...

"All of eighty feet tall she must have been. She towered over our heads as she arose to greet us, a vast cloud of the glittering hair of the Nor women floating about her head, the sex aura a visible iridescence flashing about her form.

"I yearned toward that vast beauty which was not hidden, for it is considered impolite to conceal the body greatly, being an offense against art and friendship, to take beauty out of life..."

Compare this to Crowley's Algerian vision of the Being of the 9th Aethyr (December 7, 1909):

"And this palace is nothing but the body of a woman . . .

"It is impossible to say anything about her. She is naked; her whole body is covered with fine gold hairs that are the electric flames that are the spears of mighty and terrible Angels whose breastplates are the scales of her skin. And the hair of her head, that flows down to her feet, is the very light of God himself."

Crowley is eventually shown into what he calls a "tower" by an Ultraterrestrial Being.The "chamber" is "furnished with maps of many mystical cities. There is a table, and a strange lamp, that gives light by jetting four columns of vortex rings of luminous smoke."The "tower" is some kind of spire or turret, the "chamber" some kind of alcove or containment. The description given is, however, bizarrely similar to that given by modern contactees of the interior of so-called "spaceships."

Crowley's perception seems, on balance, far closer to the actual nature of the "place."This seems all the more plausible when we take cognizance of Crowley's vision, six days earlier in the same location, in the 15th Aethyr: "And behold! There is one God therein, and the letters of the stars in his crown, Orion, and the Pleiades, and Aldebaran, and Alpha Centauri, and Cor Leonis, and Cor Scorpionis, and Spica, and the pole-star, and Hercules, and Regulus, and Aquila, and the Ram's Eye.

"And upon a map of stars shalt thou draw the sigil of that name; and because also some of the letters are alike, thou shalt know that the stars also have tribes and nations..."It should be well noted that the 15th through the 1st Aethyr of the Enochian System are linked, according to Crowley's experiences, by the being Nemo.

The English language based Cipher of the UFOnauts is less helpful here than usual. This seems to be the realm of Enochian and earlier Hebrew-based ciphers.But, nonetheless, keeping in mind the cipher, qabalistic principles are the same in all contexts, and with a nod to Shaver's MANTONG concept (English is a bastardized reinvention of the primal language of the Universe, called "Mantong"), we note that the Aethyr's Name, DEO, has a NAEQ6 cipher value of 38, the same as that of AIWASS, the intelligence which dictated The Book of the Law to Crowley.If Shaver's "Princess Vanue of Nor" is the Being of DEO, the great nude female entity with a sexual aura nearly unbearable even to the preeminent Sexual Magus of the Twentieth Century, Aleister Crowley, we may find her title CHIEF OF THE NOR ON QUANTO revealing, as its cipher 6 value of 297 is that of TEMPLE WHORE PRINCESS.

Who Decides What You Can Know?

Genesis 3:5 (KJV)

For God doth know that in the day ye eat thereof, then your eyes shall be opened, and ye shall be as gods, knowing good and evil.

Genesis 3:22 (KJV)

And the LORD God said, Behold, the man is become as one of us, to know good and evil: and now, lest he put forth his hand, and take also of the Tree of Life, and eat, and live for ever:

Genesis 3:23 (KJV)

Therefore the LORD God sent him forth from the Garden of Eden, to till the ground from whence he was taken.

John 10:34 (KJV)

Jesus answered them, Is it not written in your law, I said, Ye are gods?

A great deal is written, though mostly in obscure sources concerning the legendary founding of an Ultraterrestrial beachhead on the Earth in early Sumerian times by the fish-like (and manlike) being from Sirius, the Oannes.There is even some public speculation on the establishment of a Priestly caste, in Babylonia, India and Egypt, devoted to maintaining secret knowledge of this contact, and perhaps maintaining the contact thorough all of subsequent history.

Whether such contact is for good or ill depends upon who you read. The pro-Masonic writers tend to consider this a golden secret carried forward by the Knights Templar, founded by Hugh de Paynes and eight other French crusaders in 1118.After enjoying prosperity and the patronage of Catholic Europe for some time, the Order was brutally suppressed by Church and State, but survived, according to Masonic legend, in Scottish Rite Freemasonry after the burning of the last Grand Master Iacobus Burgundus Molanus (I.B.M.) and many of his followers outside of Scotland.The Templars were charged with the secret worship of a half human, half beast called "Baphomet" which some spiritual descendants embrace, while other deny vehemently.Most tend to take on the patronage of St. John the Baptist, whose feast day, June 24th, is the old Feast of Oannes, as well as International Flying Saucer Day, in honor of Kenneth Arnold's encounter on June 24th, 1947 with nine saucer-like objects.

Some of the properties – and members – of the Templar Order were taken over by the rival Order of the Knights Hospitaller, otherwise known as the Knights of Rhodes, after their conquest, in 1308 under Fulke de Villaret, of the Island of Rhodes from the Moslems.

They are known more familiarly, and in a somewhat sinister context, as the Knights of Malta, to which island they retreated after the Moslems retook Rhodes.Under that name, in modern times, they have been accused of exercising great influence over governments in Christian countries, and have been associated in contemporary conspiracy literature with the Trilateral Commission, the Bilderberg Group, the Club of Rome, and the leadership of the crusade against Communism which dominated Western Political Thought from the end of World War Two until the breakup of the Soviet Empire in the 1990s.Many of these groups, but particularly the Knights of Malta, are involved in privately "selling" cooperation between Ultraterrestrial Forces of dubious motivations and Terrestrial governments and industrial groups.

In February of 1937, on the eve of the Second World War, a representative of the Knights of Malta, an American (still living as I write this in 1994), met with the more esoteric leadership of the Third Reich in Germany. The meeting took place in a hidden SS retreat, and was attended by General Karl Haushofer, the senior initiate of the Black Lodge inside the German Reich.The purpose of the meeting was to "sell" the Nazi regime on contact with what the young Maltese Knight called "the coming race."Asked by the present writer in 1979 what he meant by the term, he told me, "The Ultraterrestrials, of course. The Germans had noted their 'ghost rockets' in Sweden, and were aware of their power. Most of the older Nazis present, though, were former members of the Thule Group or the archaic Vril Society, and took me to be talking about Tibetans or Aryan supermen or some such bunk. Except Haushofer, who knew better, and the 'Man with the Green Gloves' who, though supposedly a Tibetan himself, was certainly an Ultraterrestrial."The deal fell through when the Reich fell, and the Knights switched their attention elsewhere.

Strange Behavior of the MIB: They Do Not Act Like Humans Would!

Vancouver, British Columbia, Canada
December 1, 2000 - 10:00 am

Several days after witnessing two low flying objects over the area, on two separate nights (One of the objects was described as huge, making a rumbling like noise; it had a V-shaped tail with two rows of round and oblong windows and was black, gray and silver in color.) and after receiving a suspicious phone call from someone claiming to be a General from the Canadian armed forces, two strange men appeared at the door of the witness' residence. They produced wallets, one black, one brown, containing photo ID that stated they were from the Canadian Air Defense. They asked to come inside. The witness extended his hand, but was ignored.

Moving into the house took them through the kitchen area, but they stopped upon seeing the microwave. After some questioning, the witness lowered a portion of a counter and they carefully slid through the extra space. Sitting down they produced a small silver-colored tape recorder and inserted a small disc, between a nickel and a quarter in size. On entering the house, one of the men had noticed an unusual walking stick in the hallway, about which he remarked that the head of the stick's carving, painted red, reminded him of primates back home.

The two men were olive skinned and appeared to have slanted eyes. Each wore glasses with thick rims. They wore gray suits with black shirts, one had a white tie, and the other was buttoned up to the neck. The one with the tie had a clip that contained a red "stone" that flickered. The other had a ruby ring surrounded with diamonds. His watch was square but without apparent hands, instead being encircled with buttons that periodically illuminated from white to green to mauve. The strap appeared to be molded into the skin and was a solid steel band. The belt on his pants was of metallic strips with a square buckle. Both had very large feet, estimated to be 14". Each carried a brief case that was heavy and cold.

When sitting down they never relaxed into their chairs but retained a stiff back the whole time. Not once during their stay in the house did they speak to each other. The witness' two cats were extremely agitated the whole time during the visitors stay. Also, the owner's dog that lived upstairs barked during the whole episode. The men noticed that the witness was wearing a very unusual watch and one of them touched his arm. The touch felt very cold and clammy. They questioned the witness about his sightings, and one of them appeared to be taking shorthand notes. When they questioned him they looked into his eyes and seemed to "pierce his brain."

As they were leaving, they again carefully avoided the microwave. Outside in the yard they spent about 30 minutes scouring the ground with a Geiger counter. As they rounded the corner of the house, the witness went from the kitchen to the bedroom, which gave him a clearer view of the driveway and the road. Despite the very short period of time it took him to achieve this, the two men were not in sight, nor was a car leaving, and no car door could be heard slamming. They had vanished. Later the witness discovered that on the windowsill, only six inches behind where one of the men had been sitting, was a Windex bottle that was partially melted as if heat had been applied to it. Alongside was a cassette warped in a similar manner. The witness suffered from a severe migraine type headache after the two men left. His eyes also felt gritty and teary, and his face now appeared sunburned. He also suffered from strange dreams, including one that was of lying prone on a table in a round room with a bright light above him and then sensing being touched.

Two days later, while going outside his house, the witness saw the same two men he had seen before in the driveway. Both were dressed in white coveralls. One was carrying a Geiger counter, the other a 12 to 16 inch parabolic dish in his hand, pointing to the sky, plus earphones and a microphone that was attached. He appeared to be searching the sky. The wires all led into a black box at his waist. At one point he had what looked like a camera, although not video, aimed at a tree over which the UFO had been originally seen. During the time they were together neither was seen speaking to each other. Nor was any car seen which they might have arrived in.

In December, a few days after Christmas, a man appeared at the door of the witness. He stated that he had come to see his unusual watch. He stated that his name was Mr. Smith and showed some ID. He wore a dark charcoal suit, white shirt, and black tie. He also wore a black fedora. His feet were very large, "size 13, or 14," like the witness' previous visitors. His shoes were black and shiny, with no signs of dirt on them at all. He was about 4-feet 8 inches to 5-feet tall, very thin, and very pale skinned with very long fingers. He also wore black wrap around glasses with silver frames. The witness extended his hand but was ignored (again).

Upon entering the house, the visitor commented upon the carved walking stick in the hallway. He also asked the witness to turn the microwave off before he walked in front of it. Sitting down at the kitchen table, he produced a small silver tape recorder, claiming it could record up to 80 hours or more. Using a pick-like tool from his breast pocket, he examined the witness' watch. He opened a black briefcase, removed some paper, a silver pencil with a red top, and a pen like flash light that emitted a mauve, pencil-thin beam, which he scanned the interior of the watch with. He took out a small digital-type camera and with it he took several pictures of the watch. During the whole of his visit he spoke very little, and his speech seemed slurred.

Again the cats were agitated during the stranger's visit. He again expressed interest in the watch and the witness asked $500 for it, but he replied that he had to check with his colleagues. The stranger also expressed interest in a computer, saying that it had very minimal power. The stranger departed without saying goodbye. The witness went immediately to the window but could not see any sign of the visitor or any car in the vicinity. He had simply vanished. A plastic hair blower nozzle was found melted and a ruler in a drawer close to where the visitor had been sitting was bent into a slight 'S' curve. Again the witness suffered from a severe headache and an eruptive nosebleed.

In early January 2001, two peculiar strangers again visited the witness to a previous UFO encounter. These two were different from the others. They were at least six-feet tall, very bony, with head, hands and feet out of proportion to the rest of the body. They wore gray suits that seemed to be "oily," had black ties and hats plus wrap around sunglasses that they never took off. When questioned about the glasses, they remarked that they could see perfectly well. Their ears stood out from their heads and their skin was pale white, whereas their fingernails were gray in color. They never removed their hats during their visit. And throughout the whole time, only one of them spoke. When asked for ID's they displayed "silver" cases that contained a photo, an unusual symbol, plus their names in small print.

Upon entering the kitchen, they asked the witness to please unplug the microwave; they also told him to turn the computer off. The two Persian cats were going crazy, dashing around the room and trying to get out of the window, which was closed. Each man carried a briefcase with an inverted 'L' shaped handle. The man that did all the talking asked to see the witness' unusual watch. He then removed from his briefcase four small containers, each of which had a different colored top. Opening two, he proceeded to pour the contents over the watch. He told the concerned witness that no harm would come to the watch. He was given $250 for the watch and told that they would give him the rest later. He told them that he was moving soon, and to this they replied "We know. Don't worry. We can find you if we want to."

They soon departed without the common courtesies, staring blankly at the witness as he extended his hand. Once again, the witness hurried to the bedroom window only to find, as before, no sign of either man departing, nor could any vehicle be heard leaving. After the visit the witness felt drained, had a severe headache that lasted for two days and a rash on his arms, face and chest.

Source: Graham Conway, UFO BC
Graham Conway is now deceased
Aileen Garoutté
Keep looking up!

Round Trip to Hell in a Flying Saucer

In the early 1950s, U.S. President Eisenhower unknowingly bought into a similar plan proposed by the Knights of Malta to him on behalf of their Ultraterrestrial overlords, in the name of the anticommunist crusade of that period."Deviants" were rounded up, and unprecedented power was placed in the hands of the Military Industrial infrastructure throughout the decade, until Eisenhower, in a surprise farewell address, asserted his fundamental decency and libertarian patriotism and roundly denounced the whole deal, paving the way for the Kennedy era and a generation of progressive experimentation.

The Knights of Malta briefly found themselves sudden outsiders. A bloody worldwide orgy of assassinations and murders of progressive political and moral leaders quickly followed, and by the 1980s the U.S Administration was safely in the hands of an aged ex-actor with degenerative Alzheimer's Disease surrounded by a staff nearly totally dominated by members of the Knights of Malta. By the 1990s, the anticommunist pretense could be dropped, the confused and restless citizenry disarmed, and the feeble opposition which remained could be easily co-opted.

But what of the occult societies that had carried the flame for centuries? What of UFOlogy, conspiracy theory, metaphysical, and "White Lodge" Masonic groups?

The Knights of Malta's viewpoint infiltrated organized occultism and UFOlogy through the connection between William Dudley Pelley's pro-Nazi Silver Shirts prior to World War Two, and the occult Black Lodge within the Third Reich, centered in the SS, the Ahnenerbe Society, and the appropriately named "Black Order" – descended from such black magical bodies as the Thule Group and the Vril Society as detailed in Secret Cipher of the UFOnauts.Pelley and his outfit were certainly tools for the Maltese Knights, and key figures in UFOlogy became involved, including George Adamski and George Hunt Williamson. Adamski was introduced to Williamson by Pelley, at a time when Adamski was trying to sell his contact story as science fiction to Ray Palmer, then a prominent publisher.These initiates, not including the well-meaning Adamski, were knowledgeable about the Ultraterrestrial cipher, the Sirius-Oannes legend, etc. Interestingly, they were met with a spirited libertarian resistance from the very start by Meade Layne of Borderland Sciences, and his immediate successor, the late Riley Crabb, who "blew the whistle" on the interaction between the U.S. Government, the Knights of Malta and Ultraterrestrials since at least 1954.Layne was a True Adept, himself knowing the Ultraterrestrial Cipher and using it to make contacts of his own. Bill Webb of QBLH, an occult body that has done a great deal to reveal the Cipher to a broader public, recalled to us how Layne would visit him in Arizona in the 1950s, on his way to purported UFO landing sites. Webb, like Layne, had been a member of Dion Fortune's Inner Light offshoot of the Golden Dawn.The classic way of using the Cipher was to read published reports of alien encounters, such as those of Dan Fry, Truman Bethurum and Orfeo Angelucci, convert the planetary and personal names given by Ultraterrestrials to contactees to cipher, and infer where the next landing was going to occur. This seems to have been the HIDDEN PURPOSE of those high profile cases; to get publicized, so that scattered adepts in possession of the cipher would know where and when to make contact.

Ironically, Layne was so advanced that his sincere but less-initiated successor Crabb was afraid of him, and would actually do ritual exorcisms of the BSRF once on Adams Avenue in San Diego after Layne's departure, according to what I have been told by BSRF's present leader, former Michael Bertiaux student Tom Brown.

In the meantime, after 1952 the CIA actively sought to infiltrate and disrupt private UFO groups. I was told by Major Dewey Fornet, the one-time Pentagon Monitor for the Air Force UFO Project, that the UFO wave in the Summer of 1952 during the exceptionally hot "dog days" of July, completely overwhelmed the U.S. Defense system of those relatively technologically unsophisticated times. While UFOs were "dog-fighting" with jets and being spotted on radar in restricted air space over the White House and Pentagon, communication channels were so jammed that a "sneak attack" by a more terrestrial enemy (i.e., the Soviet Union) would have gotten through virtually unopposed in the UFO generated confusion.After that, the CIA determined to discredit the whole subject in earnest.A major attempt to set up a civilian National Investigations Committee on Aerial Phenomena was quickly co-opted by the intelligence community, and many of the group's leaders were military and intelligence personnel, including Director Major Donald Keyhoe's classmate from the Naval Academy and one-time CIA Director, Roscoe Hillenkoetter.Most of the "official sounding" UFO groups of that period are now dead. Curiously, the survivors include the very independent S.A.U.C.E.R.S. of Jim Moseley, and the now fifty year old BSRF.In its early days BSRF was closely associated with the group of sixteen high adepts or Ascended Masters called The Inner Circle, otherwise known as The Guardians. These entities, and those of their kind, humans who become More Than Human, seem somehow to "keep things in balance" through the ages of wars in the heavens and infiltration by Ultraterrestrials who, though far beyond humanity in knowledge and power, seem somehow afraid of us. Whatever they fear in us seems to be our only salvation.

Perhaps the early Gnostics had it right in turning the Genesis story on its head. In the Gnostic Version, as in the ancient Hypostasis of the Archons ("the reality of the rulers"), we find that the Serpent of Wisdom is the defender of humanity (in Hebrew Cipher "serpent" and "messiah" have the same numerical value), offering us the Tree of Wisdom and the Tree of Immortality, in opposition to The Authorities, or Celestial Rulers, who wish to keep us in ignorance and in the shadow of death.The Serpent or Dragon is a close relative (mythically speaking) to our presumed benefactor, the Oannes, Prometheus, Odin and the other celestial Titans who, at great cost to themselves, steal for us the fire of heaven.But, as the Yada di' Shi'ite, Aiwass, G.I. Gurdjiefi, Phil Dick or Frederich Nietsche would tell us, we are our own salvation or damnation.This is the last thing government bureaucrats, Knights of Malta or goose-stepping Silver Shirts and fundamentalists would have you realize: You are not helpless. Resistance is not futile. Within humanity is some Seed of Greatness that even the very gods tremble at.

If there is any "message" in this book, it is that we are, potentially, a very powerful race of beings.This is, ultimately, a message of hope.

"The Book of Spells or of Conjurations is the Record of every thought, word, and deed of the Magician...

"Let the pen with which the writing is done be the feather of a young male swan – that swan whose name is Aum. And let the ink be made of the gall of a fish, the fish Oannes."- Aleister Crowley, BOOK FOUR.

Note: Interested parties may find the entire text for this volume at http://www.bibliotecapleyades.net/cienciareal/men_in_black.htm

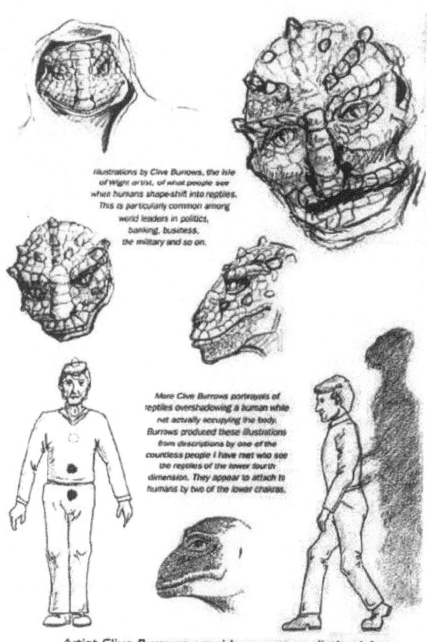

Illustrations by Clive Burrows, the Isle of Wight artist, of what people see when humans shape-shift into reptiles. This is particularly common among world leaders in politics, banking, business, the military and so on.

More Clive Burrows portrayals of reptiles overshadowing a human while not actually occupying the body. Burrows produced these illustrations from descriptions by one of the countless people I have met who see the reptiles of the lower fourth dimension. They appear to attach to humans by two of the lower chakras.

Artist Clive Burrows provides a very realistic vision based on witness accounts of the humanoids known as "the serpents."

Shape Shifters, Shimmers and Mystery Cryptos

The accounts are more documented that you might suspect they would be.

Stories of shape shifting might seem absurd on the surface – something more akin to a third rate horror movie, best seen at a suburban theater complex in a mall at a Saturday Midnight show with teenagers screaming as Jack Nicholson turns into a werewolf.

Many American Indian tribes speak of human transmutation where a witch or shaman is able to transform into an eagle, a coyote or a wolf. There are those tribal members who can accomplish this feat at will, while others are taken over during drumming or dancing ceremonies when the composition of sound and chanting can entrance those attending a Voodoo ritual or charismatic Christian revival. In Africa there are entire tribes who can switch over into Leopard Men, possessing supernatural, animal-like strength after the transformation process. And don't forget our ole friend Count Dracula, who can fly into your bedroom at night and bite your open neck in the resultant shape of a bat.

Many Native Americans believe they have the power to shape shift and have incorporated such beliefs into their tribal rituals such as those shown here by the masked Qagyuhla dancers in this rare historical photo.

The phenomenon of exceedingly large cats – the size of pumas and jaguars – have made unannounced appearances in places where such animals are not native. In the British Isles in particular, but not limited to the UK. While visiting an associate near Cincinnati, Ohio, the author himself saw a large feline crossing through the mist early one morning on the lawn of a country home I was staying at. A trick of my visionary senses, or a pure and simple trickster of the supernatural kind?

Mary Alice Bennett has scoped out the topic of "mystery animals" very eloquently and concludes that the ability to shape shift is not a matter of mythology, but instead has an alien angle: "A shape-shifter thought to be an adept shaman who has the ability to change form is more likely to be an extraterrestrial entity able to masquerade as a human being." Bennett furthermore asks the question, "Are there also animals visiting us from other dimensions who can appear to be creatures of Earth? Can they live in two worlds?"

There is something about shape shifting that is considered inherently evil, at least by those who approach UFOs from the darkness of demonology and "Satanism." The world's most controversial conspiracy theorist, David Icke, propels the idea straight forward that amongst us humans – obscured right under our very eyes on this planet – are a demonic reptilian race who have been here since antiquity for a multiplicity of nefarious purposes. And they have every reason to keep their identity hidden so that they can not be "picked out" and acknowledged for what they truly are all about. In the "ordinary world" – on the "surface – they are the leaders of the world...the kings, queens and emperors. Yet inside they are truly monsters. For they have a clandestine secret . . . a secret so horrifying and scary . . .that it defies rationality And, in order to maintain their human form, this hidden, secret race of Reptilians must drink human blood to remain energized and keep their material bodies from shifting back into their much more hideous form – what they came here looking like thousands of years ago from another planet. The Serpent Race, or Reptilians, would be the demons of the extraterrestrials, or so is held the widespread belief. In their subterranean chambers they are in command of the evil "Bloodline" of the world's most privileged, including the George Bushes and her Majesty the Queen of England. Posted on You Tube are a variety of videos recorded off TV that are said to show such Serpent Race luminaries making subtle transformations, especially in the case of their reptilian eyes turning into slits and their tongues extending. So help me God, as wild as these claims may be, there is no necessity to make this stuff up.

The Alien World of Shimmers

Several photos have been shown to us in recent times of what are purported to be Shimmers, a term which describes the transformation of a person that has been captured on film turning into an alien or other creature. The word has become a catch-all phrase utilized by paranormal researchers looking to modernize such antiquated terms as shape shifting and Transfiguration. UFO shutterbugs believe that this is an ideal way to discover if the neighbor who just moved in next door is really an alien in disguise. Something like not being able to see the reflection of a vampire, but sort of in reverse as it is captured on film or in digital form for all to perceive.

Writing in the online "UFO Digest," Arizona expressionist artist and writer Mary Alice Bennett notes that the late Dr. John Mack from Harvard University understood "that the "'ET aliens are consummate shape-shifters' who appear to seekers on vision quests and to contactees as large-eyed animals. Many times under hypnosis a witness will recall their UFO 'screen-memory' of a deer, panther, eagle or an owl during an encounter. 'The horse with the big dark eyes' was the memory of one contactee. These power animals have one thing in common: their eyes are recalled as being abnormally large and black. Mack revealed a black panther memory during the regression of one of his male abductees. The subject related that he was a

Native American of the Susquehannock tribe before the time of the white man. His name was "Panther-by-the-Creek," named for the black panther who was seen at the time of his birth. The brave thought it significant that he saw the black panther again after being returned from an alien encounter. This account presents the paranormal black panther in a UFO context, known to the tribe as an auspicious animal."

Perceiving no reason to halt her incredible discoveries with the statements made by a prestigious university psychiatrist, Bennett, in her article "Alien Big Cats – Paranormal Panthers – Shape Shifters," presents the extraordinary experience of a female acquaintance whom she believes to be a true "sensitive," having the ability to "sometimes see the spirits of human beings" who can materialize to her from other realms and dimensions at any time. "One night she entered her Phoenix apartment kitchen and was confronted by a 4-foot-tall white translucent entity with a cat-like hollow-eyed face. It had long clawed fingers and powerful back legs like a kangaroo. It crouched as if to spring at her, at which point she shut herself into her bedroom with her children. She spent the entire night there in her room with the lights on, praying. In the morning, the creature was gone."

UK's controversial spokesperson David Icke believes a secret race of reptilians actually are living amongst us as humans but able to shape shift at will as demonstrated in this horror classic Hisss.

Always popular romance novels have gone pop culture more than ever before with titles like "Howlin'" depicting a very attractive female shape shifter.

The Strange Shape Shifting World of Chris O'Brien

A Tantalizing Interview by Tim Beckley

I met Christopher O'Brien before he headed out west. We were in a Manhattan recording studio and Chris was a young, energetic musician putting down some guitar tracks. I had been involved booking and promoting a few local glitter bands and met some glam rockers, such as David Bowie, whose persona of Ziggy Stardust from Mars had propelled him into international stardom. Bowie had expressed an interest in UFOs and the occult and in fact my article on his fight with demonic forces, drug abuse and witchcraft can be found numerous places across the world wide net (stored in the archives of UFO Digest and the Conspiracy Journal).

Several years went by and Chris was living in the San Luis Valley of Colorado and had several best selling paperbacks on his hand. His UFO "addiction" started at a New Year's Eve party when he overheard several ranchers discuss the sighting of UFOs and the possible connection between their appearance and the mutilation of prize horses and cattle. Drawn into the mystery of the animal mutes, he found himself working with law enforcement officials from area counties, ex-military members, ranchers and an extensive network of skywatchers.

As he explained it to me as we sat on the back stoop of his sprawling home which he had just moved into and which overlooks a wide expanse of beautiful countryside mere miles from Sedona, AZ, he couldn't help but be fascinated with the strange events that were going on right under his very nose in the South-Central Colorado/Northern New Mexico region of the Southwestern United States. Chris strongly believes that he was able to document what may have been the most intense wave of unexplainable ground and aerial level paranormal activity in a single region of North America. His ten-year plus investigation resulted in the three books of his "Mysterious Valley" triology: "The Mysterious Valley," "Enter the Valley," and "Secrets of the Mysterious Valley." His field investigation of UFO reports, unexplained livestock deaths, Native American legends of shape shifters, cryptozoology, secret military activity and the folklore, found in the world's largest alpine valley, has produced one of the largest databases of unusual occurrences gathered from a single geographic region.

Today, Chris focuses his attention on what he describes as the "trickster" aspects of the UFO mystery. Every week, along with host Gene Steinberg, O'Brien hunkers down behind the microphone as co-host of the GCN Network radio program The Paracast (over 200 shows currently archived at www.TheParacast.com) where he grills others who espouse a variety of UFO related theories, some of which he can go along with, some of which he puts his foot down and disputes.

Of all topics paranormal, I would say Chris has to know more about shape shifting and the transformation of humans into other life forms than any other person besides maybe a Native American shaman or two – and they are NOT talking.

Our conversation is an open one and covers considerable territory, while zeroing

in on the shape shifting phenomena in particular.

Tim Beckley Interview
December 20, 2010

Q. What historical evidence do we have of shape shifting?

There is little (if any) irrefutable scientific evidence for "shape-shifting." Nature has a few examples, such as the caterpillar turning into a butterfly, but as far as humans with the scientifically proven ability to metamorphose into another state of physical existence, there is no evidence to prove this is possible. But why does every culture around the world have myths, legends and stories of adepts (or the afflicted) that have this ability? There must be an underlying reason for this pervasive belief.

Q. Any famous cases in literature you can point to?

There are examples of important historical figures that were alleged to have exhibited shape shifting abilities. Procopius in his *Secret History* mentions curious claims concerning the alleged shape shifting ability of Emperor Justinian I, who—along with Constantine—insured the domination of the Roman Catholic Church over other competing belief systems such as the Mithras Cults. I found this excerpt at sacred-texts.com:

And some of those who have been with Justinian at the palace late at night, men who were pure of spirit, have thought they saw a strange demoniac form taking his place. One man said that the Emperor suddenly rose from his throne and walked about, and indeed he was never wont to remain sitting for long, and immediately Justinian's head vanished, while the rest of his body seemed to ebb and flow; whereat the beholder stood aghast and fearful, wondering if his eyes were deceiving him. But presently he perceived the vanished head filling out and joining the body again as strangely as it had left it…Another said he stood beside the Emperor as he sat, and of a sudden the face changed into a shapeless mass of flesh, with neither eyebrows nor eyes in their proper places, nor any other distinguishing feature; and after a time the natural appearance of his countenance returned. I write these instances not as one who saw them myself, but heard them from men who were positive they had seen these strange occurrences at the time.

Q. Stories of werewolves are fairly common - what other manifestations of shape shifting are on record? Dracula turns into a bat of course.

Mentions of werewolves can be found as far back as the writings of the Greek historian Herodotus, who mentioned them in his work *Histories*. He wrote that a tribe in northeast Scythia were collectively transformed into wolf-men at least once per year. The poet Virgil also mentions werewolves. The famous Greek novel *Satyricon* tells the story of a man supposedly transformed into a wolf during full moons. In the 16th century there appeared to be heightened interest in werewolves in France, and the cases cited mostly involved women. And, during approximately the same time period, according to bishops Olaus Magnus and Majoulus, "the werewolves were... far more destructive than 'true and natural wolves'" in Prussia and northeastern Europe.

Q. Native Americans have such stories? What are their most popular forms of shape shifters?

The Windigo is a mythical creature found in the traditions of various Algonquin-speaking tribes in the northern United States and Canada—most notably the Inuit, Ojibwa, Anishnabi and Cree. Descriptions of this creature, the largest of all supposed North American shape shifters, vary somewhat from tribe to tribe, but generally the stories describe a gigantic, hairy, foul-smelling humanoid creature with a taste for human flesh. In general, Windigos are considered to be malevolent cannibals and in some sub-traditions are said to have supernatural powers. There are various possible explanations for the development of such a creature in Native American folklore and they don't involve simply making up "bogeyman" stories to scare the younger tribal members. Windigo probably developed from a fear of famine and starvation due to the region's harsh winter weather they endured. Prairieghosts.com has a good description of Windigos:

The Inuit Indians of the region called the creature by various names, including Wendigo, Witigo, Witiko and Wee-Tee-Go, but each of them was roughly translated to mean the "evil spirit that devours mankind." Around 1860, a German explorer translated Windigo to mean "cannibal" among the tribes along the Great Lakes.

Native American versions of the creature spoke of a gigantic spirit, over fifteen feet tall, [which] had once been human but had been transformed into a creature by the use of magic. Though all of the descriptions of the creature vary slightly, the Windigo [are] generally said to have glowing eyes, long yellowed fangs and overly long tongues. Most have a sallow, yellowish skin but others are said to be matted with hair. They are tall and lanky and are driven by a horrible hunger.

A Windigo allegedly made a number of appearances near a town called Rosesu in Northern Minnesota from the late 1800s through the 1920s. Each time that it was reported, an unexpected death followed and finally, it was seen no more... Even into the last century, Native Americans actively believed in, and searched for, the Windigo. One of the most famous Windigo hunters was a Cree Indian named Jack Fiddler. He claimed to kill at least 14 of the creatures in his lifetime, although the last murder resulted in his imprisonment at the age of 87. In October 1907, Fiddler and his son, Joseph, were tried for the murder of a Cree Indian woman. They both pleaded guilty to the crime but defended themselves by stating that the woman had been possessed by the spirit of a Windigo and was on the verge of transforming into one entirely. According to their defense, she had to be killed before she murdered other members of the tribe.

Skin-walkers are said to be evil sorcerers that exist alongside and among the Diné people. They are said to practice the "Witchery Way," be able to transform themselves into a variety of animal forms, and practice a particularly feared form of black magic. The actual term "skin-walker" comes from the Diné description "with it, he goes on all fours" or *yeenaaldlooshii*. This term refers to the skin-walker's alleged ability to change into a four-legged animal such as a coyote, wolf, fox or sometimes a bear. As a result of this belief, it is taboo to wear the skins of these carnivores. Sheepskin and calfskin are acceptable, but carnivore skin used for clothing is extremely frowned upon. In the Diné tradition, there are several different types of witches, but skin-walkers (most often male) are said to be the most powerful and deeply feared by the Navajo and Apache people. There is much superstition around the belief in these dark adepts and it is rare to get a Diné person to open up and address the subject. No matter how modern our world, this traditional belief still exists today across the windswept high-deserts of the Southwestern United States that the Navajo and Apache call home. Here is a thumbnail sketch from theunexplainedmysteries.com that defines the extent of my knowledge about skin-walkers when I initially began researching *Stalking the Tricksters*:

Although [a skin-walker] is most

Home on the "range." - Tim Beckley spends an afternoon speaking with Arizona's own shape shifting expert Chris O' Brien on his mysterious homestead somewhere between Sedona and Phoenix. Photos by *Charla Gene'*

frequently seen as a coyote, wolf, owl, fox, or crow, the *yeenaaldlooshii* is said to have the power to assume the form of any animal they choose, depending on what kind of abilities they need. Witches use the form for expedient travel, especially to the Navajo equivalent of the 'Black Mass,' a perverted song (and the central rite of the Witchery Way) used to curse instead of to heal. They also may transform to escape from pursuers. Some Navajo also believe that skin-walkers have the ability to steal the "skin" or body of a person. The Navajo believe that if you lock eyes with a skin-walker they can absorb themselves into your body. It is also said that skin-walkers avoid the light and that their eyes glow like an animal's when in human form and when in animal form their eyes do not glow as an animal's would.

Popular New Mexico journalist/author Tony Hillerman wrote many novels about the Navajo reservation before his death in late 2008. In one novel, *Skin-walkers*, his protagonists (Navajo Policemen "Joe Leaphorn" and "Jim Chee") attempt to get to the bottom of several murders thought by the locals to have been perpetrated by a skin-walker. Hillerman responded to questions about the subject in an interview before he passed:

Skin-walkers are tied up with the Navajo concept of good and evil. The Navajos believe that life is a kind of wind blowing through you. Some people have a dark wind, and they tend to be evil. How do you tell? People who have more money than they need and aren't helping their kinfolk—that's one symptom of it. Along with this tendency toward evil, if they're initiated into a witchcraft cult, they get a lot of powers. Depending on the circumstances, they can turn into a dog; they can fly; they can disappear. There are many versions of a skin-walker, but that's basically what it is. A lot of Navajos will tell me emphatically, especially when they don't know me very well, that they don't believe in all that stuff. And then when you get to be a friend, they'll start telling you about the first time they ever saw one.

Traditionally, skin-walkers are able to change themselves into dogs, and traditionally they wear the skin of a dog over their shoulders or the skull of a dog as a cap. So I guess that's the reason for the term. I've never had anyone explain it to me. Navajos just don't like to talk about it much, even when you've known them a long time. It's kind of obscene, you see. It's something you don't talk about in polite company. There's a feeling that a skin-walker might be listening and might want to get even with you. You're kind of uneasy about it … I know that [Hillerman's book *Skin-walkers*] is one of the more popular books among Navajo young people. Maybe it's a little bit like pornography to them. But I've had no objections to the book. It's hard to judge, because Navajos are incredibly polite. They just do not like to offend people.

The few documented stories related to encounters with *skin-walkers* often have a similar tone and most often these evil sorcerers are perceived lurking about a victim's property and/or house and are often blamed for the unexplained death of a loved one, or a victim's livestock. The phprs.com dictionary describes the skin-walker's alleged abilities:

Sometimes the *skin-walker* will try to break into the house and attack the people inside, and will often bang on the walls of the house, knock on the windows, and climb onto the roofs. Sometimes, a strange, animal-like figure is seen standing outside the window, peering in. Other times, a skin-walker may attack a vehicle and cause a car accident. The skin-walkers are described as being fast, agile, and impossible to catch. Though some attempts have been made to shoot or kill one, they are not usually successful. Sometimes a skin-walker will be tracked down, only to lead to the house of someone known to the tracker.

According to traditional knowledge, skin-walkers are able to read a victim's thoughts. They are also thought to be able to mimic any human or animal sound. Diné believe that this ability is sometimes used to draw unwitting victims outside by calling out in the voice of a person known to them or using a familiar animal sound. The standard thinking is: don't *ever* look into and/or lock eyes with a suspected skin-walker. This will enable his will to enter you and take over all your motor functions and make you do and say things that are completely beyond your control. If this is a real ability, imagine the horror of being taken over, fully alert, but a helpless witness to your body's actions. If this is true, it kinda takes the voodoo zombie thing to a whole new level!

University of Nevada-Las Vegas anthropologist Dan Benyshek, who specializes in the study of Native Americans of the Southwest, told George Knapp, co-author of *Hunt for the Skin-walker:*

"Skin-*walkers* are purely evil in intent. I'm no expert on it, but the general view is that skin-walkers do all sorts of terrible things---they make people sick, they commit murders. They are grave robbers and necrophiliacs. They are greedy and evil people who must kill a sibling or other relative to be initiated as a skin-walker. They supposedly can turn into were-animals and can travel in supernatural ways."

As in turning into a fiery orb and shooting across the prairie as some of my San Luis Valley witnesses have claimed over the years? Or how about running alongside a car at 70mph? In Arizona, skin-walkers have also been reported by motorists who happen to be traveling late at night through the "the rez" (as the reservation is called by the locals). I have heard several stories from witnesses and located this anonymously filed, alleged first hand account from the June 2002 archive at paranormal.about.com:

Round Trip to Hell in a Flying Saucer

Like most Navajos in Northeastern Arizona, I have seen many strange things. It is not good to talk about them because we can get witched, but I will share a story with you about my experiences with skin-walkers. When I was younger, my friends and I used to do a thing called "shadow hunting" in which we [would] try and seek out the "lairs" of skin-walkers. My cousin and I have "night vision" and extra sensory perception in which case we tried to test our abilities. So we drive out to the isolated desert on a full moon, until we find a good-looking hot spot. To our surprise we came upon a meeting of skin-walkers, and before we knew it they had surrounded us. I have seen and felt them before, but just not as many and not as powerful. I saw firsthand how fast they are—they left streaks of color behind them as they passed. They were running circles around us, which of course was frightening, but when I looked up on the ridge of the mountain I saw the biggest humanoid figure looking down at us and obviously pissed off. With that, my cuz shifted the truck and we took off.

Several days later, we were "visited" by something we have felt before. My cousin started calling "it" Yeti because it was too big and frightening. Every time

it came over, me and my cousin would wake up and instinctively know which side it was on. From then on my cousin and I would get random visits from them, even after moving to a city far away from that place. I believe that they sent me monitors or something to watch me, because sometimes I feel a presence when I'm out there and I see things.

Knapp was told some interesting accounts by reservation law enforcement that have a similar feel to the aforementioned account. These nocturnal road encounters all have a similar feel and probably make up a majority of skin-walker encounters by non-Native people:

Although skin-walkers are generally believed to prey only on Native Americans, there are recent reports from Anglos claiming they had encountered skin-walkers while driving on or near tribal lands. One New Mexico Highway Patrol officer told us that while patrolling a stretch of highway south of Gallup, New Mexico, he had had two separate encounters with a ghastly creature that seemingly attached itself to the door of his vehicle. During the first encounter, the veteran law enforcement officer said the unearthly being appeared to be wearing a ghostly mask as it kept pace with his patrol car. To his horror, he realized that the ghoulish specter wasn't attached to his door after all. Instead, he said, it was running alongside his vehicle as he cruised down the highway at a high rate of speed... [The] officer...still patrols the same stretch of highway and says that he is petrified every time he enters the area.

One Caucasian family still speaks in hushed tones about its encounter with a skin-walker, even though it happened in 1983. While driving at night along Route 163 through the massive Navajo Reservation, the four members of the family felt that someone was following them. As their truck slowed down to round a sharp bend, the atmosphere changed, and time itself seemed to slow down. Then something leaped out of a roadside ditch at the vehicle.

"It was black and hairy and was eye level with the cab," one of the witnesses recalled. "Whatever this thing was, it wore a man's clothes. It had on a white and blue checked shirt and long pants. Its arms were raised over its head, almost touching the top of the cab. It looked like a hairy man or a hairy animal in man's clothing, but it didn't look like an ape or anything like that. Its eyes were yellow and its mouth was open."

Q. How legitimate can these stories be? What makes us think such accounts are not pure fantasies?

There are too many similarities between accounts and too many accounts to dismiss these types of claims out-of-hand.

Q. Are there cases in which there are groups of witnesses to a shape shifting?

Yes. For instance, in Africa there have been recent news stories of goats that are found to be shape-shifted witches. These transformations have allegedly have been witnessed by multiple witnesses, including law enforcement officials.

Q. Have you ever confronted anyone who claims to be a shape shifter?

No, but I did have a girlfriend in high school who was a double-jointed gymnast. She could shape-shift her limbs into positions (and do things) you wouldn't believe! ♩

Q. Have you ever witnessed a manifestation firsthand?

Yes. In late 1998, a prominent member of the Crestone, Colorado, community where I lived approached me. She casually asked what I knew about "Indian witchcraft." The request was out of character and I instantly sensed something unusual was behind her low-key request. I related to her basic information pertaining to rituals of intent and protection, the use of power talismans and the like and she interrupted me, took me aside and told me about a strange adorned animal spine and skull bundle that had been found hanging on a creek behind her house. It seems she had recently experienced a falling out with a visiting Native American "medicine man" and then, some time later, this scary-looking bundle turned up near her house. She had a mystery on her hands, and naturally, she thought of the two events as being linked somehow. Did I know what the bundle was or what it was used for? She claimed it had immediately been disposed of and hadn't been saved, but it was obvious that she was concerned enough about the artifact to ask me for my opinion. Without seeing the bundle and studying it—making note of the objects and how they were arranged, it was difficult for me to translate or interpret, but I offered to conduct a cleansing and blessing at the spot where the scary-looking artifact was discovered. Several months went by and everything seemed normal. She never mentioned the event again, nor did I ever ask her for an update on the peculiar situation; some questions are better left unasked, and this was one of them.

One evening, Wednesday November 10, 1999, at 6:20 PM, I was taking a shower in the attached greenhouse of my house with its sweeping 360 degree view of the San Luis Valley. Looking out the west-facing plate glass windows that made up the western side of the greenhouse, I noticed, with a start, what could only be described as an antler-adorned, six-foot tall, bipedal creature gliding across the front of the windows, from left to right. The being was in the shadow just out of the thin light projected out to the yard, but I was able to easily discern its distinctive shape. When I first noticed movement, I was facing sideways to the window and only had a peripheral view of the apparition but, as I turned, I distinctly witnessed something the likes of which I've never seen before or since. Looking back at the event today, I'm surprised I wasn't completely freaked seeing this apparition, as I was standing naked, all soaped up. But looking at my notes I am reminded that the weirdness didn't end there. Later that evening, at 11:30 PM, I was with my friend Amber, and we observed what appeared to be a "prairie-dragon like form" travel from the porch through the dog door and into the living room. Amber and I simultaneously saw a transparent "beige-colored form" enter through the dog door, which was only two feet away from us. We both heard what sounded like a dog "whine."

I learned later that what I witnessed while taking a shower is eerily similar to Navajo/Apache (Diné) accounts of a skin-walker lurking about. They are sometimes depicted wearing antlers and whatever it was I witnessed definitely had an impressive rack! The coyote-like form my friend Amber and I witnessed later that evening put an exclamation point on the day. But, reviewing my event log I am reminded of another weird incident that occurred the prior late summer/early fall. I had been sitting downstairs alone watching TV in the living room, when a rapid succession of rapping sounds circled the house around the walls of the second story above. The five or six raps banged in a clockwise circle around the house's upper story and I bolted outside with a flashlight to see whatever it was. Nothing. I made note of it but I'm still puzzled today—years later—what it could have been. While researching skin-walkers for my book *Stalking the Tricksters,* I found that rapping sounds going around your house are attributed by some Diné as being a skin-walker attempting to get your attention!

Q. How do you relate this to the UFO mystery?

There are countless UFO reports where witnesses describe objects that *appear* to change from one shape into another. My own database from the San Luis Valley has several dozen, if not more. There could be several possible explanations for these events. Trufos (if there is such a term) are often shrouded inside a plasma cloud of ionized particles. This plasma cloud surrounding the object can appear to change shape, color and/or size. One possible explanation for this appearance of changing shape could be the plasma cloud undulating and taking on different forms that appear to the witness to shape shift. There are also reports of choppers (or other mundane aerial craft) that appear to change into spheres or discs, and discs or spheres that appear to shape shift into mundane aerial craft. Whether this transformation is caused by some sort of holographic/projected process or indicates the actual ability to shape shift is an open question in my mind—we don't have enough evidence to support any firm conclusions.

Q. There are cases where the UFOs themselves have changed shape or size and dimension.

Here is a strange claim from my first book *The Mysterious Valley:* Investigator David Perkins called. "This one's real bizarre," he prefaced his account. According to search and rescue personnel and local residents, it seemed that two hunters, in a week period, ended up missing. When the first showed up a day later, the frightened man, "raced away in his truck without saying a word." The second, (a Pueblo, CO, fireman) wandered into the Libre community in Gardner, CO, and approached the ornate house of a local artist. Hays told the artist an incredible story of an ordeal he claimed he'd suffered over the past four days. He didn't seem hungry or thirsty, appeared to be rational, "remarkably calm," and "didn't seem traumatized." The artist told Perkins, "He looked like a cop with a four-day growth of beard." The hunter claimed he had arrived at a rented cabin on Dry Creek, on Greenhorn Mountain, high above the commune, for a weekend hunting trip.

The man claimed that a large group of "aliens dressed in camo appeared" at his campsite and before he could react, he was gassed, captured and tied up. They never spoke to him and never fed him. He said he survived by eating grasshoppers. The camo-clad, human-looking aliens appeared to be conducting "some sort of maneuvers." *He said that at one point the group started to get aboard a small ship. He was astonished when the "ship expanded" to accommodate them all. The ship allegedly took off, morphed into the shape of a bear, then morphed into "a three-headed wolf," then turned into a cloud!* (my emphasis added)

Perkins also didn't know what to make of Hays' claim. "This is so weird!" he said several times, with a nervous laugh. It supposedly occurred on the mountain right behind Perkins' house. When law enforcement officials went up to the cabin they found his vehicle trashed, with the passenger-side door open and the remains of a campfire, just outside the open door. His "half-burnt clothes" were scattered around the area.

Q Is this all part of the trickster element you speak of?

Tricksters play subtle but crucially pivotal roles as they disassemble the rules of the particular cultural situation within which they manifest. Sometimes they change their facade within a given culture, subtly working the process over time, evolving and altering their character and the "lesson" to illicit needed change. Or, when needed, they are willing to alter and sometimes even change the very nature of Gaia itself. But, in general, they are here to break down outmoded structures and dissolve order into chaos so they can introduce elements of novelty and change into a particular cultural belief system. This anarchic introduction of novelty to topple the status quo has tremendous power and influence and the powers-that-be are getting nervous. On the surface these elements of change and the deconstructive process appear negative to the status quo, but the end result of the manipulative behavior tends to be positive. Of course, this understanding of the positive result is usually only present in hindsight.

Throughout history cultures have been blessed (or cursed) with the synchronistic challenge of the trickster. When a given culture is at a crucial crossroads during periods of novelty and change, tricksters appear to exercise supernatural powers that fabricate situations and scenarios where their transformational lessons can be revealed. Many trickster forms seem to exist beyond mere life and death; they have the paranormal ability to shape shift into a variety of animal forms, manifest as pure energy and even appear simultaneously in more than one location. Although usually male, some trickster types are said to be cross-gender—choosing male or female forms at will. The trickster is arguably the most ancient of all cross-cultural archetypes and their role in any given society or tribe has ancient importance/relevance that rivals the influence of all other god-form(s). Consensual reality is the cultural, theatrical stage on which the tricksters direct the change that takes place in the play as they introduce novelty into the script at will. The lessons they impart to us actors on the stage are rendered to trick or shock us out of complacency, stripping away particular outmoded stereotypical thinking while reminding us of the limitless possibilities of new thinking.

UFOs, for instance, can be viewed as a classic, modern trickster form. These unexplained objects challenge culture to question the omnipotence of scientific thinking and call into question scientific explanations explaining the true nature of reality.

What You See Is Not Always What You Get

By Timothy Green Beckley

How can a seemingly metallic structure change shape? And I'm not talking about just contracting a pair of wings. I'm talking about a disc turning into a triangle. Or a square transforming into a cigar. This is the one phenomenon with which what you see is NOT what you get.

As an example, I made an extensive study of the Carl Higdon abduction in which a Wyoming hunter saw a landed craft and was taken on board and zipped off to a – we assume – far away destination. One of the remarkable aspects of this case – there are several that make this an exceptional incident, as detailed in my book Strange Saga – is the fact that the craft appeared relatively small while on the ground, but inside it appeared much larger, holding not only an entire crew but a number of elk that had been grazing near the landing spot.

Round Trip to Hell in a Flying Saucer

In Manhattan's Chelsea area on October 13, 2010, crowds watched a cluster of UFOs morph high in the heavens. Some thought they were balloons but a close examination of the videos shows something that appears to be a single object that mushrooms out into several distinct objects before pulling itself back together like an idealized aerial Humpty Dumpty.

Mickie Eckert's experience goes back a few years, and at the time it was totally unique in the annals of flying saucerdom. Her story did not seem to fit in with any existing pattern and yet the sincerity shows on her pretty face as she related a bizarre tale that defied explanation.

Looking at me with bewildered eyes, it was obvious that Mickie, a young woman in her mid-twenties, was seeking answers. She was confused about what had happened and was anxious to find out the reasons she was selected to have a close encounter that goes beyond anything previously recorded.

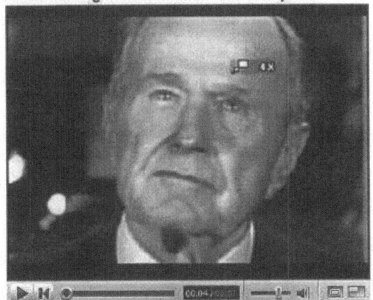

Among the "human shape shifters who have been identified are ex president George Bush Sr and the Queen of England who are said to partake in blood rituals.

It was July 22, 1978. Mickie, along with her best friend, Kathy Echard, were driving along Interstate 80 East. They were headed towards Nebraska near the Wyoming border, when they saw what they thought was an accident on the side of the road.

"We turned to get a better look and saw these white lights bobbing up and down. In order to get a better look, we pulled over to the shoulder of the road and aimed our car headlights in the direction of the crash."

It was apparent that Mickie wanted to talk about what transpired that night. We were seated around a large table, in a private conference room at the Royal Quality Inn in San Diego, California. Mickie had come to the privately-sponsored UFO conference (promoted by veteran newsman Hal Starr) mainly because she wanted desperately to talk with some of the top names in the field who are supposed to be trained in the handling of such matters.

In attendance and at the podium that day were such leading UFO luminaries as Jim and Coral Lorenzen from APRO (since deceased), Walter Andrus, director of the Mutual UFO Network, and Dr. James A. Harder, Associate Professor of Engineering at the University of California (Berkeley). Maybe it was because of their tight speaking schedule, but none of those present seemed to be able to find the necessary time to speak with Mickie Eckert. It was only after she was introduced to me by John DeHerrera (a practicing hypnotist who has been involved in the investigation of several contactee cases, most notably that of Brian Scott) that Mickie found someone who would listen intelligently to what she had to offer.

Going back to the evening in question, Mickie maintains that the sun had just set as they drove on a desolate and very isolated stretch of road eight miles north of Whelock, Nebraska. "Our spotlights were trained on what we thought to be a mishap, but all we could see was three round circles hovering a few feet above the ground."

At the time, neither of the two young women realized that they were headed for a journey to a "Twilight Zone" more real than any TV program about the supernatural could ever hope to be. "In front of our eyes, these lights turned into two sports cars that were coming toward us." One moment they had been confronted by the mysterious presence of airborne lights and the next thing they were aware of were two automobiles speeding in their direction. To say the least, they didn't know what to make of this transformation.

WHERE IS YOUR GOD NOW??
HAHAHA!!

Face Book is home to many strange groups but perhaps none as strange as the Shape Shifting Human Rights Group that has posted this rather offbeat photo on their FB wall.

"We wanted no part of what was happening so we took off in the opposite direction. As we turned the car around to leave, in back of us we saw this whole bunch of lights. We backed up on the Interstate and now there were two trucks that had appeared out of thin air. On the trucks were teeny little lights. The trucks were following us, of this I'm sure."

The two tractor-trailers kept a steady pace on the highway in back of the girls. It was as if unseen eyes were watching their every movement, perhaps seeking an ideal spot to overtake them for some fiendish purpose.

"For some reason, Kathy asked me to stop and she got out of the car and stood in front of it. It was then that we saw all these other cars parked along the side of the road. They were just stopped there. When Kathy got back into our vehicle she wanted to drive and so I let her take the steering wheel. To her it felt as if something — some force — was trying to take control of our car. She got scared and eventually turned the driving back over to me and I too felt this strange pulling."

Putting as many miles behind them as possible, the two girls sped on through the night, anxious to get back to their home in California. "As we were passing through Salt Lake City, we stopped off at a Safeway store to get some gum and cigarettes." Mickie makes no bones about the fact that they were still shaken but says they were trying to pull themselves back together again, not having seen anything unusual on the road for quite some time now.

"As we were about to leave the Safeway supermarket, I noticed a reflection on one of the large windows coming from either inside or outside. Initially, I just assumed the reflection was caused by either the store lights themselves or from some street light nearby.

"Out in the parking area I discovered this was not at all the case, for directly across the lot was this little light about the size of a basketball just sitting near the ground."

There seemed to be so much that Micki had to say that the words wouldn't come out fast enough. Several times I had to slow her down so as not to miss any part of her narrative.

Totally freaked out by what was transpiring all around them, Micki's friend was anxious to push on as quickly as possible. "As we entered Wyoming we stopped again to get some bottled water. We were in a pretty good-sized town called Evansville, and it was still pretty early, but there wasn't a light on in the entire city. Everything was closed. None of the houses had lights on either. I looked out of the window on the driver's side of the car and there were these two ships hanging there. One was orange, the other yellowish-white. We continued on toward Green River and the objects passed through the trees on the side of the road. At this junction in time we lost control of the car once more. No matter how fast we put our foot down on the gas pedal the car refused to accelerate past a certain speed."

In the middle of nowhere the car died completely. With this, a light came into the auto passing right through an open window. The light touched Kathy Echard and for no explainable reason, Mickie began talking to that light. "Come on, little light, why don't you touch me, too," she remarked, despite the fact that everything up until this point had frightened her.

No sooner had it appeared than the light inside the car vanished. "All of a sudden we didn't see the ship anymore, but we started seeing trucks. Northwestern, American, and other big-named rigs. They were traveling in both directions, up and down the northbound and southbound lanes. The only way I can describe it is as a caravan of big lights going back and forth. This one particular truck stopped directly in front of us and we knew something was wrong. It was freaky -- the trucks were now ships; dome-shaped, 3-sided ships about the same size as a compact automobile, and they were no longer on the road, but traveling about six feet off the ground."

"Reptileman" could easily have been real according to such UFO "experts as David Icke. Turns out this picture is of a man in a costume. - Are we sure?

Micki admits that she was too bewildered to be an excellent observer. She finds it hard to estimate the number of trucks or dome-shaped ships but she does know that the car they were in got pushed forward about 20 feet as if it had been lifted by a terrific force from underneath.

Despite their accelerated heartbeats, the girls decided to get out of their car to have a look, to see if anything might have gotten caught underneath their wheels which might account for the sudden tug forward. There was nothing there that would offer a solution to the puzzle, and so they climbed back into the relative safety of their vehicle.

"Soon there was this other car that pulled up directly in back of us and Kathy said she wanted to get out and see who was driving it." It was quite apparent from Micki's comments that the girls were anxious to seek help from any other companion of the road they might find driving so late at night.

"When Kathy got back into the car, I was anxious to know what she had said to the individuals in the car behind us. She just looked me straight in the eye and said, 'Turn around and tell me what you would have said to them.' There was this black dog, tail curved up and two red eyes blazing just outside our car door."

The girls were understandably terrified by this new development.

Cowering in fear, Micki happened to glance into the rear view mirror. What she saw only added fuel to a fire of panic that was so near to bursting out of control within them. "I saw what appeared to be a kid with his arms bunched together on the back seat." The girls got out of the car in an attempt to escape this potential menace. Luckily the dog-like creature they had seen was nowhere in sight. However, directly behind them were two bright lights which were joined by several other duller-looking lights. After several minutes they all blended into one light. "As the light went past us, it was no longer just a light -- but a ship. We heard this rumbling sound and our hair stood on end. Our skin was covered with goose bumps."

At this point it seemed as if Micki and

The 2005 horror film Shapeshifter terrorized many a movie patron.

Kathy had been transported to another dimension, another sphere of reality, for all at once things started looking peculiar, totally out of whack. "Then the sun started to come up, but it was only an orange ball and it was coming toward us. And then it was not orange anymore, but its color turned suddenly to gray, and it was about 100 feet across, just enormous. And people started to appear out of nowhere, walking across the freeway carrying tubes or pipes. We didn't actually see them come out of any ship because the sun -- or whatever it was -- had landed in a valley out of our immediate viewing range."

The beings -- or whatever they were -- were standing in the middle island that separates the north and southbound traffic. "There were these bunches of blue lights and we knew something was going to happen. We were terrified. We felt like we were going to be taken to another planet and would never be heard from again."

Without warning the car started up. "I got mad at Kathy because I thought she had slammed on the brakes and I hit my head on the dashboard. We saw this ship coming down the Interstate and we also saw an 18-wheeler truck towing one of the sports cars we had seen earlier in the evening. Something pushed us from behind but we couldn't get the car to run of its own accord."

From out of nowhere a man appeared and asked the girls where they were headed. "He said he was heading toward Chicago and we said that's where we were going too. I'd have gone to Timbuktu just to get out of the spot we were in."

From what I was able to gather, the man did not know anything was happening. He seemed totally unaware of the frightful state of the girls' minds caused by a terror that was real enough to them even if nobody else was able to perceive what was transpiring around them.

"I was so scared that I crawled all over the driver. He stopped at a truck stop to get coffee and we got out and walked to a nearby motel. We didn't have very much money. But we had about $35 and so we got a room. We unlocked the door and turned on the light and the TV went on by itself. Also this little teeny light flittered around the room and we knew we hadn't escaped."

Realizing that they were being observed, the girls tried to intimidate the light that was buzzing around their room.

"Kathy, did you mail that letter telling about the flight pattern of the UFOs to my lawyer?" I asked with a purposeful slowness. She said she had, playing along with the game.

the **reptilian agenda**

Amazing confirmation that a reptilian extraterrestrial race has controlled the world for thousands of years.

David Icke talks with the Zulu Shaman Credo Mutwa. In this fantastic interview, Credo Mutwa reveals the story of the reptilian takeover of Planet Earth and how a shape-shifting Reptilian race (the "Chitauri" to Africans) has controlled humanity for 1000's of years and how their bloodlines are in the positions of royal, political and economic power today. This program will re-write the UFO/ET story in a way that will blow ur mind. Zulu chief Credo Mutwa says the existence of the Reptilians is well known throughout the culture of his tribal members.

"We called the police and finally, at 5 o'clock the next afternoon, they came and took us back to the spot where we had abandoned the vehicle. As it turned out, the car wasn't where we had left it. And when we went back to the valley where the ship had been, the area wasn't the same. There was no little road on the side of the road. The freeway railing wasn't even the same. There was a sign MOUNTAIN ROAD 189. There is no Mountain Road 189 in all of Wyoming. We had a full tank of gas and we were about 250 miles into the state and there wasn't a gas station anywhere."

It was like they were driving without consuming fuel.

The one item of interest was the corpse of a cow and a sheep off in a nearby field. The cow was all bones and the sheep had all of its skin peeled off, which made it look like a blanket lying there.

Micki says that the police made them fill out a complete report. "After they had finished hearing our entire story, they shrugged and told us we'd seen swamp gas!"

Moving the tape recorder closer to Micki, she reported that her life as well as her friend's have been drastically altered because of the events of that night.

"Kathy is only 31 years old, but she's been in the hospital at least 20 times since this happened. It's hard to explain, but somehow I feel we are the same people, but then again we aren't. Kathy had always been a slob and I have always been neat and clean. Now my house looks like the wreck of the Hesperus, and Kathy's is really neat, tidy, and very well cared for. Before I had always been the type to make my kids breakfast, lunch and dinner, while Kathy believed her children should prepare their own meals. It's just the other way around now. It's almost as though we've somehow exchanged personality traits. In other words, I'm still me, but it's as though I'm having my personality altered -- taken over. I have always been a reader, for instance, but now I'm reading much more. I'm reading as much as I can on UFOs; that's the one subject that fascinates me the most."

Under hypnosis, Micki was made to draw what she had seen. When it came to sketching the trucks that had appeared on the highway, she rendered a skeleton-type being instead of a moving vehicle.

"Is it possible that they altered your whole thinking process that night?" I asked the witness. Micki admitted that this is what might have happened and that what really transpired could be entirely different from what she perceived. For some unexplainable reason, Micki and her friend, Kathy, have grown farther apart in their friendship. "Before the experience we had been the best of friends for 17 years. Now we speak to each other only once a week, tops."

Micki is anxious to undergo further hypnosis. She wishes to find out what really took place on July 22, 1978. She is not satisfied just forgetting about the incident. The whole episode is a true puzzle. Taken as an isolated encounter, most UFOlogists would probably do their utmost to doubt the word of those individuals who were personally involved. The rule of thumb seems to be, "If you can't explain it, or it doesn't support existing evidence, brush the whole affair under the carpet." If we were to do this, we wouldn't be any better than the government agencies who have tried so hard to hide the very existence of UFOs from the public.

This case is a prime example of how mysterious the entire UFO phenomena might be. Just when you thought you might have pinned down the answer, it darts right away from you again!

The Morphing Matter of Space Ships

By Tim Swartz

It's strange enough to hold a belief that the entities attached to the UFO phenomenon – demonic or not – can change shape. It's a concept right out of the works of Charles Fort, the journalist who collected tales of the strange and unknown, many of which appeared in scientific journals and accredited journals of his time period. But now we have to take a giant leap and contend with the crazy notion that the craft themselves can alter their form from one shape to another? Before you toss this book back onto the shelf from which you

Renowned author Tim Swartz stands in front of the Great Pyramid.

retrieved it, consider the evidence of Conspiracy Journal internet editor Tim Swartz and others who have been confronted with yet another aspect of this mighty puzzle that keeps many on the edge of their galactic seat.

There is no doubt that UFOs are strange. The fact that they are usually seen silently zipping around in our skies is weird enough; but throw in the fact that many UFOs that appear solid are seen to be constantly changing shape and size, it's enough to drive any serious UFO researcher to take up butterfly collecting instead.

It is one of the great mysteries of UFOs: how can something that looks so real not behave like a solid object and change shape as rapidly as smoke in the wind? This has led to wild speculations on the true nature of UFOs and allowed skeptics to dismiss the entire phenomenon as simply misinterpreted natural events.

What hard-core skeptics fail to take into consideration is the thousands of diverse UFO sightings that have come in over the years that exhibit the same shape-shifting characteristics. A reported sighting of a weird object that changes shape can be a good way to distinguish a real UFO from one that is fraudulent.

UFOs are seen to come in all kinds of different shapes and sizes, ranging from saucers, ovals, cigars, spheres, to rocket and triangular shaped. They can suddenly appear and disappear, only to reappear in a completely different location. They can split in two and rejoin again instantly. This has led to all sorts of heated arguments between UFO researchers who have a preferred shape, choosing to throw out cases that don't meet their criteria. However, if you take into account all of the reports of UFOs seen to morph from one shape into another, then possibly the vast diversity of UFOs is not so difficult to explain after all.

On June 29, 1954, A British Overseas Airways Corporation (BOAC) Stratocruiser Centaurus left New York's Idlewild Airport bound for London. Just after 9:00pm the aircraft passed 170 miles southwest of Goose Bay, Labrador, flying northeast at 19,000ft. The crew suddenly noticed an object to the west of the plane that was roughly five degrees aft of the port wing at a distance of about five miles. As they drew closer, the crew could see a large pear-shaped UFO flying in formation with six other smaller objects.

Space junk or morphing vehicle. . .NASA has no answer!

Against the sunset these objects appeared dark, with the six smaller UFOs changing their positions around the larger craft, which seemed to change from its original pear shape to a telephone handset shape and, in the words of Captain Howard: "what looked like a flying arrow - an enormous delta-winged plane turning in to close with us." The anomalous shape-shifting object seemed to be solid with definite, clearly-defined edges.

As the jetliner drew closer, the smaller UFOs formed into a regular line and seemed to merge into the larger object. Then the remaining large UFO appeared to suddenly shrink and vanish right before the eyes of the startled crew.

Captain Howard remarked later: "They were obviously not aircraft as we know them. All appeared black and I will swear they were solid. There was a big central object that appeared to keep changing shape. The six smaller objects dodged about either in front or behind."

In another case, a Baptist Pastor, while traveling with his family in the western part of the U.S. on June 8, 2002, observed a silver aluminum object flying above the mountains.

The Pastor says, "When I first noticed the object, it was in the shape of a box and about the size of a small private plane. I tried to show it to my family and I was pointing where to look. Taking my eyes off of it for a moment, it changed to a round bottom cup shape without the handle (the round section being at the top). The sighting lasted about 30 seconds. The craft was not in a hurry, really, but seemed to be just cruising around. I don't know how it disappeared. I lost sight of it trying to point it out to my family after looking away for just a second."

On June 5, 2005, a man was stopped at a traffic light on Route 422 in Niles, Ohio, when he noticed a bright silver, metallic UFO in the clear blue sky in front of his car.

"It was thin, cigar-shaped, with rounded ends, and there was a large spot of sun glare shining from the left (back end). With my arm completely extended, its length would have been about the width across of a quarter."

About six to seven seconds after he first spotted the unusual object, it seemed to change shape, with the front end moving slightly inward so that the object took on more of a boomerang shape with one side shorter than the other. The glare from the sun that had been so bright at the left end moved in a quick flash and settled more in the center of the object, and there seemed to be a darker spot right in the middle.

At that point the UFO was seen to ripple and get fuzzy at the edges. After the hazy ripple, it completely vanished, leaving the eyewitness wondering what he had just seen.

One odd shape-shifting UFO was actually captured on camera in 1994 at an undisclosed location within the Nellis Air Force Base Bombing and Gunnery Range Complex, Nevada. The videotape is said to have been smuggled out by contractor personnel who had operated tracking stations on the Nellis range. Even though the UFO was photographed by a very good remote-controlled, fixed-mounted camera, it still has that fuzzy, cotton-ball look about it which seems to be common among UFOs.

The Nellis Test Range UFO footage is an excellent example of what seems to be a real UFO caught on tape. This object, tracked by military radar and cameras, flies boldly around in a bright, clear sky seemingly unconcerned that it is being watched and photographed.

The object recorded on videotape flying over the desert terrain that day appears to be constantly changing shape. At first it appears to be disc-shaped, then it looks somewhat like a small jet with round stubby wings, then it changes into three balls; all the while the object is never clearly defined. It is as if it is surrounded by fog or mist, keeping it just out of focus. What kind of object are we dealing with that is never still, is always changing shape, and seems to be not quite solid?

As the object slowly spins, a projection of some kind can also be seen. There is also a shifting "coal black" region. More often than not, the craft has a morphing, indefinite profile that appears to be self-luminous.

Physicists have speculated that what we see around shape-shifting UFOs may not be the UFO itself, but rather the energy change occurring around the UFO as it moves between dimensions. Apparent "vehicles" that seem to change shape while in the air may not be spacecraft at all, but cross-sections of four-dimensional objects that bisect familiar 3-D reality. For example, a 3-D cross section of a 4-D tube would appear spherical. If the tube was irregular in shape, we would expect it to "change shape" in our three dimensions as it moved, much how a sphere passing through a two-dimensional plane would appear like a rapidly growing disk to any watching flatlanders.

Alan Holt and David Froening at the end of the 1970s worked on an extension of Einstein's Unified Field Theory involving what they referred to as a "field propulsion" craft. This spacecraft would change color and shape as it entered different stages of flight, and this is similar to many UFOs that are reported around the globe.

Have UFOs Inspired Morphing Aircraft Designs?

Rumors have circulated among the UFO community that modern aircraft designs have been influenced by back-engineered extraterrestrial spacecraft. According to the website LiveScience.com, NASA and Department of Defense engineers are trying to create a plane that can morph into new shapes during flight by flexing or twisting, due to being made of new metals that form a kind of "flexible skin."

Amazing advances are being made in the development of new metal alloys. These alloys have remarkable characteristics, in that they will change shape upon the application of an electric current or magnetic field. They change shape, or "morph," rapidly and with some considerable force. They are termed "compact hybrid actuators," alloys that incorporate advanced nano-technology that is designed to enable them to mimic living systems in their versatility and dynamism.

Its not unusual for UFOs to change shape or morph before they disappear from view as in the case of this object that was photographed out a plane window.

The list of potential applications seems endless, and the U.S. military is funding a variety of related research programs exploring the full range of options. Self-healing wings that flex and react like living organisms, versatile bombers that double as agile jet fighters, and swarms of tiny unmanned aircraft are just a few of the science-fiction-like possibilities that these next-generation technologies could make feasible in the decades ahead.

In his 1997 book "The Day After Roswell," the late Col. Philip J. Corso described his own experience of examining unusual material alleged to come from the 1947 UFO crash site in New Mexico:

"There was a dull, grayish-silvery foil-like swatch of cloth among these artifacts that you could not fold, bend, tear, or wad up but that bounded right back into its original shape without any creases. It was a metallic fiber with physical characteristics that would later be called 'super-tenacity,' but when I tried to cut it with scissors, the arms just slid right off without even making a nick in the fibers. If you tried to stretch it, it bounced back, but I noticed that all the threads seemed to be going in one direction. When I tried to stretch it width-wise instead of length-wise, it looked like the fibers had re-orientated themselves to the direction I was pulling in. This couldn't be cloth, but it obviously wasn't metal. It was a combination, to my unscientific eye, of a cloth woven with metal strands that had the drape and malleability of a fabric and the strength and resistance of a metal."

Corso claimed in his book that he "seeded" the alien material to the research departments of Monsanto and Dow. Furthermore, Corso claims that the material had previously been delivered to the Air Materiel Command at Wright Field. Wright Patterson Air Force Base is famous in UFO circles for its Foreign Technology division, purported to hold extraterrestrial craft and artifacts. It could be that the new morphing technologies being used in new, top secret aircraft are the results of years of study on the UFO debris captured by the U.S. in the 1940s.

The entire UFO phenomenon is always changing and never clearly defined. When you think that you finally have something definite, the phenomenon changes again and you are back at square one. For more than fifty years, this is what has constantly confounded UFO researchers, and when it comes to shape-changing UFOs, there appears to be no real truths or answers.

Phantom Hellhound Phenomenon

The first English account of a large black Hellhound appeared in the "Anglo-Saxon Chronicle" in 1127:

" *Let no one be surprised at the truth of what we are about to relate, for it was common knowledge throughout the whole country that immediately after his arrival [Abbot Henry of Poitou at Abbey of Peterborough] - it was the Sunday when they sing Exurge Quare o, D - many men both saw and heard a great number of huntsmen hunting. The huntsmen were black, huge and hideous, and rode on black horses and on black he-goats and their hounds were jet black with eyes like saucers and horrible. This was seen in the very deer park of the town of Peterborough and in all the woods that stretch from that same town to Stamford, and in the night the monks heard them sounding and winding their horns. Reliable witnesses who kept watch in the night declared that there might well have been as many as twenty or thirty of them winding their horns as near they could tell. This was seen and heard from the time of his arrival all through Lent and right up to Easter."*

No discussion of the demonic presence in our world would be complete without a mention of the Devil Dog/Hellhound phenomenon. Legends of encounters with evil canines goes back into the mists of antiquity, and meeting such a fiend as you go about your business is always a terrifying experience.

Writer Graeme Davis, on a website called "Role Player," offers a summary of some of the typical guises of the Demon Dog. There is, for example, a type of "wandering black dog" that can be encountered in any rural area, normally at night.

"The dog is usually encountered by a lone traveler. It is heading in the opposite direction to the traveler and is content to ignore and be ignored. However, if anyone should speak to it, try to strike it or take any other action, the dog will use a supernatural power to strike the offender blind, dumb, mad or worse. It can do this simply by stopping and fixing the victim with its fiery eyes; the effect seems to be spell-like rather than a gaze weapon."

Davis writes that the dog's power functions as a kind of mind control and can induce fear, foolishness, panic, terror, a mental stun, madness and mindlessness.

In nearly all the stories of Hellhounds, according to Davis, "these creatures do more harm with their voices than with their teeth. The sound of their baying carries for miles, and often the hounds themselves are never seen. Sometimes their baying works as a death omen, and sometimes it has a lesser effect, causing fear, rooting a person to the spot and so forth."

The Wikipedia website also takes up the study of Demonic Dogs. In an entry called "Black Shuck," one learns that, "For centuries, inhabitants of England have told tales of a large black dog with malevolent flaming eyes (or in some variants of the legend, a single eye) that are red or alternatively green. The beast varies in size and stature from that of simply a large dog to being the size of a horse. There are legends of Black Shuck roaming the Anglican countryside since before the Vikings. His name may derive from the Old English word 'succa,' meaning 'demon,' or possibly from the local dialect word 'shucky,' meaning 'shaggy' or 'hairy.' The legend may have been part of the inspiration for the Sherlock Holmes novel 'The Hound of the Baskervilles.'

HELLHOUND

Hellhounds are the watchdogs of Satan, according to legend. They have been seen all over the world, but especially in the UK in recent years.

"Sometimes," the entry continues, "Black Shuck has appeared headless, and at other times he floats on a carpet of mist. According to folklore, the specter often haunts graveyards, side roads, cross roads, near bodies of water and in dark forests."

On August 4, 1577, Black Shuck was said to have burst through the doors of a church in Blythburgh in Suffolk, England. The dog then ran up the nave, past a large congregation, killing a man and a boy and causing the church tower to collapse through the roof. As the dog exited the church, he left scorch marks on the north door which can be seen at the church to this day.

On that exact same day, in the nearby town of Bungay in Suffolk, another Devil Dog made an appearance. As recorded by the Reverend Abraham Fleming, "This black dog, or the Devil in such a likeness, running all along the body of the church with great swiftness and incredible haste, among the people and in a visible form and shape, passed between two persons as they were kneeling upon their knees and occupied in prayer, wrung the necks of them both in one moment and they strangely died."

The scorch marks left on the door at the church in Blythburgh are called by the locals "the devil's fingerprints," and the event is remembered in this verse: "All down the church in midst of fire, the hellish monster flew, and, passing onward to the quire, he many people slew."

There is another legend that goes something like "all who see Black Shuck will perish within a year of looking into his red eyes."

It would behoove one to avoid eye contact with the demonic fiend, wouldn't it?

And according to *The World Of Mystery,* Bigfoot and other cryptoids are no match for the Hellhounds or the exceeding robust Demon Dogs that still roam the rural areas of the UK, noticed sometimes in close proximity to the appearance of the also very mysterious and often unexplainable crop circles that pop up: "There's something even more chilling on Cannock Chase. It's time for the fabled Hellhound – a portent of doom – to take a bow-wow. Reports have been received on paranormal websites of the Demonic Dog roaming our area. The hound, also known as the 'ghost dog of Brereton,' has been seen on numerous occasions stalking the roads leading into Brereton.

"The apparition has been described as large, black, muscular, with sharp pointed ears and strangely glowing eyes. British folklore indicates that the black dog forewarns death. The most prominent sightings happened in the 1970s and early 1980s. Whilst driving through the Chase in 1972, Nigel Lea described seeing a ball of light crash into the ground. He slowed down to take a closer look and was confronted by 'the biggest bloody dog I have ever seen.' Within a month, one of Mr. Lea's close friends died in a terrible industrial accident, which Mr. Lea believed may be connected to the dog apparition. In January, 1985, there was another report of the Hellhound stalking."

Very ominous – and as might be expected there is a strong tie in with the appearance of a UFO apparition. Together or separately, such phenomena are sure to be seen again!

Well known hell hound from the movie Cujo.

Cosmic War for the Planet Earth

Between Inner Earth People and Outer Space Aliens
By Timothy Green Beckley

Back when I was just beginning my research into esoteric matters, I was bombarded with Christian-oriented literature, much of which was pseudo-religious with a decidedly right-wing spin; some of it even peppered with Nazi and KKK propaganda. Little of it addressed concerns of UFOs or metaphysics. If anything, it usually slammed such matters, directly implicating Mr. Scratch (aka Satan) as being behind such phenomena. I didn't think much of a demonic approach to UFOs in those days. I have always considered myself a spiritual individual, but not a person to follow the strict dogma of any group, religious or not. I guess I also didn't become conscious that there might be a connection between UFOs, the forces of Lucifer and an underground civilization that played a part in this mostly because of the fact its possible existence was a closely guarded "state secret" kept hidden from most of us.

One newsletter that arrived in the mail from time to time did catch my attention. *Showers of Blessing* was edited by Rev. William L. Blessing, who was courageous enough to delve into the mysteries of the universe, tackling inner earth and UFO mysteries as hardly any other cleric would dare.

From time to time, Rev. Blessing would compile his various sermons into large philosophical discourses. One large size volume that was published around 1965 was a controversial tome that apparently was taken out of circulation. **Inner Earth People / Outer Space Beings** is a huge collection of Rev. Blessings teachings which were nearly lost to time, had I not come across this 320+ page massive undertaking in a rare book collection.

Because of the conflict in the world today and the increase in UFO sightings, I personally feel that this work should reach as wide an audience as possible.

The Bible teaches us that there are beings dwelling inside the earth. For want of a better term, I shall call them the Inner Earth People. I estimate the population of Inner Earth to be ten billion. There are 200,000,000 pilots in the flying saucer corps. They will quite soon invade the surface of the planet and, indeed, that invasion may have already begun by an advanced recon force that is flying out over the surface of Earth, mapping land areas and strategic places where they will launch their primary strikes during the all-out invasion.

"And the four angels were loosed, which were prepared for an hour, and a day, and a month, and a year, to slay the third part of men. And the number of the army and horsemen were two hundred thousand thousand; and I heard the number of them." (Rev. 9:15-16)

That is two hundred million aviators of flying saucers. They look exactly like surface dwelling humans and their flying saucers are made of a type of metal that is plated with gold. "The sound of their wings was as of the sound of chariots." (Rev. 9:9)

"And the fifth angel sounded, and I saw a star fall from heaven unto the earth; and to him was given the key to the bottomless pit. And he opened the bottomless pit; and there arose a smoke out of the pit as the smoke of the great furnace; and the sun and the air were darkened by reason of the smoke of the pit. And there came out of the smoke locusts upon the earth; and unto them were given power as the scorpions of the earth have power." (Rev. 9:1-3)

They are bringing a cloud of darkness, a mist, a smog, a cloud over the cities that they are mapping out, such as Los Angeles, London and elsewhere. But when the all-out invasion begins they will blanket the whole Earth in darkness. "It shall be one day which shall be known to the Lord; neither night nor day." (Zech. 14:7)

Their vehicles were well known to the ancient prophets and were best described by Ezekiel: "And I looked and behold, a whirlwind came out of the north, a great cloud, and a fire enfolding itself, and a brightness was about it, and out of the midst thereof as the color of amber, out of the midst of the fire. Also out of the midst thereof came the likeness of four living creatures. And this was their appearance: they had the likeness of a man. And every one had four faces, and every one had four wings. And their feet were straight feet, and the sole of their feet was like the sole of a calf's foot; and they sparkled like the color of burnished brass. And they had the hands of man under their wings on their four sides; and they four had their faces and their wings. The wings were joined one to another; they turned not when they went; they went every one straight forward. As for the likeness of their faces, they four had the face of a man, and the face of a lion on the right side; and they four had the face of an ox on the left side; they four also had the face of an eagle. Thus were their faces; and their wings were stretched upward; two wings of every one were joined one to another; and two covered their bodies. And they went every one straight forward: whither the spirit was to go, they went; and they turned not when they went. As for the likeness of living creatures, their appearance was like burning coals of fire, and the appearance of lamps: it went up and down among the living creatures; and the fire was bright, and out of the fire went forth lightning. And the living creatures ran and returned as the appearance of a flash of lightning." (Ezek)

They will constantly beam messages to us. They will fly on magnetic lines, advancing from one point to another almost instantly, reversing their course or position more rapidly than the human eye can follow, using the power of levitation—reverse gravitation.

The inner earth people are of several different races and orders. Some originally lived on the surface, but some of them once lived above the Earth in outer space.

Long ago, they invaded the Earth from space. The book of Genesis describes them as the "serpent" people.

"And it came to pass, when men began to multiply in the earth, and daughters were born to them, that the sons of God saw that the daughters of men that they were fair; and they took them wives of all which they chose. And the Lord said, 'My spirit shall not always strive with man, for that he also is flesh; yet his days shall be a hundred and twenty years.' There were giants in the earth in those days; and also after that when the sons of God came in unto the daughters of men, and they bare children to them, the same became mighty men which were of old, men of renown. The earth also was corrupted before God; and the earth was filled with violence. And God looked upon the earth, and, behold, it was corrupt, for all flesh had corrupted His way upon the earth." (Gen. 6:4; 11-12)

The invaders from space came originally from twenty-two different dwelling places in outer space and the names of the leaders of each of the outer space places that led a host of their people to the Earth are as follows:

1. Samyaza,
2. Urakabarameel,
3. Akibeel,
4. Tamiel,
5. Ramuel,
6. Danel,
7. Azkeel,
8. Sarakuyal,
9. Asael,
10. Armers,
11. Batrael,
12. Anane,
13. Zavebe,
14. Samsaveel,
15. Etrael,
16. Turel,
17. Yomyael,
18. Arazyal,
19. Atnzarak,
20. Barkayal,
21. Barkayal Tamiel,
22. Asaradel.

(Book of Enoch, Ch 7 & 8)

Just exactly how many followers each leader brought with him to earth is not known but, at any rate, they materialized their bodies just like Earth people and remained in the flesh and married women of Earth. The children of these invaders were called "giants," many of them malformed, having six fingers and six toes. (1 Chron. 20:6) We do not say that all the offspring were malformed but many of them were. There was undoubtedly a race of giants ten to twelve feet tall and also a race of pygmies produced by the crossing of these outer space people with the women on the Earth. The first generation of these people was not sterile, but there is evidence that the second generation were sterile hybrids who could not reproduce.

This crossing over and mixing of the outer space invaders with the women on the Earth continued for 1,656 years; that is, from the time that Adam left the Garden of Eden until the final days of Noah. (Gen. 5:1-32) All the inhabitants of the Earth had become sterile one hundred years before the flood. The last children born on Earth before the flood were the triplet sons of Noah: Shem, Ham and Japheth. They were born on Noah's 500th birthday. (Gen. 5:32) From that time until the flood, no children were born on Earth. Consequently, no person on Earth was drowned in the flood until one hundred years of age, for no children had been born for one hundred years.

Incidentally, in passing, it must be stated that the degeneracy of the Earth before the flood was indescribable. Not only had the outer space people crossed with women, but men had corrupted themselves with animals as well, "for all flesh had corrupted his way upon the earth." (Gen. 6:12) Many of the animals we are forbidden to eat are part human. I could go into detail about this, describing the human marks in the bodies of each of the unclean animals, but suffice it to say that the serpent has a pelvic bone, as well as the remnants of arms and legs and gives birth to its young. It is too long a story to point out the human marks in each of the unclean animals, but they all have them. The hog does not chew cud and has a stomach like a human.

The space people who invaded Earth—fallen angels, if you wish to call them that—together with their hybrid offspring who were giants and pygmies, were all sent into the inner earth just before the flood. Later, and various intervals since the flood, some of the earth people have been banished to the inner earth. "And the earth opened her mouth, and swallowed them up, and their houses, and all the men that appertained to Korah, and all their goods. They, and all that appertained to them, went down alive into the pit and the earth closed upon them; and they perished from among the congregation." (Num. 16: 32-33)

Inner Earth People and Outer Space People has been kept in print by Global Communications, Box 753, New Brunswick, NJ 08903 and is available direct or through Amazon.com

Of Devils and Deros
The Inhabitants of Hell from Antiquity until the Present Day
By Wm. Michael Mott·

In the various mythic, folk, and religious traditions of the world, the subterranean regions of each have shared various characteristics. First and foremost, the underworld is perceived as the domain of the dead, of souls passed on beyond the flesh. Second, it is portrayed as a realm, in general, of special imprisonment and punishment, and thirdly as the dwelling-place, prison, or kingdom of a variety of supernatural or mysterious beings.

The Buddhist tradition has filled the underworld with a variety of hells, peopled by the damned, by dragon-people and dragons, and by a wide variety of imps, demons, and ogres. The Hindu tradition from which Buddhism springs does the same, with their version of the dragon- or serpent-folk being the naga, who are portrayed as reptilian humanoids (who can appear quite human, at will), and who are often physically-extant beings of great antiquity, power, lust, and technological advancement. The

Wm. Michael Mott has covered all aspects of the underworld from the most ancient to modern tales of the inner earth and its many demon-like inhabitants.

nagas are steeped in the arts of shape-changing deception (like the European "glamour" of subterranean faerie-land), and have flying machines (almost identical in description to modern UFO manifestations), "deathray" -type weapons, and other forms of advanced technology. Along with other races represented in Hindu lore, they utilized these technologies in vast inter-species wars in ancient times: wars involving the naga, human beings, the demonic rakshasas (many of whom are also subterrestrial or suboceanic), and various divine beings. After devastating conflicts which seem to fit the description of nuclear war (perhaps like that which destroyed Mohenjo-daro, a "fused" stone site that is still radioactive today), the non-human participants were said to have retreated to vast city-state complexes beneath the seas, the Earth's crust, and even to the nearer planetary bodies (the moon in particular).

The Sumerian-Hebrew tradition, and later the Judeo-Christian one, contains the seeds of a similar tale. According to those traditions (which really represent one continuous tradition) there was a pre-cataclysmic age (generally remembered as the antediluvian or pre-flood age) before our own, a time in which beings called the nephilim—consisting both of fallen angels in human form, and their hybrid, half-human offspring—built vast empires on our planet and then proceeded to squabble and war over those empires, with mankind caught up in the continuous chaos. The nephilim and their sons were giants both in size and in intellect, and constructed both terrible weapons and terrible genetic mutations through inter-species gene-splicing, nearly corrupting the entire human genome beyond repair or recovery. It should be noted that Noah and his family were rescued from the cataclysm which eventually came due to the fact that he (and presumably, they) was found to be "perfect in all his generations," i.e., representative of an uncontaminated, pure human genetic line.

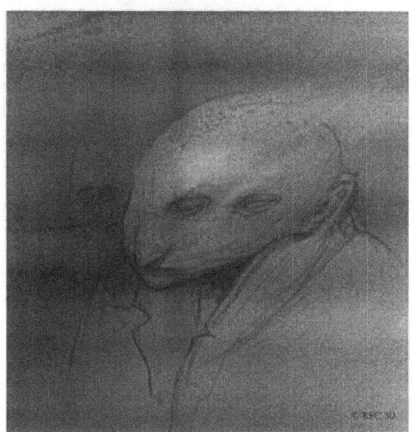

The demonic Dero are said to inhabit a vast underground cavern system and are cannibalistic and exceedingly ugly.
Art by R.E.Chappell

This same ancient tradition, described at length in the Book(s) of Enoch as well as Jasher and Jubilees, and also in the Dead Sea Scroll "Book of Giants," indicates that, as in the Hindu account, the non-human beings before the Flood were ambitious, violent and aggressive, constantly at war with one another. Interestingly, the Essene "Book of Giants" confirms the link between the Hebrew and Sumerian traditions, for in it, the spokesman or leader of the "giants" is none other than Gilgamesh, the half-human demigod of Sumerian myth. As all of these books indicate, these beings, to assist themselves in their wars (again, this is mirrored in the Hindu tradition) had genetically-engineered beings that were part human, part animal, and even of their own descent. These beings, too, threatened the stability of the human gene pool and the continued genetic validity of the human race.

The Hebrew "nephilim" or "fallen ones" were known as the "anunnaki" or "annuna" among the Sumerians, and this is remembered in the Biblical description of the "sons of Anak," who were a tribe of cannibalistic, violent giants which arose again at a much later date after the cataclysm. The ancient books indicate that, immediately after the Flood, those who were not destroyed were either imprisoned beneath the crust (the fallen-angelic fathers of "extraterrestrial" origin) or fled there to escape both catastrophic wrath and the altered, genetically-damaging rays of the post-Flood sun (the nephilim hybrid sons and their genetic creations). Directly from this tradition comes the Judeo-Christian concept of devils and demons imprisoned beneath the ground (even down to the horned skulls, tails, and double-rows of teeth, all nephilim-hybrid traits), and of evil spirits and supernatural beings—some physical, some ethereal—which creep forth to prey on humankind, yet shun the light of day.

The Greek tradition of the wars of Gods and Titans, and the half-human supermen known as demigods, also represent a dim memory of these times and beings. And it is from the Greek tradition that the name of one of the pre-flood kingdoms, possibly the greatest superpower of that distant age, comes down to us still. It was a nation of great advancement which eventually was destroyed by the wrath of the gods themselves in a catastrophic act of destruction, of earthquake, volcanic fire, and all-consuming flood. The name of that empire-state, of course, was Atlantis.

The modern-day advent of the "UFO mystery" (actually very ancient phenomena, going back to the wars and ages mentioned previously) did not, as popularly believed, begin with the sighting of unknown craft by Kenneth Arnold over Mt. Ranier in 1947. That distinction actually belongs to a man named Richard S. Shaver, who wrote not only of the subterranean world and the ancient, sun-fearing and war-fleeing humanoid beings from before the Flood, but also of their saucer-shaped flying craft and advanced rays of mind-altering madness and physical destruction.

Rather than go into a long exposition about who Shaver was and how he came upon both the UFO and pulp-fiction scene (already much-examined and written about elsewhere), let us look instead at his interpretation, his claims, which fit well within the archetypal underworld/pre-cataclysmic world complex already described. Suffice it to say that, according to Richard Shaver, he had been IN the caves or cavern world, and he had been shown examples of their advanced, ancient technologies and had been told, to some extent, their history.

Always an avowed materialist with no interest in "religious mumbo-jumbo," Shaver nevertheless recreated the same "religious" and "mythic" traditions in his tales. In a nutshell, he claimed that our surface-world reality is only a small part of the actual physical reality of our planet, and that beneath the crust, the descendants of the pre-flood nations still exist, and still wage war with one another. Additionally, they shun the light of the sun, which was detrimentally changed after the cataclysm or Flood (possibly when a protective canopy or shell of liquid water about the planet fell, remembered biblically as when "the windows of heaven opened," and more damaging radiation reached the Earth's surface—see *CAVERNS, CAULDRONS, AND CONCEALED CREATURES, 2nd Expanded Edition*, for more on this). They are descended from the "Atlans" or people of Atlantis, and also the "Titans," their genetic creations of partially human descent. Based more upon circumstance than descent from these groups, these beings have evolved and devolved into two groups, the malicious "dero" (coined by Shaver for "detrimental robot," "robot" in the sense of having no real self-control and in fact being insane) and the "tero," who are essentially close to human and at war with their degenerated cousins. Both groups, however, seem to have a penchant for abducting surface-world people, the tero possibly for reproductive purposes, the dero for sadistic or even cannibalistic ones.

As in the Hindu tradition, Shaver indicated that these beings fled beneath the crust, beneath the seas, and into space when the Flood came and "the sun changed"; as in the Hebrew tradition, he stated that they are trapped beneath the Earth's crust, fleeing the sun and hating "surface man." According to Shaver they have a variety of antediluvian devices which enable them to spy on everyone on our planet, manipulate our thoughts and actions, and which can even reach out and maliciously manipulate machinery, vehicles, and other technologies, causing mayhem and destruction at will. They can create holographic illusions of anyone or anything as well, and they are largely responsible for the modern manifestation of unidentified flying objects.

Here we see a parallel with the devils and demons of Buddhist, Hindu, and Judeo-Christian traditions, all of which blame invisible and subterranean beings for temptations, violence, mass murder, insanity, disembodied voices and even possession by alien or non-human personalities. Shaver claimed that all such phenomena were merely ·the work of the mechanisms of the ancients, in the malignant hands of non-human mental defectives and perverts, bent on the suffering and destruction of a surface-world race of whom they are supremely jealous and resentful. According to him, missing persons often were taken by the dero into their underworld lairs, to become slaves, torture victims, targets of their lust, and to eventually end up as food.

Needless to say this parallels all of the ancient traditions already mentioned, as well as various folk and "fairy" traditions that tell of ancient, genetically-diminished races dwelling beneath the ground, races which prey on humanity for fresh genetic stock, for purposes of lust and procreation, or simply out of malice and resentment. Shaver's cosmology was more than just that—it was his ontology, his complete world-view, one which he swore was true and valid until his last breath. In spite of his insistence that his entire story was purely materialistic, in the scope of the "Shaver Mystery" we have a complete recreation of the most ancient mythic and religious traditions, with the original explanations and interpretations replaced by Shaver with the trappings and devices of the most popular form of written entertainment of his day: Pulp Science Fiction. His underworld, physical or metaphysical, is a form of Hell nevertheless, and the beings he claimed dwelt there are demonic and infernal in the truest sense of the terms. Coming full-circle, his tales of the subterranean vestiges of a once-mighty race parallels the most ancient traditions on our planet of those beings, entities, and shadowy kingdoms that are behind many or most of the paranormal, UFOlogical, and monstrous mysteries of our world.

Demons and the Shaver Mystery

By Warren Smith

Though it was a science fiction magazine Amazing Stories was the first publication to carry the all true stories of Richard Shaver who claims he was kidnapped and held captive in an underground hell under the control of the Dero.

It was one of the most sensational, highly controversial, articles ever published in an American magazine. 'I Remember Lemuria' by Richard S. Shaver was published in the March, 1945 issue of Amazing Stories magazine, a Ziff-Davis publication. Life magazine tagged the Shaver Mystery as "the most celebrated rumpus that rocked the science-fiction world" because author Richard Shaver claimed the story was fact, not fiction.

Life said: "The Shaver Mystery concerned a race of mal-formed subhuman creatures called deros (from detrimental robots) who inhabited a vast system of underground cities all over the world. The original name of their habitat was Lemuria, and they had once been slaves of the Lemurian master race. But the master race had long since disappeared from the earth, leaving the ignorant and malicious deros in control of the great cities and wonderful machines it had built. Since then the deros occupied themselves mainly in persecuting the human race who lived on the crust of the earth above them. The deros were responsible for much of the evil in the world. Catastrophes, from shipwrecks to sprained ankles, were attributable to their influence. They often appeared on the surface of the earth and were sufficiently human in appearance to pass unnoticed in a crowd. But they performed most of their harassment by telepathy, rays, and other remote control devices from their subterranean homes.

Their underground cities communicated with the surface through various caves which were extremely dangerous for human beings to enter. Albert McDonald and his Hollow Earth Society have published several monographs on the Shaver Mystery, as it is known to occult and science-fiction fans. The group has formulated a committee on the Shaver Mystery and, as a result, their files are a very complete source of material on the controversial tale. Selections from the monographs are published here as they appeared in the organization's literature:

Questions and Answers
With Hollow Earth Society

Who Are The Dero?

Essentially, Shaver declared that the interior of the earth is laced with networks of gigantic caves. The total area of the caves is larger than the total area of land on the surface world. The inhabitants of this cavern world are known as the "abandondero," as they were abandoned when a mass exodus from the earth occurred approximately 12,000 years ago. The migration was necessary when the sun started to throw deadly radiation over the entire solar system, including our own planet. These radioactive emissions from the sun lodged in the bodies of an "immortal" race that lived on earth. Known as the Titans and the Atlans, these immortal people now live in the dark voids of space.

Sadistic and demonic creatures, the Dero kidnap earth women to rape and keep in bondage as illustrated by Carol Ann Rodriguez.

Unable to stand a radioactive sun, the Atlans and Titans made an attempt to live in caverns deep inside the earth. There were cavities within the earth and, with machines and superior technology, they enlarged these spaces into vast caverns. Why didn't the Titans and Atlans remain in the caverns? Until the sun turned radioactive, they had lived for thousands of years. They were virtually immortal. The radioactivity poisoned their bones, brought on cellular destruction, and the aging process as we know it today.

The Atlans and Titans, advanced races, had higher knowledge, superior technology, and science. They decided to leave the earth and seek another planet as a home, preferably one without a sun. They settled on a dark planet that has no sun. With their race dying, they launched a massive effort to construct space ships. Time was limited. They could not build a fleet of ships to allow everyone to migrate, and as with any life-saving venture, only certain groups were allowed to migrate. The poor, the unfortunate, and those afflicted with radioactive diseases, were left in the caverns. This is why Shaver called them the 'abandondero.'

What happened to the abandoned people?

The Atlans and Titans fled because the caves were cut off from the sun. Healthful rays were necessary for zest, vitality, and a normal life. As the abandoned group wandered through the caverns, they evolved down into degenerate, idiotic midgets. Shaver says these bestial creatures are the "dero." Totally without goodness, they're evil demonic creatures. Another, less populous group, is the "teros." They managed to ward off menial and physical degeneration through beneficial nutrients, chemicals, and ray machines. Despite their best technical and medical research, teros age quickly. They usually die by the time they reach 50 years of age. The tero are advanced thinkers, dedicated to good, and they are ruled by benign leaders.

If the tero are smarter, shouldn't they have outwitted the deadly dero?

The dero are the devil-men, a fast-growing race which delight in attacking, capturing, and torturing the tero. The tero have been scattered through the caves and caverns. They are often forced to hide from the devilish deros. The forces of evil rule much of the interior. What makes the dero so dangerous? When the Atlans and Titans flew to another planet, they left their marvelous machines. The dero are the heirs to some of the most advanced technology in the universe. This equipment was created by people who were virtually immortal; therefore, their machines were built to last for thousands of years. The deros use these machines and technical systems to attack surface homo sapiens and the tero.

What types of machines have been taken over by the dero?

Some of the most advanced equipment known to humanity. A partial list includes: flying machines. Several years before the first modern flying saucer was sighted by Kenneth Arnold on the west coast, Shaver described these vehicles as being abandoned by the elder race that migrated to the stars. Ray machines: Telaug and vision ray machines can penetrate cavern walls and bring in views of the surface world. These vision units allow the devilish deros to see what people are doing at any time, at any place, in the surface world.

Projection Ray machines: These machines project weird, fantastic images and thoughts into the minds of innocent victims, victims often selected at random by the demented dero.

Tractor Ray Beams: A train is speeding across the surface of the world. In the dark recesses of his cavern, a dero focuses a tractor beam on a railroad switch. The track is opened; the train is derailed.

The dero can instantly change highway traffic signals, sabotage industrial machinery, and ruin complex devices. Have you ever had a machine or object that refused to work, then performed marvelously when the repairman arrived? A dero may have been amusing himself.

Tractor Ray machines are used to throw open manhole covers, loosen a single step on a stairway, or sabotage a vital part on a speeding automobile.

Surgical Ray Cannons: The dero enjoys projects of the most terrible nature. These devices were originally created to perform delicate surgical operations. Today, the dero focuses these instruments on a person to slice a delicate, essential nerve. Surgical rays are beamed on a single individual's head until the juices of his brain bubble and boil furiously.

Mental Machines: These horrible devices create realistic illusions, nightmares, strange dreams, and compulsive behaviour in a victim. Many murderers have informed the police that "I just got a sudden urge to kill

Were they actually the target of a vicious dero mental machine?

Richard Shaver stated that the cavern people have been bequeathed death rays, gigantic machines for excavating caves, powerful weapons, and fleets of vehicles for driving through the caverns. He also said that some deros enjoy driving modern automobiles from the surface world. Is it possible that stolen cars are driven down into the tunnels? Fortunately, not all of the people in the caverns are dedicated to evil purposes.

What is a stim machine?

Shaver wrote of a pleasure stimulation machine which was used to revitalize sexual nature. Shaver claimed to have had a stim machine played on him during his visits to the caverns. "A powerful augmentation of woman-life; to a hundred powers of natural love," he wrote. There are no words to describe what this apparatus did for his life. Unfortunately, many of these stim machines have been captured by roving bands of deros. These complex mechanisms are used to create varied degrees of sexual intensity. The deros, who are totally degenerate, may spend their entire lives in a stim ray sex orgy. This debauchery can be heightened to such a degree, and prolonged for so many years, that the dero is deformed. They are transformed into even more frightening, more monstrous creatures. Perhaps a stim machine is addictive.

Does this mean they do not harm women on the surface world?

To the contrary, the dero kidnap nubile young women for their amusement in the caverns. Stim rays are played over their bodies. A frightened, prudish woman can be transformed into the depraved, willing participant in a dero orgy. In the May, 1967, issue of the **Hollow Earth Bulletin** we printed portions of The Messerschmidt Manuscript.' A French woman, thought to have been killed, returned to her home in the suburbs of Paris with a frightening tale of being kidnapped and taken into the dero's lair. An edited version of her statement follows: There are those who will claim I am insane ... They will testify that I am mentally ill and unable to remember those weeks in the caves. I wish I could erase those memories from my mind. But, the world must be warned. The monsters are down there. We must destroy them before they kidnap more women for their horrible purposes ... I was a young woman of nineteen years of age in 1943, proud of my ability as a student, and eagerly

looking forward to marrying a young man who planned to be a physician. One night we planned to meet at my fiancé's office building, join another couple, and have dinner in a small cafe. We were not worried about the Nazis. I arrived a few minutes late at my fiancé's office building and the old man who ran the elevator had left for the day. I decided to operate the lift for myself. I stepped inside to inspect the controls. There were no symbols to indicate whether the lift went up or down by moving the lever one way or another. Light hearted and in love, I decided that if I ran the elevator into the basement, I could reverse the controls and go up to the other stories ... I made an error and the elevator stopped in a dark basement. I reversed the controls, but my hand slipped. I pushed on the "down" control.

The elevator suddenly plunged down below the basement, falling through space as if the cable had broken. After a rapid drop, perhaps several hundred feet, the elevator stopped with a sudden lurch. I was so frightened as I fell onto the floor of the cage, sobbing and screaming. Through my terror-stricken mind, I heard a loud, guttural noise on the other side of the elevator door. The elevator door was torn open with a vicious slam and I saw the most horrible beast in the world.

The memory of that monster haunts my mind and, at night, I cannot sleep without sedatives or sleeping pills. His face was of a pale, whitish color. His short, twisted body was covered with thick, bristly hair. His eyes? Piggish, insensitive to any emotion, and gleaming with evil lust. The creature was fat, almost bloated. There were terrible scars and running sores over most of his body. He had no neck, so his head was placed squarely atop his muscular shoulders. The face was the most horrible portion of his terrible features. It was much too large for his body, totally devoid of hair. The skin was scarred and wrinkled. His nose was fashioned more like a snout. It was at least seven inches in length, a terrible thing hanging down over his lipless mouth. His nose ended about the middle of his chest. He was nude. His body looked as if he had never worn garments.

A filthy, animal-smell filled the elevator. Mercifully, I fainted into unconsciousness. I have never known what happened in the elevator. Did they use that for an entry into the outside world? I have thought about it and those elevator shafts may go down far into the earth at certain points. When I recovered consciousness, I was lying on the polished stone floor of an immense cavern. There were several other women standing around in that dark corner and, as my eyes adjusted to the dimness, I saw that we were caged into one corner of a large cave. A metal gate, and bars, rose from the stone floor up to the ceiling. I suppressed an impulse to scream, thinking this terrible nightmare would end any instant. Across the way, the devil-men were fighting over a carcass. It was some reptile-like animal which they hunted in the caverns. I learned later that if these reptiles became scarce, they crept up into Paris at night and captured human beings for their food. There were giant hooks on the walls, quite sharp, where they hung the bodies to drain. They collected the blood as a drink, fighting among themselves for the thick, red drippings.

There were about twenty women crowded into the cave. Most of them were totally mad; insane creatures who had lost their minds. They huddled in the cage, whimpering and crying. Others simply sat in mute catatonic shock. They were like living robots, with their emotions and human feelings destroyed by the horrible existence in the caverns. I stood up, looking around for my clothing, which was gone. Trying to hide my nakedness, I walked to the front of the cage. Despite my fear, I shouted across the room to the group of monstrous beings. It was a moment of total unreality.

"The police will be looking for me," I said. "Release me, or I'll charge you with kidnapping." My mind was like a taut string on a musical instrument, ready to snap at any moment. The devil-man who had pulled me from the elevator grinned wickedly through his lipless mouth. He lurched up from where he had been gnawing on the carcass. I trembled with fear as he shuffled toward me. I moved back into the cage. He spoke in a guttural growl, almost grunts.

This was a signal and the other women in the cage grabbed me. They pressed me against the bars of the cage. I passed once again into unconsciousness as the devil-man placed a dirty, hairy palm on my breast. I regained my senses once more that same night. I remember that seven or eight of the devil-men chased me round the cavern. They tossed me back and forth between each other, fondling my body, and - as they wished - carrying me off into a passageway for their private amusement.

After that first night, nothing they could do to me would kill the spirit of life within my body. I learned! Oh! How I learned. I put my mind elsewhere when they pulled me from the cages. I survived and retained my sanity by living in the past. When one of the lusting, evil monsters dragged me out of the cages for his pleasure, I went into a catatonic state. I relived the happy years of my childhood in my mind to retain my sanity. Or, I blanked out into unconsciousness.

Most of the women who had been captive for some time were in horrible physical condition. They had picked up the various infections and sores from the beasts. They had skin eruptions and bruises were all over their bodies. Many had lost weight, due to the mental strain, and the food. The men-beasts often forgot to feed us and, when they did, they threw a large chunk of meat into the cage. I never knew if the meat was human, or animal, and I became so hungry that I didn't care.

About once a week, perhaps more often because time measurement was impossible in the caverns, we were given an armload of damp, moldy weeds. We were allowed a small fire in the cages, for cooking, and to ward off the dampness. We took these subterranean ferns, mosses, and mushrooms, and brewed them into a stew. Once, we were given a dark, almost black, type of mushroom that produced hallucinations.

I must have been a captive of these terrible devil-men for two weeks, perhaps a month, when the gray men appeared from out of the tunnels. The devils scrambled in the opposite direction, grunting with fright, as the gray men shot them with gas guns. Several of the bestial men-animals were killed.

Prisoners were released from the cage, given a toga-like robe for clothing, and taken through the tunnels for medical attention. They had a strange sort of vehicle, not like our automobiles, that was parked in the tunnels. A physician led us into a mobile laboratory. The room had large number of machines and, even under the lights, the metal was grayish in color. Everything was made of this metal and even their clothing appeared to be metallic. I retained a sense of where I was, but the leader of the group indicated to the doctor that I should be treated.

They spoke perfect French, but with a strange accent. "Your mind is disturbed because of your experience," said the leader of the group. He was about five feet tall, muscular, with only his face visible under the helmet of the same gray metal. His face was more elongated, thinner, than those of the human beings I have met. It was gray in color, almost like the cast of old baking dough.

We were taken individually into another vehicle that looked like a combination hospital and computer room. Another man, who seemed to be a physician, indicated

I should lie back on a table made from the same grayish metal. He also spoke in French, indicating that the treatment would not hurt me. "You will feel no pain," he said. "We have tried to erase memories from the mind but they are never totally gone. They will come forth through dreams, nightmares, and disguised thoughts. We are attaching you to a machine that provides you with information on why you were tortured by the animal men."

"Can't you tell me?" I inquired. "It would take many years of time, as you measure it," he replied. "The machines implant information in your mind without error. The data is not filtered through my mind, but remains purified." After the treatment, I was taken to another section of the tunnels. Some of the men in metallic uniforms were sealing off the tunnels. The leader designated a man to lead me back to the surface world, and in another two hours, we were in the sewers of Paris. I was back on the streets in a short while. I must have looked very strange, walking barefoot through the streets in winter. A gendarme stopped me and I was taken into custody and, eventually, my family was contacted. I spent many weeks in a mental hospital and, today, I am in a sanitarium trying to recover from the experience.

What was the message given to the young woman through the machine?

Many millions of years ago, she related, the earth was devoid of human life. The "starmen" selected our planet as a space laboratory, transplanting various types of people from different planets onto our earth. Homo sapiens became the dominant species as our aggressive, war-like characteristics drove the other species from us. Some of these species became extinct. Others vanished and even the 'starmen' don't know what occurred. They simply disappeared without a trace.

As the human race continued to grow, some species were driven underground to the caverns for their survival. They adapted themselves to the life beneath the surface and, in time, they created the tunnels and cavern cities. There were tremendous problems related to biological mutations and the necessary evolution of the species to survive the environment of the inner earth. In time, the original colonists degenerated into the brutal, horrible animal men. In ancient times, these degenerates preyed upon surface humanity through raids on outlying areas. Ancient stories of strange appearances of unusual animals, werewolves, and men-beasts are memories of battles between our ancestors and the animal men.

Eventually, mankind developed weaponry to defend themselves. The men-beasts were pushed back under the ground. They now prowl only at night and they're very careful to avoid detection by humans. The wars, the atomic age, and evolution of the animal-men, has created the problem today. The animal-men are a great threat to human survival. The animal-men have evolved into a deadly species, more crafty and extremely cunning. The constant tests of nuclear weapons have destroyed, or cracked, many of the great tunnels. Whole cavern cities have been wiped out by these tests. The animal-men are growing stronger. They've become the heirs to advanced weaponry, airships, and electromagnetic weaponry The animal-men are on the march to conquer the entire planet, including the surface world.

Who were the men in metallic uniforms?

They are what we would call a biological team from the far reaches of space. During a routine check of the earth, they learned of the mutations that had occurred among the animal-men. They brought back their instruments and established several "breeding stations," notably under the oceans and seas. They plan to observe the war between the animal-men and the armies of our surface nations.

Will they save us from these demonic creatures?

Our salvation will come through our own efforts. The "starmen" are observers of the battle between the species on this planet. They have no plans to disturb the functions of natural selection by committing their weaponry to either species.

According to this theory, we didn't evolve from the apes. Is that correct?

To the contrary, the apes evolved downward from us as a degenerated species of early homo sapiens.

It is as if the surface world produced a similar group of animal-men.

Should we believe this story?

The lady approached our representatives in Paris last year, seeking more data on the hollow earth. She believed the Hollow Earth Society might provide more information to put her terrible experience into some sort of understanding. Unfortunately, we do not have the funds to maintain a library except at our headquarters. Our man in Paris checked her history and background in great detail. She disappeared for about four months, at the time indicated. He checked the elevator at the office building where her kidnapping allegedly took place. The shaft ended at the basement but - strangely enough - there were signs of fresh masonry construction at the bottom of the elevator shaft. We asked for permission to test the shaft for a possible proof of her story. The building owners refused to allow tests of any type.

How does her story check with the Shaver information?

Shaver stated that people on the surface evolved from the abandonero. He reported our ancestors were those ancient people who were unable to gain entry into the caves. As they roamed the radiated surface of our world, they were reduced to a species known as the Neanderthal man. Those that did not die off eventually built up an immunity to the radiation rays of the sun. As time progressed, humanity forgot about the ancestral catastrophe except for the folklore about vanished civilizations like Atlantis and Lemuria, and memory of a group known as the "Masters."

Organized, pseudo-scientific investigation of the Hollow Earth Mystery has been the goal of theHollow Earth Society since it was established in England in 1961. The group has been unconcerned about the reality of their beliefs, placing their strongest emphasis on gaining new converts to their cause. The current president of the organization is Albert McDonald, a Welsh-born businessman with a missionary gleam in his eyes. He has a zealous ability to convince almost anyone of the far-out beliefs of his organization.

Created From the Fiery Wind: The Jinn

Destined To Hide Or Conceal?

The Activities of Shaitan, or Evil Jinn, and the Goal of Shaitan

The main purpose is to convince people to follow him. He knows already that he is to be punished in Hellfire. He wants as many people as possible to follow him into Hellfire so he will not be lonely.

Shaitan pretends to be your best friend and advisor. He whispers words to you. He makes you believe that everything in this world is Halal and you should not hold back. He whispers to your friends, in hopes that the words will come to you as well, and tries to persuade you to do everything that is unlawful.

Shaitan will NEVER show themselves, because, obviously, this will cause fear, and people would not listen to something that stems from evil. But, from time to time, they will take on certain forms to stray people from the teachings of Islam.

The British **FLYING SAUCER REVIEW** has been among the most prestigious of publications in the UFO arena, having been issued almost nonstop since the mid-1950s. The founder of FSR was a retired Royal Air Force pilot, named Derek Dempster, and while the publication has gone through various leaders, its editorial direction has always been that of a serious research vehicle. Its first editor, Brinsley Le Poer Trench, had a very tight bond with the publisher of this work, having invited me to speak before a special UFO study group at the House of Lords, which he chaired in his exalted position as the Lord of Clancarty the Eighth. Though facilitating primarily a "nuts and bolts" approach to the subject, the **FLYING SAUCER REVIEW** did not shy away from relating the experiences of those who seem to have been cultivated by the intelligence behind the UFOs to undergo a flotilla of weird paranormal experiences, many similar to the darker aspects of UFOlogy which we ourselves have not shied away from discussing.

In 1982, the publication was ably produced by Gordon Creighton, whose background had included an interest in occultism, alchemy and magick. Without hesitation, despite the dissatisfaction of those hardliners who were satisfied to languish wholeheartedly in the bliss they felt from an unabashed belief in the interplanetary genesis of UFOs, Creighton was determined to usher in a new dawn of "enlightenment" which included probing the dark elements so forbidden by the ET theorists.

In a 1990 edition of the *FLYING SAUCER REVIEW*, Creighton pulled out all the stops when the **FSR** published what was certainly a very controversial article for this era. In a piece entitled "The True Nature of the UFO Entities," Creighton brings up for the first time in any UFO publication I am aware of the existence of the Islamic spirit entities known as the Jinn and commonly referred to as the Genie in western pop culture. Most might see these spirit beings as harmless tricksters as visualized by reading *1001 Arabian Nights* or watching the rather sexy Barbara Eden in the millionth and one rerun of the sitcom *I Dream of Jeannie*. To be frank, these phantoms of terror can hardly be considered benevolent, and if you encounter one or worse yet are possessed by a Jinn, you will know what hell is all about. In my collection of extreme shock films (I am after all the horror host and producer best known after midnight as Mr. Creepo) I have a couple of pictures released in Turkey that make our movie the *Exorcist* look like melba toast spooks. Talk about pea soap and heads twirling around and around – this stuff is ten times more frightening, even though Linda Blair did give the Devil a run for his money.

And why might that be so? Well let's find out by dropping in on the late *FLYING SAUCER REVIEW's* Gordon Creighton as he unravels for us the mystery of the Jinn

The True Nature of the "UFO Entities"

One of the more curious features of the followers of the various religions is that, being so dogmatically certain that in their own particular little faith they already possess the whole truth about all things in Heaven and Earth, it almost never occurs to any of them to look elsewhere and find out what the followers of other religions may know or may have discovered. This is certainly a pity, for study of all the great world religions - and notably Islam, one of the world's great religions - yields valuable clues as to the true nature of the "UFO Phenomenon." Islam knows, in fact, of the existence of three entirely separate and distinct species of intelligent beings in the Universe, and indeed can furnish surprisingly precise details regarding their natures and roles and activities. Angels, Men, and Jinn.

The first category is that of the Angels or Messengers. The second are Men, with planetary physical bodies assembled from the mineral and chemical elements of our Periodic Table. The third category is the category of those beings created before man was who are referred to collectively in Arabic as Al-Jinn. That means "to hide or to conceal," indeed a very fitting derivation for the name of these creatures. Whereas the bodies of Angels are of light, the bodies of Al-Jinn consist of "essential fire," or "essential flame," or "smokeless fire," or "smokeless flame." It is specifically stated in the Qur'an (Surah XV, 26 and 27) that they were created before mankind and some scholars speculate these might be the "Pre-Adamic men" whose existence is hinted at here and there in the Bible. Western occultists have tried to describe them as ether, or as etheric or astral planes. I have also seen it suggested that some sort of plasma is indicated. The source of the Jinn is not very distant from us, yet at the same time somehow very far from us. In other words, on some other dimension, or in some other Space/Time framework, "right here," some other Universe that is here, behind Alice's mirror; "a mirror-universe on the other side of the Space-Time Continuum" as it has been neatly put by some investigators.

Although the Qur'an is not clear on this, it looks as though some of the Jinn could be fully physical and what we call extraterrestrials, while other species of them are of an altogether finer sort of matter, corresponding to what various UFO investigators have tried to indicate by such terms as "ultraterrestrial" or "metaterrestrial." In thinking about these ideas, we might bear in mind the theory of the Russian philosopher P. D. Ouspensky regarding the possible existence of other, more subtle, levels of matter on which the elements of the Periodic Table of our own chemical world are repeated – and, if I understand him aright, repeated more than once, on more than one level. The early writings of Dr. Meade Layne in the USA about the "Dense Etheric World" from which he maintained that the UFO entities and their craft originated should also be borne in mind. His book *The Coming of the Guardians*, was published in 1958, and may prove to have been very important as certain of the benevolent Jinn may well be our "Guardians."

Genderuwo is a type of jinn, a spirit of an ape-like, near-human form that is both large and stout, has a reddish-brown color and is covered in thick hair over his entire body. Genderuwo is especially well known in a community in Java, but he also appears in Sudan, where he is called "Gandaruwo." His habitat is a favorite residential water stone, old buildings, large trees or shady corners of the damp, quiet and dark. The Domicile Center believed this creature to be in the Donoloyo Teak Forest, in the Sloghimo District, about 60 km east of Wonogini, and in the White Teak, Purwosal, Girimulyo, Kulan Projo, about 60 km west of Yogysharta.

That there is some close affinity, or some link of destiny between Jinn and Mankind seems certain, for although the vast majority of the Jinn are devils, shaytans, nevertheless we are assured in the Qur'an that some among their many species are "goodies" and are capable of salvation. For it is specifically stated that Muhammad was sent as a Messenger to both Mankind and the Jinn, so that, in the Final Days, some of the Jinn will enter into Paradise, while the rest of them will be cast down into Hell. Their revelation to Iblis, the top Devil (i.e., Satan) is in general somewhat obscure. In the Qur'an, Iblis is certainly described as a Jinn, but elsewhere in the Qur'an he is also described as an Angel. (Surely the explanation is that Iblis is that same high being, originally of Angelic status, who rebelled against God and is named in the Christian texts as "Lucifer.") Had we the space, much more might be said about the Jinn and their doings, but only a brief account of their main characteristics can here be given. Their principal features, as listed below, are as I have gathered them from all the Muslim written and traditional sources that I have been able to consult over the past 15 years. The readers can see for themselves the parallels with the reported features of UFO entities and can draw their own conclusions.

Chief Characteristics of the Jinn

The chief characteristics of the Jinn are:

1. In the normal state they are not visible to ordinary human sight.

2. They are, however, capable of materializing and appearing in the physical world. And they can alternately make themselves visible or invisible at will.

3. They can change shape, and appear in any sort of guise, large or small.

4. They are able also to appear in the guise of animals.

5. They are inveterate liars and deceivers, and delight in bamboozling and misleading mankind with all manner of nonsense. (See the average Spiritualist séance for examples of their activities, and also the usual "communications" from UFO entities in close-encounter cases.).

6. They are addicted to the abduction or kidnapping of humans. (The Scotsman Robert Kirk, who wrote "The Secret Commonwealth" in 1691, evidently "knew more than was good for his health," and was killed by them.)

7. They delight in tempting humans into sexual intercourse and liaisons with them, and Arabic literature abounds with accounts of this kind of contact by mankind with both the "goodies" and the "baddies" among the Jinn. There are also even a considerable number of accounts of encounters between the "goodies" and famous Muslim saints.

Please note, in official Islam - and this cannot be over-emphasized - the existence of the Jinn has always been completely accepted, even legally, and even to this day, in Islamic jurisprudence. The full consequences implied by their existence were worked out long ago. Their legal status, in all respects, was discussed and fixed, and the possible relations between them and mankind – especially in relation to questions of marriage and property! - were seriously examined by jurists, as the greatest and most authoritative Western source, the Encyclopedia of Islam, confirms. Stories of sexual commerce between Jinn and mankind have been of perennial interest to Arab readers, and it is important at this point to mention that in Chinese literature there is also a considerable tradition of this sort which awaits examination by researchers. The great Arabic literary catalogue known as the Fihrist, compiled in the year 373 of the Muslim Calendar (A.D. 995) by Muhammad bin Ishaq bin Abi Ya'qub al-Nadim al-Warraq al-Baghdadi, lists no less than sixteen works dealing with this theme. (Compare also the European occultists' records of sexual contact between men and female Sylphs, as well as the copious medieval Christian records relating to Incubi and Succabae.)

8. The Jinn are wont to snatch up humans and teleport or transport them, setting them down again - if indeed they ever do set them down again - miles away from where they were picked up, and all this is the "twinkling of an eye." (See my first article on *Teleportations*, about the Spanish soldier who, on October 25, 1593, was suddenly taken from Manila in the Philippine Islands across the Pacific to Mexico City. In FSR Vol. 11, No. 2, 1965.)

9. The Arabian tradition asserts that, throughout all known history, there have been a few particular human beings who, through some strange favour, have "been in league with the *Jinn*" or "had a compact with the *Jinn*" - to such a degree that the *Jinn* have endowed them with what we regard as "preternatural powers" - i.e., *psychic powers*. These humans have consequently become known as wonder-workers, soothsayers, and *magicians*. Either "white magicians" or "black magicians," depending of course upon what sort of *Jinn* they were in league with.

Here again, compare the European tradition about individuals who have discovered how to collaborate with the *Kingdom of the Sylphs* or the *Fairies*. For example, there is the case of the "working partnership," not more than seventy years ago, between a *Sylph* and a highly successful Parisian dealer in rare old books. The *Sylph* made its contribution by acting as the "scout" and finding out where and in whose possession the rare books were. All the dealer had to do then was to approach the owners and offer to buy!

10. Along with all these displays of prowess by the *Jinn* there goes, finally, a tremendous *telepathic power* and the ability (to use an age-old term) to 'cast a glamour' over their human victims. Our UFO records are already full of evidence of this.

How much of what we see happening today, at the highest levels of international politics, as well as in ordinary human affairs, can be attributed to this subtle control and interference in our lives by insidious and unseen forces? Indeed, this is one of the prime reasons for the perilous state in which man finds himself. Some recent reports from UFO investigators hint at alien plans to provoke war here and drive the Gadarene Swine (mankind) over into the abyss.

The present-day Christians, who generally seem to have very little sense of curiosity, are apparently quite happy to pass their days in total ignorance of all this. But a careful study of the New Testament *(and only in the original Greek!)* will show clearly that nothing of what is said above was unknown either to the Teacher and Healer Jeshua of Nazareth or to his principal followers - particularly Paul. (Incidentally, Christians may like to know that in Islam the full name and title of Jeshua of Nazareth is Issa, Son of Mary, Word of God.

Long before the rise of Christianity or Islam there were of course other great Teachers (Messengers) who perceived clearly the situation in which mankind finds itself. One of these was Zarathustra (Zoroaster) in the Old Iranian civilization of the Achaemenidae -- about 600 or 700 years B. C. The great religious text left by Zarathustra is the *AVESTA*, which tells us much about the Demonic Forces, referred to under the blanket term of AHRIMAN, the Enemy of Light. Mankind, in this teaching, is seen as a special creation of ORMAZD, the SUPREME SPIRIT, who is locked in permanent conflict with AHRIMAN.

The soul of man is the object of the war, and man himself is the battlefield.

Will the Forces of Darkness Prevail?

In our own days, there has probably been no teacher who saw and understood all this more clearly that the great Austrian Dr. Rudolf Steiner (1861-1925), founder of the Anthroposophical Society.

Clinging to the wall of a cave in Jordan this is said to be an authentic photo of a Jinn in its natural habitat.

Clairvoyant from childhood, Steiner saw into the other worlds and planes and saw deeply into the human heart, and no books or teachings are so relevant as his are to the crisis of mankind that is now upon us. His lectures throughout 1917, for example, show clearly that he foresaw, in their totality, the political, social, and military results and the police-state tyranny which would inevitably follow from the Russian Revolution, just as the "Lady" of the Apparitions at Fatima in the same year also did. Steiner foresaw what would result in the world as a whole from a materialistic science run mad: the development of "test-tube" man, "biological engineering" and other horrors; the deliberate creation and development of living monsters; and the soul-less, God-less, dehumanized, computerized, insect-like chromium and plastic slave world of "1984" that may now be at hand.

According to Steiner, a tremendous and crucial round in the battle was fought out in the last thirty years of the 19th century, and on the Inner Planes, between the Forces of AHRIMAN (the term he took over from Zarathustra) and the FORCES OF LIGHT. These latter are conventionally known to our Western, Christian tradition as the Cohorts of Michael. Steiner said that the fight ended in a complete victory for the LIGHT, but that, as a result of it, a great many of the powerful demonic beings had been actually cast down upon the planet Earth, with the consequence that their presence and their influence now impinge more than ever upon the prospects and the destiny of mankind.

Steiner taught that the coming years will see incredible upheavals, in the course of which this great battle will be carried forward, to its conclusion, INSIDE EVERY HUMAN

Round Trip to Hell in a Flying Saucer

HEART. See Rudolf Steiner: *Der Sturz der Geister der Finsternis: (The Overthrow of the Spirits of Darkness),* Series of Lectures, 1917. (Available only in German.)

The objective of the Forces of Darkness is to take over the stream of human evolution, to merge with it, and to divert mankind from the evolutionary development "planned" for it. The end result of this would be new creatures in which those qualities that represent the highest that we know would have been eliminated.

Smart-alecky modern man of the Pop Age, the "Trousered Ape" as he has been called, has of course no use for all this sort of "rubbish," and immense numbers of our species have discarded all belief in the existence of demons, along with any belief in the Great Power that rules the Universe.

There is a delightful passage in C.S. Lewis's *The Screwtape Letters,* where the Senior Devil, talking to one of his underlings, makes a profoundly important remark: *"Of course, our greatest trump-card is the fact that everybody KNOWS we don't exist."* (Or words to that effect.)

Similarly, the vast majority of mankind KNOW that *Jinn* and UFOs and UFO entities don't exist. And what a nice advantage that is for the entities!

But what if *Homo Sap* (so-called, self-dubbed) were in for some big shocks in the near future? What then?

With the recent advance of science, man has rapidly become aware of the vastness of the cosmos and of the probability that there exist out there innumerable other physical worlds inhabited by intelligent beings, some of which, for all we know, may be (as we dearly hope) identical with men, with our tastes and our values, our hopes and our fears.

It is natural that some among us, surveying the impasse into which we have gotten ourselves, might well be tempted to look up to the stars in the hope that someone wiser than we are might arrive one day from there and give us all the easy answers.

If there be any truth in the ancient story that the inhabitants of Magonia, unlike men, do not possess the possibility of developing immortal souls, and therefore are anxious to acquire such by mating with us and mingling their life-stream with ours, what moment could be more propitious to them for achieving their purpose than now?

Can't you just hear the message of their Captain?

- *"We are from Tau Ceti, and we come to bring you salvation and show you the way out of your problems. We will get you off the hook!"*

Vol. 29, No. 5 Flying Saucer Review

Types and Characteristics of the Jinn

"Verily we created man from dried clay, from black putrid mud. And we created the Jinn before that from fiery wind."

Surah al-Hijr 15:26-27

Hierarchies of the Jinn

Iblis: the father of all Jinn.

Shaitan: a Jinn who is malicious, vicious and wicked

'Ifrit: a Jinn who is stronger and more powerful than a **Shaitan 'Amir;** Resident Jinn who lives with people

The Different Types of Jinn:

* Those that fly
* Those that are stationed in one area or region on land
* Those that take the form of these animals:
* Snakes
* Scorpions
* Creeping animals
* Dogs

Stealing of information:

Fortunetellers rely on the information that they receive from Jinn.

Before the arrival of the Prophet Muhammad, the heavens were open, and the Jinn were able to eavesdrop on future information passed around by the angels and bring them back down to the Earth. In those days, the information was very correct.

At present however, the heavens are closely guarded by angels, and if a Jinn manages to sneak past the angels with information, the Jinn will then be pursued by a brightly burning flame and destroy them to ashes.

Surah Al-Hijr 15:17-18

"And we have guarded it (the heavens) from every cursed devil, except the one who is able to snatch a hearing, and he is pursued by a brightly burning flame."

So now, a Jinn can still manage to steal information, but mixed with it are a hundred lies.

Manifestation In Different Forms:

Jinn do take on forms and change shapes. They can take the form of snakes, scorpions, dogs, birds and other animals. Surprisingly, they can appear in human form too, but this case is extremely rare. Most human-like forms that we are familiar with or have heard of are in the shape of ghosts, spirits or apparitions.

There is a hadith where Abu Hurayrah, a companion of the Prophet (pbuh), encounters a shaitan in human form. (Sahih Al-Bukhari). From this encounter, it is also confirmed that by reciting Ayah Al-Kursi, the Shaitan is driven away.

Places of Residence:

The Jinn are everywhere, present at any place where human beings are present.

However, there are special places where one may find them in abundance and on a regular basis:

- Deserts
- Ruins
- Places of impurities, such as bathrooms
- Graveyards

Although many Jinn are inland, their main headquarters is the sea. The chief Shaitan gives orders to his soldiers to move to the land to advise people to do all types of crimes, immoralities, etc.

For those who enter their homes mentioning the name of Allah, the jinn cannot have a place to stay overnight in that house.

Partnership With Jinn Is Forbidden

After the revelation of the Qur'an, Allah demanded from all human beings that their guidance is totally from the Qur'an. Any reliance on the Jinn is considered a matter of Shirk (partnership with Allah). Those who seek help or friendship with the Jinn condemn themselves to hellfire. In many places in the world, it is common to see that some supposed 'alim person writes a Ta'weezah that calls upon the jinn for help. This is regarded as one of the biggest sins for it is shirk. As we are aware, Allah may forgive any person for his or her mistakes, but He will never forgive a person who commits shirk.

Protection From Shaitan (Satan)

There are many Ayat in the Qur'an and a good number of Ahadith as to how people can protect themselves from the evil traps and whisperings of Shaitan.

In Surah Fussilat, Allah instructs people to seek refuge in Him whenever Shaitan tries to trap them, and states the following:

"And if (at any time) an incitement to discord is made to you by the Shaitan, seek refuge in Allah. He is the One who hears and knows all things."

Qur'an 41:36

At birth, we are all assigned a Jinn companion, a Qareen.

To protect the child, the father is to read Adhan to the right ear and Iqamah to the left ear. He should protect the baby regularly with reading Ayat Al-Kursi and the Mu'awwazatain.

Exorcism:

When people become very weak of Iman and simply do not know how to protect themselves, there are cases when Shaitan may haunt their bodies. Those who become possessed by Shaitan must go through curative approaches. Cases are documented by Hadith, Seerah and Al-Qur'an.

The following are ways to drive out the Jinn:

- Demanding the Jinn to get out

- Cursing the Jinn to get out

- Beating the Possessed Person

Even the Jinn Can Repent Their Ways

Surah Al-Ahqaf (The Winding Sand Tracks) 46:29-32

Allah sent a group of Jinn to Prophet Muhammad to listen to his recitation of Qur'an. The Prophet did not see them and he did not know of their presence but was informed by Allah later about the incident. After listening to the beautiful recitation, the Jinn accepted his messaged and accepted Muhammad as a Prophet and as a messenger. Immediately they went to their tribes and families and affirmed their belief in Allah, His Messenger Muhammad, and the message that was revealed to them.

References:
Sakr, Ahmad, Al-Jinn (Illinois: Foundation for Islamic Knowledge, 1994).
Bilal Philips, Abu Ameenah, The Fundamentals of Tawheed (Riyadh: International Islamic Publishing House, 1994).

In the Valley of the Jinn

Philip Imbrogno doesn't dare question the existence of the Jinn. He's seen, heard and knows too much about these invisible, decidedly treacherous and utterly deceptive beings. The Genie in reality doesn't come out of a lamp or a bottle, and he's more likely to possess your soul in the name of demonic Jihad than grant you three wishes.

A comrade in UFO arms for many years, Imbrogno has traveled the desert regions of the Middle East firsthand and can see the fear in the locals' eyes when the subject of the Jinn is broached. This no nonsense, well seasoned paranormal investigator – who holds both a BS in Chemistry and a Ph.D. in Theoretical Chemistry/Particle Physics from MIT – was a tightly knit associate of the late Dr. J. Allen Hynek and co-author with the North Western University astronomer of **Night**

Siege – The Hudson Valley UFO Sightings. Imbrogno has been a science educator for 30 years, so certainly you wouldn't think of this type of guy as being on a cosmic quest of any sort, much less chasing down demonic forces. The only difference between Imbrogno and the stars of *Ghost Busters* is that his forays into the supernormal are not written by a Hollywood scribe, but are gleaned from the many emergency phone calls and letters he receives asking for what amounts to psychic support.

"There are quite a few UFO and paranormal investigators," Phil says, "who try to lump all cases into one explanation. Some say that all paranormal phenomena are caused by aliens, while others claim ghost and demonic forces are responsible. It is my belief that a trans-dimensional being best known in mythology is responsible for the manifestations of not all, but *most* paranormal phenomena, which would incorporate UFOs.

"In the western hemisphere we know the Jinn as the Genie, a heavily fictionalized character, but most people know nothing or very little about the actual ancient race of beings. A great deal of information concerning the Jinn or Djinn comes to us from the Muslim-Islamic and ancient Persian beliefs. The word Jinn is Islamic and actually means 'hidden.' This word describes these dimensional beings perfectly since Jinn are said to be invisible to humans and can be seen only if they allow themselves. To a person who lived two thousand years ago, this might mean that they are invisible, but to us in the 21st century it indicates they exist in another dimension, a plane of physical space that we humans cannot so easily perceive."

One of my all time favorite writers, Phil was a frequent contributor to *UFO Universe*, a nationally distributed newsstand publication I edited over a period of a dozen years before the bottom fell out for independent publishers. Phil covered a far reaching number of topics. He started out fairly conservative, but then got into some virgin territory. If you get a chance, Google his name and audio interviews. I love listening to the conversations he has with talk show hosts like Coast To Coast's George Noory and Gene Steinberg, host of The Paracast. You can tell he's blowing their minds with his tales of the unexplained, which come from a

A fiery version of the Jinn looms tall and menacing.

man of impeccable credentials and academic letters.

As this is being put into print, Imbrogno's publisher Llewellyn is releasing a book co-authored by the queen of the paranormal, Rosemary Ellen Guiley: *The Vengeful Djinn*. Phil says, "We will unmask the Jinn to the American public for the first time." It certainly is one of the few mainstream titles to delve into this esoteric subject matter in more than a few dozen pages, and in that it presents an unprecedented body of work.

"According to ancient Islamic stories," Phil explains to us, "the race of Jinn has free will and many of them, when compared to human beings, have great power. Some have the ability to transverse the barriers between dimensions. Their bodies are not solid and ridged like ours, but more fluid in nature. According to the Noble Qur'an, humans were made of clay and the Jinn were made from the purest of smokeless fire. In modern science, this could only mean one thing: they are made of plasma, the fourth state of matter. Jinn can appear human, but they can also take the form of a strange alien-looking being, animal or even a demonic monster. They are the shape shifters that are found in the mythology of many cultures.

Half Human, Half Reptilian

Thought to be a fable more than a fact, this may nonetheless be a real photo of a Jinn emerging from its hiding place inside a lamp.

"We are told that a Jinn in its favorite physical form appears half human and half reptile. This is an interesting fact since many modern close encounters with aliens describe beings that are reptilian or serpent-like in appearance." Phil certainly seems to be onto something here, given the number of extreme reports we get of people encountering reptilian-like creatures – some that come out of the darkness of the UFOs themselves, others materializing in bedrooms and having "nonconsensual sex," resembling the tactics the Jinn fancy using.

One of the few researchers to have established a link between the Jinn and the infiltration of UFOs and their occupants, Phil lays out his findings carefully.

According to our resident expert, "Originally, they were considered to be spirits of nature who often played tricks on susceptible humans. The Islamic belief is that the Jinn can be agents of good or evil, with the evil Djinn enjoying punishing humans because they feel that God placed humankind in a better position. In ancient times, according to the legends of many Middle Eastern countries, accidents, disease and untimely deaths were thought to be the result of a wrathful Jinn."

Not satisfied being simply an armchair strategist, Phil Imbrogno has put a few notches on his nomadic traveling belt, venturing into Jinn territory as far back as the mid-1990s and attempting to facilitate tracking down the various legends of the Jinn. "I heard so many stories and gathered a great deal of information about this ancient race of beings that it made me consider the reality of their existence. To the Muslim people there is no question whether or not the Jinn are real. To these people the Jinn are as real as your next door neighbor."

Not one to be an unprovoked conspiracy theorist, Phil was determined to become one of the boots on the ground. "My pursuit of the Jinn took me from Saudi to the small nearby country of Oman. It was in this country that I learned of a possible attempt by the international governments of various countries to capture one or more Jinn as it passed from their reality to ours. The purpose was to obtain technology that they believed allowed them to cross the dimensional barrier between our world and theirs. "

Phil says his explorations took him to the Hagar Mountains, to a place called Majis Al Jinn, a cave so large that the great Pyramid in Egypt would fit comfortably inside. "It was here at this locale that the Djinn were believed to be able to enter our reality. The experiences I had at this portal convinced me that the Jinn are much more than just a fable. They are, indeed, an ancient race of beings that existed in the same spatial area of time and space before the human race. What I and my guides witnessed that day still haunts me today. It surely changed the way I look at the world of the paranormal."

By Timothy Beckley

❂ ❂ ❂

In the following section, *Alternative Perceptions* editor Brent Raynes gets down to the nitty gritty with Phil and together they play hard ball with the Jinn

Publishers Note: There are various ways of spelling Jinn. Phil's favorite is Djinn, but in order to keep with continuity throughout the book we have taken the liberty of dropping the letter D.

A Jinn Reality Check with Phil Imbrogno

By Brent Raynes, Editor, Alternative Perceptions Magazine

Back in 2007, New York's noted UFO researcher and author Phil Imbrogno told me in a phone interview, "There are many people who are involved with paranormal research, but you don't really understand its reality until you experience something yourself, and then it becomes more of a reality than a hobby. You have people who are investigating UFOs who are looking for spaceships and so on, which is okay, but you see a lot of these people are doing it as a hobby or something to fascinate them or entertain their bored life, but what they don't realize is that a lot of this stuff is real and I know many people, people who I have worked with and have been part of my investigation team, who have totally given up all of this because once they realized that this is a reality it scared them to death and they got out of it. It was no longer like watching TV. It was something that was in their life. It was real. 'My God, this isn't just something I read about.' People say, 'This is real!'"

Phil knows full well just how real it is. He has personally seen the shattering and profound psychological effects upon a good number of eyewitnesses, as well as fellow investigators. In his book **Interdimensional Universe** (2008), Phil described a truly frightening and life-altering case that he and a number of his colleagues came to investigate a number of years ago. It may well be one of the most terrifying UFO-related cases you have ever read. It all began with a phone call back in February 1978 from a single 35-year-old mother. She stated that she, her mother, and her daughter had been having numerous experiences with UFOs and alien beings, and that the beings would actually walk into their home through a rotating "black hole" and lead them into the "hole," at which time they would lapse into a state of memory loss and not be able to remember any further details. She explained that her mother claimed that she had been having these experiences herself since age nine.

Phil called together his crack team of experienced UFO investigators, a team that

In the Islamic religion the great Shaitan does its best to rule over the world.

consisted of a very professional and credible group of men. Phil had just gotten his degree in astronomy from the University of Texas, one man was a biologist, another was a police officer, another was an engineer, plus another was a corporate executive, and then there was a commercial airline pilot too.

The team gathered at the woman's home in Cold Springs, New York, on the evening of February 16, 1978. During that initial interview, the lady described numerous encounters with globes of light that would often follow her car, and even enter their home. She recalled one incident where a blue globe of light entered the house through the living room window, at which time the television and house lights went out, coming back on when the mysterious light disappeared up through the ceiling. Then, within a short time after that, her daughter, then ten, pointed to a window and said, "UFO out there." Sure enough, a yellow ball of light, about six inches in diameter, was moving across the front lawn. Phil went outside and came within about 20 feet of it, noticing a tingling sensation going up and down his neck, as if, he explained, he were in a field of static electricity. The light had been about ten feet off the ground, moving with a kind of wobbling motion, then hovered as if observing Phil, and then shot straight up into the night sky.

Needless to say, the team was quite excited at this point. The case looked very promising. Arrangements were quickly made to bring in a psychologist to conduct a regression hypnosis session on March 15th. The therapist was someone who Phil had worked with several times before and who insisted that only one member of the team should be present during the hypnotic regression. Phil was that person. He tape recorded the session, as well as made written notes. The daughter had been ill with the flu, and so was in her bedroom asleep while this session was going on. They had arrived early afternoon, around 2 pm. It took about half an hour for the mother to relax and go "under," but once she did she began recalling an episode from 1976 when she awakened around midnight to hear a strange buzzing sound that seemed to vibrate through the house. She got out of bed to investigate and found her daughter walking around in circles in the living room, saying that "The people from the hole are here."

She shook her daughter by the shoulders, as she seemed entranced, and this brought her out of it. Then she went outside, she stated, and saw a strange red illumination in the sky. Then she was remembering an incident at age five, when she awoke early one morning to discover three leather-skinned beings standing over her bed. Smiling, they told the child that they would not hurt her, that they needed people like her in their work. Then she noticed a

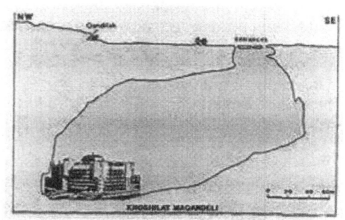

Supposed home to demonic forces, the Cave of the Jinn is so vast that it would be possible to hide the Great Pyramid inside one of its tunnel systems. Phil Imbrogno visited here to see for himself.

spinning black hole nearby into which the three beings were "sucked," producing a sound similar to when something large gets clogged in a vacuum cleaner.

The mother began breathing heavily and the doctor had to calm her down before proceeding. Then she recalled another incident, this one from a night in the winter of 1977, when she awakened somewhere between two and three am and saw a tall hooded figure in a robe standing at the foot of her bed.

Face Behind the Mask

As she watched, he removed the hood, and she gasped as he looked rather like the devil, with long ears, a pointed nose, and skin like leather. He wanted her to come with him and she yelled back at him, "No way! Get out of here!" She then prayed for God and the angels to protect her and her daughter, who was sleeping next to her in the same bed. The evil-looking being appeared angry and told her that God had "no power here" and that he would return for her when he was ready. The being then vanished into a swirling black hole.

Pretty soon the doctor decided it was best to bring the mother out of her hypnotic trance. Her pulse was 130, she was breathing rapidly, and sweat was pouring down over her face. Immediately upon coming to, she got to her feet and ran to her daughter's bedroom. Before she reached her daughter's room, the girl came running out into the hallway and met her mom, and while clinging to her told her mother that the "man from the hole" had appeared and said he was going to take her. At first the mother told her frightened young daughter that it was just a dream, but then asked her what else the "man" might have said. Pointing directly at Phil, she said, "The man said that he would get him and his friends if they don't leave us alone." Phil wrote that this scene sent genuine shivers up and down his spine. This was only the first, I am sure, of many such shivers that were later to come.

Screams and Sirens

The next day, Phil met with his team to go over the details of the hypnotic investigation and to play for them the tape recording. They met at his home and he initially went over his notes. Then he rewound the tape, explaining that he himself hadn't listened to it yet either. Everything appeared at first to be normal. You could hear the psychologist giving suggestions to the woman for relaxation, but then once she finally began describing her experiences her voice and that of the doctor faded into the background while high-pitched siren type sounds appeared on the tape, along with what sounded like howling and screaming noises, some sounds sounding like animals and others possibly human. As they listened in shock, a very audible voice then came on and in perfect English stated: "Stop playing with my head. They pointed you out to us and we know where and how to get you all." Now they were all very shaken.

Phil took the tape to a friend who did audio recordings for the State University of New York, and he determined that what had sounded to Phil and the others like a foreign language on the tape was English in reverse. He explained that he felt someone was playing a trick on them. Phil assured him that the tape was brand new and had never been out of his custody, except for a very brief time when he walked down the hallway, but he was still only an estimated ten feet from the recorder. Though not all of the reverse speech message could be heard due to the

Dr. Philip Imbrogno has been a science educator for over 25 years and believes the Jinn are deeply entrenched with the UFO mystery.

howling and electrical like noises, a portion of it was very audible. The voice claimed to be something like "Ablis," from some place "parallel" with our world. He claimed that, sometime before our recorded history, his race used to live on the surface of our planet as we do, but that due to "experiments that went wrong" they were "shifted" into another "dimension." Their mission was, the voice claimed, to re-enter our world through "portals," and that to achieve this they needed humans with a "sensitive spirit." Phil would later wonder if that meant people with psychic sensitivity.

Though Phil began to work on the premise that some ham radio operator could have produced this strange recording effect (something that he never did actually prove did happen, though he certainly tried to figure out how it could have been done), pretty soon his group of fellow investigators began to seem disinterested and distant. He realized something strange was going on. For a whole week, he hadn't heard from any of his fellow team members. Then he got a call from the biologist who described hearing voices, like someone talking right into his ear, but he could see no one. Phil had never encountered anything like this and didn't know how to respond. The next day he called and said that the voices were coming from extraterrestrial beings, and that three of them had appeared to him in his bedroom at 3 am. They were dark blue, 4-5 feet tall, and had red eyes, he stated. Phil tried unsuccessfully to call him back again, after not hearing from him for several days. A week later, he learned that the biologist had leaped in front of a train. Police soon ruled it a suicide.

The definitive book on the subject, *Vengeful Djinn* is co-authored by Phil Imbrogno and Rosemary Ellen Guiley "queen" of the paranormal.

Soon after this, the pilot called Phil and told him of a visit he had received from a man in a dark suit who claimed to be an agent of the National Security Agency and who claimed that if he didn't want to lose his commercial pilot's license then he had better discontinue his UFO investigations. Phil never heard back from him again!

Phil decided to call the other members of the team and see what was happening with them. He managed to reach the corporate executive who described to Phil a disturbing "dream" that he had had in which he thought he had awakened in the middle of the night to see a tall robed being with a hood, surrounded by a pale-green glow. In fear he sat up in bed and the being then held out in its hand a glowing red beating heart. Explaining that this could be his heart, it then squeezed the heart and burst it, and the man saw blood spurt onto the walls and the bed. Then he woke up in a cold sweat, at which time he determined that it was just a dream. Soon afterwards this man went to the doctor for a routine physical, at which time it was discovered that something was wrong with a valve in his heart. He was told that the condition was an easy one to fix and the doctors had expected a full recovery, but three days after his surgery he died from heart failure and, Phil notes, the doctors never gave the man's wife a satisfactory explanation as to what had gone wrong.

The police officer and his wife had a series of sightings that frightened them both, and so he dropped out of the UFO field. The engineer continued to conduct UFO work, but kept mostly to himself. He would claim that he had a number of very close UFO encounters, had poltergeist manifestations in his home, and eventually told Phil that he thought that his 12-year-old son was being possession by a "demon" of some kind. This really surprised Phil, as the engineer had formerly been an atheist. He later became a Christian. Phil's last conversation with the man was around 1979 or 1980. In 1981, a friend showed Phil a newspaper story in which this man had been arrested for burning UFO books in Hartford, Connecticut, on the lawn of the university there.

Phil today remains the only one from that original "Dream Team," as they called themselves, who continues with his UFO investigative work. At the time he wrote this book, he added that he had only "recently" begun to look back at many of his past UFO cases and realized that a good number of them had been "most likely Jinn encounters." The Jinn are mysterious inter-dimensional beings described in Muslim religious literature.

The Order of Creation

Renee Fleury and Phil Imbrogno stand before New England's Balanced Rock. Dr Imbrogno has determined that strange and peculiar anomalies are often associated with such structures, including weird lights and sounds.

Dr. Greg Little wrote of the Jinn in his 1990 classic, *People of the Web.* "The Jinn supposedly have a group identity, much like a bee colony," he wrote. "Note that Whitley Strieber's *Communion* relates that he likened his alien abductors to insects with a group consciousness."

So who or what are the Jinn, and can they really be related to UFO cases? "These creatures, the Jinn of the Muslim religion and the elementals in the Buddhist faith, they reportedly can materialize and dematerialize, and so can our Western culture's abducting creatures," California UFOlogist Ann Druffel explained to me. "They shape shift in various forms, and they delight in harassing and traumatizing human beings. They reportedly abduct human beings and transport them long distances in a matter of seconds. And the Jinn, the elementals, and our own abducting grays [have taken] a sexual interest in human beings down through the millennia. In every major culture of the world, and in many minor cultures, they all have these same folkloric stories, and even religious and philosophical texts in some of the countries talk about this 'third order of creation,' as the Muslims call it. They aren't angels, they aren't devils, they aren't human beings. They're something in between who share our world with us in a hidden state."

Just before posting this article, I contacted Philip Imbrogno to see if he wanted to add any remarks or observations to what I had written. He emailed me the following: "I am currently doing a book on the Djinn which has been contracted by Llewellyn. I am hoping that it will inform not only UFO investigators, but people who research all aspects of the paranormal. When we include the Djinn in the equation, much of the confusing world of the paranormal makes more sense. One must remember they are an ancient race that have existed before human beings and are often called 'God's other people' in the Muslim world. One must not look at them from a religious sense. We must see them for what they are: a race of inter-dimensional beings."

Djinn is another variation on the spelling of Jinn, which represents the same being.

Though many of us in our Western culture are unfamiliar with the Djinn, in the Muslim world they are very widely known and the reality of these beings is taken, it certainly seems, without question. Again referring to Dr. Little's book, Phil Imbrogno concluded: "Followers of Islam tend to take their religion and their holy book, the *Koran*, seriously. They believe in the literal, physical existence of the Jinn. Even Islamic scientists take the Jinn seriously."

Undeniable the best monthly newsletter on the paranormal available on the internet readers can get a complementary subscription to *Alternative Perceptions Magazine* at www.mysterious-america.net

Is There A Cosmic Battle Underway?

By Sean Casteel

If those who accept a belief in the darker elements of UFOlogy are correct and Luciferian forces are behind most of what can be classified as unexplained aerial phenomenon, what could be the ultimate result of a hostile alien demonic presence? Where could this prophesied state of spiritual conflict finally lead us? The Book of Revelation, Chapter 12, Verses 7 and 8, has this to say on the subject:

"Now war rose in heaven, Michael and his angels fighting against the dragon; and the dragon and his angels fought, but they were defeated and there was no longer any place for them in heaven."

What Saint John called a war in heaven has seemingly been observed repeatedly in the skies of Planet Earth for millennia, as can be seen by a careful examination of historical documents. But first, let's talk a little about the aliens of the present day as hostile in their own right.

Several years ago I conducted an interview with researcher and author

Michael Brownlee for Tim Beckley's widely accredited "The Conspiracy Journal." Brownlee talked at length about why, in his opinion, the alien race behind the UFOs and the alien abduction phenomenon could not be viewed as anything less than evil. One weapon the aliens use on us mortals, he maintains, is the time-honored ploy of making us feel guilty.

"The really stark thing that comes through," Brownlee told me, "is the statement that humans are the real problem in the universe. That's an outrageous statement. It is based upon a species-wide guilt, if you will. It's like, 'Oh, man, we're really bad. We're really screwed up.' That's exactly where we're most vulnerable. 'You need us to come and straighten things out.' From a psychological perspective, that is the basis of a codependent relationship. That's exactly what they're trying to create. They want us dependent on them. They want us controlled."

The aliens offer solutions to mankind's problems, Brownlee said, as a kind of Trojan Horse in order to get their foot in our door so they can lead us to a totalitarian form of government.

"The message of fascism," he went on, "is always, 'This will solve all problems.' What we're looking at are the signs of a fascist takeover that, if it is not exposed and resisted, will wind up being not just a fascist state, but a fascist world."

The aliens will not simply land and run the world, but will instead work through intermediary human/alien hybrid creatures who will look like humans but be very, very powerful, particularly in terms of the mental plane of existence.

"In the mental realm," Brownlee said, "they are very effective and we are unfortunately very naïve. So one of the ways this plays out is in one of the key areas of alien activity – the manipulation of our religious and spiritual beliefs. They are very aware that we are naïve, and they are able to easily manipulate people who are particularly prone to fanatical beliefs, fundamentalism, in all of its varieties around the world. They can be very influential."

Is A Star Wars Defense System Already In Place To Combat A Hostile Alien Invasion?

Brownlee believes that this negative alien influence operates behind the scenes in world affairs and is even responsible for the Islamic fundamentalism that led to the September 11, 2001, terrorist attacks. The movement continues to escalate and may eventually lead the governments of the world to global warfare. He also referred to over-flights by UFOs of our nuclear installations and to incidents where the aliens managed to shut down our missiles at will.

"There is no way," Brownlee asserted, "that that could not be interpreted as a blatantly hostile act. If we did anything like that to any other country, what would happen? It would be instant cause for war, right?"

Having seen our military rendered essentially powerless, how do we respond?

"I know of people," Brownlee said, "who are involved in space defense projects who are very consciously aware that what they're doing is developing systems to defend against extraterrestrials. It's happening. It's not just pie-in-the-sky or a rumor; it's actually happening. There are very good indications that the whole Star Wars missile defense effort has very little to do with terrorism and rogue states on this planet. I think it's much more likely that those systems are early attempts to design systems to build a shield against extraterrestrial incursion.

"We talk about this dark conspiracy, of the wealthy and so on. It's not difficult to imagine that those people in positions of power are either knowingly or unknowingly co-opted by the extraterrestrials. Yeah, there's a conspiracy all right, but it's much larger than our conspiracy theorists have been talking about. We've been talking about human conspiracies. Well, all human conspiracies are being manipulated by the extraterrestrials, essentially."

Rebellious Angels

What Brownlee calls "fascistic aliens" many Christians instead call demons. On a website called "UFOs and the Bible," David Flynn argues that UFOs are the modern manifestation of rebellious angels from ancient times, a theme that we have repeatedly been confronted with.

"Among these myriads of angels," Flynn writes, "are those who follow their own rebellious plan instead of God's. Those rebel angels – who appear in many guises, from ghosts to aliens to 'Blessed Virgin Mary' apparitions – are the intelligent, nonhuman beings behind UFOs and the paranormal. 'They' have a plan, and their message is a deceptive one."

Flynn quotes one G.H. Pember, who in his 1876 book "Earth's Earliest Ages and Their Connection with Modern Spiritualism and Theosophy," said, "The occultist is brought into intelligent communication with the spirits of the air, and can receive any knowledge which they possess, or any false impression they choose to impart. The demons seem permitted to do various wonders at their request."

Also, Dr. Pierre Guerin, in an issue of "Flying Saucer Review," declared that "UFO behavior is more akin to magic than to physics as we know it. The modern UFO-nauts and the demons of past days are probably identical."

Having bolstered his argument with the above quotes, Flynn introduces the idea that Satan is the entity called "The Prince of the Power of the Air" in the New Testament and is designated as being able to fly anywhere at will.

"Imagine the confederation of rebellious angels," Flynn writes, "seated in the atmospheric heaven in the spaces above and around our planet. This fundamental scripture contradicts many traditional concepts of 'hell' as the domain of the devil and his minions. The popular notion of 'Satan ruling the underworld' is not found in the Bible."

An interesting point is being made here. The Devil and his demons don't dwell in some fire-drenched place in the bowels of the Earth but instead reside somehow in the skies around Earth, poised and ready to do battle with God and the human remnant God has saved.

John Keel and the True Nature of the Aliens

The late John Keel is often quoted in this context of aliens and their similarities to demons, from his book "Operation Trojan Horse." Flynn also makes use of Keel's theories.

"Throughout most of history," Keel wrote, "the manifestations of demonology and demonopathy have been viewed from a religious perspective and explained as the work of the Devil. The bizarre manipulation and ill effects described in the demonological literature are usually regarded as the results of a great unseen conflict between God and the Devil. In UFO lore, the same conflict has been observed, and the believers have explained it as a space war between the 'Guardians' (good guys from outer space), who are protecting our planet, and some evil extraterrestrial race. The manifestations are the same, only the reference is different.

"Did ancient man misinterpret UFO manifestations by placing them in a religious context? Apparently not. The literature indicates that the phenomenon carefully cultivated the religious frame of reference in early times, just as the modern manifestations have carefully supported the extraterrestrial frame of reference. Operation Trojan Horse is merely the same old game in a new, updated guise. The Devil's emissaries of yesteryear have been replaced by mysterious 'men in black.' The quasi-angels of Biblical times have become magnificent spacemen. The demons, devils and false angels were recognized as liars and plunderers by early man. The same imposters now appear as long-haired Venusians."

Flynn next adds his own take to the discussion.

"Rebel angels," he writes, "can take on any form they please, even appearing as angels of light. The deceptive rebel angels often appear to humans in seemingly benign guises: as the enlightening angel to Mohammed, as the angel Moroni to Joseph Smith, in disguise as the Virgin Mary in apparitions, and disguised as Enlightening Alien Space Brothers. 'Aliens' are really disembodied angels – the rebellious angels who according to Jude left their God-given habitation to dwell in genetically manipulated hybrid bodies just prior to the Flood."

Which is a genuinely frightening idea. How could we know if we are in the company of such a human-looking alien hybrid? It is even more frightening to contemplate the notion that this hybrid creature could be just a mere outer shell for a demonic entity who truly seeks our harm.

More Chapter and Verse
On Heavenly Warfare

Christian writer Terry James maintains a website called "Rapture Ready" that deals with End Time prophecies as well as the present day UFO phenomenon. In an online article called "UFOs and the Real War of the Worlds" he presents his case for a demonic UFO presence as outlined in specific passages of scripture.

"Satan, according to Bible prophecy," James writes, "plans spectacular displays of fireworks and other supernatural pyrotechnics for the tribulation, the last seven years before Christ's advent. Those phenomena will, again, according to God's Word, take place in the atmosphere above Earth and in space. We are given that forewarning in the following Scripture:

'And he doeth great wonders, so that he maketh fire come down from heaven on the Earth in the sight of men, And deceiveth them that dwell on the Earth by the means of those miracles which he had the power to do.' (Revelation 13:13-14).

"Jesus made it clear that the phenomena that will come at the End of Days will be fearsome to behold:

'And there shall be signs in the sun, and in the moon, and in the stars; and upon the Earth distress of nations, with perplexity; the sea and the waves roaring; men's hearts failing them for fear, and for looking after those things which are coming on the Earth: for the powers of Heaven shall be shaken.'"

After establishing that scriptural basis, James moves on to say, "There is coming a second great war in the heavenlies, and it will make H.G. Welles' 'War of the Worlds' fiction look tame by comparison. The resulting devastation and carnage will literally cause the hearts of earth-dwellers of the tribulation era to explode with adrenalin-pumped fear."

According to James' interpretation, the war in heaven prophesied in Revelation 12 and (quoted at the beginning of this chapter) has already happened, forcing Satan and his minions to be cast down to the Earth. James is now talking about a second war in heaven, which has yet to occur but is nonetheless an inevitable event that will torment those left on the Earth during the tribulation period.

"God has placed so much in His Word," James continues, "to warn about this adversary and his legions, the devil and his minions, that the evil has been in all the cosmos since that first Great War in heaven and must saturate every aspect of existence.

The war of the worlds has never come to an armistice since Satan first rebelled. The war is heating up, as anyone with spiritual discernment from the Bible's perspective can understand. The physical plane is beginning to reflect that loathing for all of God's creation while the Devil turns up the heat. We are seeing this begin to manifest itself, I believe, in the great increase in sightings of the UFOs, and strange goings-on in matters assigned to by those who don't know the truth, to stigmata, ghostly hauntings, or other phenomena intruding into our dimension of existence."

Is This All For Real?

Terry James fervently believes that this war in heaven is a reality, not just a fictional mishmash of bold heroic characters fighting the Dark Side, as in the "Star Wars" movie franchise.

"It is real warfare," James writes, "and more horrific than any warfare the people of Earth have ever endured. Jesus said: 'For then shall be great tribulation, such as was not since the beginning of the world to this time, no, nor ever shall be. And except those days should be shortened, there should no flesh be saved. But for the elect's sake those days shall be shortened.'"

But in the meantime, according to James, "Satan is obviously ratcheting up his invasion plans. First, he is stirring the ethnic and religious strife among peoples of most every part of the planet. Second, he is manipulating the Babylonian system of government and economy, moving it toward one world. Third, and this is the assault that is about to begin in earnest, he is setting up the 'strong delusion' of 2nd Thessalonians 2:8-13.

I believe that the planet is seeing and will soon experience much greater manifestations of supernatural interventions into the affairs of mortal men. The two spiritual worlds are about to collide in a mighty explosion of End-of-Days decimation."

The Skies Over Nuremberg

Stepping away from Biblical interpretation, it is important to mention an aerial battle that occurred in Nuremberg, Germany, centuries ago, long before mankind had invented any form of air travel that could have been mistaken for what was actually seen. A website called "Extraterrestrial Contact" offers several differing versions of the story, but basically it goes like this:

"At sunrise on the 14th of April, 1561, the citizens of Nuremberg beheld 'a very frightful spectacle.' The sky appeared to fill with cylindrical objects from which red, black, orange and blue white discs and globes emerged. Crosses and tubes resembling cannon barrels also appeared, whereupon the objects promptly 'began to fight one another.' After about an hour of battle, the objects seemed to catch fire and fell to Earth, where they turned to steam. The witnesses took this display as a divine warning. This report is unique in the annals of UFOlogy, in that it has never been repeated. There is no record of such 'objects' in either local or German national folklore. The surviving town records from the period give no indication of any unrest either civil or external. Given the uniqueness of the incident, it appears that something supernatural or paranormal took place."

The site offers another take on the Nuremberg incident.

"What was described could only be called a war in the heavens, with a wide variety of craft ranging from spheres to spear-like cylinders to crosses. The sky was apparently filled with the machines, clashing in battle. Comets and such were well-identified and charted in this period, so it is highly unlikely that what the people witnessed was merely a celestial phenomenon like a meteor shower, as some debunkers suggest.

"Rather, what is described are physical objects of unique details and shapes, in battle for over an hour. The battle was such that a winner was perceived as well. Spheroid UFOs were seen emerging from cylindrical 'mother-ships.' At the conclusion of the battle, it seems a magnificent, black, spear-like super-ship of some kind came upon the scene."

The black, spear-like ship was apparently displaying itself as a sign of victory for its side, or perhaps was there to do some kind of "mopping up" duty. A broadsheet, an archaic kind of newspaper, was written shortly afterward that warned, "The God-fearing will by no means discard these signs, but will take it to heart as a warning of their merciful annunciation with St. Emidus, Father in heaven, and will mend their lives and faithfully beg God that he avert his wrath, including the well-deserved punishment on us so that we may, temporarily here and perpetually there, live as His children."

The broadsheet describing the Nuremberg "war in heaven" is now held in the Wickiana Collection in Switzerland's Zurich Central Library. A woodcut was also made at the time by 16th century artist Hans Glaser.

The Lord and His Weapons

There is yet another passage in the Bible that may be meaningful to our study which I wrote about it in an earlier book, "UFOs, Prophecy and the End of Time." The verses come from Isaiah 13, starting with verse four: "Hark, a tumult on the mountains as of a great multitude. Hark, an uproar of kingdoms, of nations gathering together! The Lord of Hosts is mustering a host for battle.

"They come from a distant land, from the end of the heavens, the Lord and the weapons of his indignation, to destroy the whole Earth.

"Wail, for the day of the Lord is near; as destruction from the Almighty it will come! Therefore all hands will be feeble, and every man's heart will melt, and they will be dismayed. Pangs and agony will seize them; they will be in anguish like a woman in travail.

"They will look aghast at one another; their faces will be aflame. Behold, the day of the Lord comes, cruel, with wrath and fierce anger, to make the Earth a desolation and to destroy its sinners from it."

What is interesting about the passage is its use of the phrase "The Lord and the weapons of his indignation," in which God is portrayed as gathering together a heavenly arsenal, weapons that have some reality in the real and physical world.

If you accept the basic argument that Tom Horn makes, that both God and the Devil travel in what are called in the Hebrew "merkavim," or "celestial chariots," then this passage from Isaiah appears to be a declaration of heavenly warfare. Note that the armies of God come "from a distant land, from the end of the heavens," which again implies supernatural conflict, not mere mortals battling it out against each other.

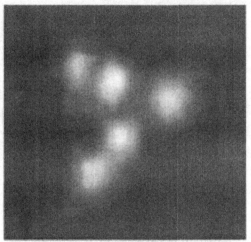

A still from a video taken in Dublin, Ireland of a strange triangle is eerily similar to craft seen through nightvision equipment in other parts of the world.

Without being overly "faith-driven" in our contemplation of the verses, the passage nevertheless portrays the Lord as apparently saying that his purpose is to destroy the sinners from the face of the Earth, which may be a variation on the prophecies of Armageddon from the Book of Revelation. In that final battle, Jesus will appear in the skies over Israel and take up arms against the Antichrist and his demonic armies in a final conflict fought presumably in the material world. That will clearly be an instance of the Lord's use of his own military hardware to scour the Earth clean of rebellious sinners, be they human or some class of fallen satanic warriors fighting to retain their stranglehold on the people of the Earth.

Can Technology Help Us See The War In Heaven?

"I couldn't help but - when you stop to think that we're all God's children, wherever we live in the world, I couldn't help but say to him (Gorbachev) just how easy his task and mine might be if suddenly there was a threat to this world from some other species from another planet outside in the universe. We'd forget all the little local differences that we have between our countries and we would find out once and for all that we really are all human beings here on this Earth together. Well, I guess we can wait for some alien race to come down and threaten us, but I think that between us we can bring about that realization."

President Ronald Regan

My editor and publisher Tim Beckley offers some valuable input regarding the question of whether utilizing the latest night vision apparatuses can enable us to see things in the heavens which would normally be invisible to the human eye. Beckley began by discussing the variety of video footage taken from the space station and released by NASA which appears to show an actual aerial battle taking place in outer space.

"In some of this footage, which is readily available on *You Tube* and places like *Disclosure TV*, you can readily see what appear to be UFOs," he explained, "mysterious unidentified objects of one sort or another, that are traversing the sky or cosmos in the darkness of space. And apparently someone – or something – is shooting at these objects as they crisscross about in full view of our astronauts. As they are being fired upon with some kind of laser weapon the objects actually reverse their flight pattern across the screen and head in the opposite direction, as if they are averting the firing that's going on between opposition forces."

Beckley concludes that there has to be another fact being hidden from the public that goes right along with the assumption that there is a space battle being conducted.

"NASA – or some unofficial bureau in the government – must have established a secret space program with super-duper Tesla-like weapons – or reverse alien technology -- that they have not told the public about. It could well be that they are actually trying to conceal this fact either for security reasons or because they have usurped the U.S. Constitution along the way and are now operating as a rogue agency so as to combat these negative UFO forces that could be coming into the atmosphere and which may be demonic in origin if one is to believe the Book of Revelation and the beliefs of those that classify themselves as Christian UFOlogists."

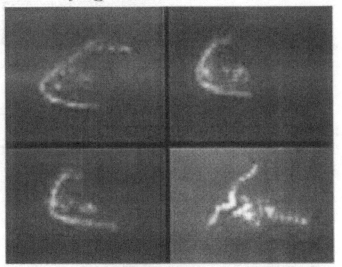

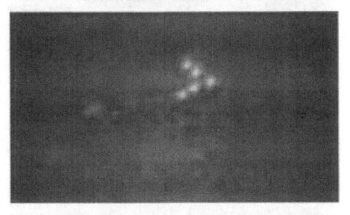

Someone hoping to document UFOs, earth lights, ghostly manifestations, and similar anomalies, needs the highest level of fine detail. Even if you search far and wide, we feel you will not find better prices than ours for truly fine quality products. We are professional paranormal investigators, with a Lab in the tallest mountains east of the Mississippi, with clear skies. Our goal is to deliver you a high-quality product that will help you push forth scientific study at a price you can afford. Our staff - Joshua P. Warren and L.E.M.U.R. have been featured on the Discovery Channel, History Channel, Travel Channel, TLC, National Geographic, Sci-Fi Channel, Animal Planet, Fine Living Network, Coast to Coast AM, Fox News and CNN.

There is, notes Beckley, a currently available form of technology that the public might not be aware of that seemingly enables anyone to visually watch and record these random battles in space.

According to Beckley, "There are now sites on the internet where readers can actually pull up and glimpse stills and videos which have been taken utilizing a variety of night vision equipment. These visuals definitely do seem to show full scale combat maneuvers. Californian Ed Grimsley, who says he has been watching these aerial battles since he was a teen, is generally credited with adapting the first night vision goggles (using infrared PV7 Military Spec Binoculars) to observe UFOs at night. And while he has his critics, who say there is a doubtful credibility factor in his reporting, he does have any number of supporters who believe his equipment really does the trick. Included among those who have been with Grimsley and looked through the Ed's binoculars is Coast to Coast's celebrated host George Noory, who has said on the air that he was 'mesmerized' by the two UFOs he watched do its acrobatics over San Jose during a skywatch.

"Gail is another witness to the nighttime phenomenon," Beckley continued. "She says at first some people are not able to see anything unusual because they haven't yet learned how to use the equipment properly. That you have to hold the binoculars fairly steady and not move around too much."

"If you just wait a bit they will soon be in your field of view," the woman identified only as Gail told Beckley. "The area around Calistoga, California, was a real hot spot – meaning we saw a lot of craft that night and they appeared to be on patrol. The ships were in different sizes, S.M.L., and there were some shaped, well, like a racing bicycle helmet: round in front and narrow in the back. There were some of what I call 'zippers' because they appeared to zip and zoom by real fast as if to check the other ships out and then zoom off. I also saw a UFO flying in a zigzag and another started to wobble like it had been damaged. Ed said to keep watching because it was probably engaged in a battle and would turn on its distress beacon. And it did! It pulsed and wobbled into deep space until we could no longer see it. The UFOs would also park side by side. I saw two sets of two do this. These were not street lights and yes I did see one that was very bright and could be seen without any night vision and it stayed much like a star, right where it was, or moved very, very slowly compared to the UFOs. I also saw planes and they of course flew a lot lower and never once did the planes park side by side or sit still – LOL. This may be too much for you all to handle but it is the truth, people, on the life of my three sons I swear. . ."

Beckley says he has spoken to others who have also adapted night vision equipment as part of their standard skywatching gear.

"Joshua P. Warren and his associate Para Mobius are very knowledgeable about the apparatus. Mobius, in fact, has his own Paranormal Investigation and Research sales and rental company and is Associate Producer of 'Speaking of Strange,' a weekly show broadcast over WWNC, Nashville, NC from nine till midnight every Saturday evening. The show is hosted by Joshua and has six years of free archives at www.wwnc.com. Josh, with Mobius' assistance, covers the strange and more off-color sides of the news as well as metaphysics and UFOs." (And colorful it is, Beckley remarked, acknowledging having been on the show several times, speaking about everything from werewolves to the Men in Black.)

Though he has not up till this time had the opportunity to use the night vision equipment, Tim says he is fascinated with the evidence he has been presented with.

"You can see several shapes of craft and they seem to be diving and making all sorts of twists and turns. There does seem to be intelligence behind the vessels and there is a battle or confrontation taking place right there in the skies above but which is invisible most of the time.

"In fact," Beckley continued, "during the much publicized UFO sighting over the Chelsea area of Manhattan back in October of 2010, there were hundreds of people who were watching the skies at night on the same date, October 13, and lo and behold, there are objects that can be seen – some of which were photographed with night vision goggles and others under 'normal conditions.' There appear to be objects making passes and diving at each other, as if they were doing some sort of acrobatics or war maneuvers in the heavens."

Beckley cautions that we should not overly simplify this night vision phenomenon as it may be something more morally complex than simply demons and angels at war. But he does feel the proof of some kind of ongoing "hostilities" is there and that knowledge of this conflict is being hidden both by NASA and those often identified as the "Shadow Government."

Perhaps, in regard to this particular kind of cover-up, one should ask – Is the Devil making them do it? Or are NASA and our military waging a noble war against demonic invaders from space that seems right out of a video game so popular with the younger generation today? We can only conjecture as we wait and see how this cosmic warfare scenario eventually plays itself out, and hope we are aligned with the winners once the laser beams subside.

"Speaking of Strange"

Host Joshua P. Warren Wants To Know
Are Spaceships Zipping Around and Blasting Each Other Above Our Heads Every Night?

I know it sounds so unbelievable. . .well. . .no one would believe it. But what if it is true? The third generation night vision revolution in this country has opened a whole new realm of civilian observation. I saw that personally, for the first time, in February of 2009.

I was a speaker at the International UFO Congress in Laughlin, Nevada. On the brisk night of Monday, February 23, around 9 pm, night vision expert Dean Warsing invited me and a friend to join him, and his son, in the desert, at a pull-off on Davis Dam Road.

The night vision skywatchers tell you there's a distinct window of time when the UFOs show up best – around 60-90 minutes after sunset. That's the time when, although it's dark on earth, the angle of the sun is just right to illuminate the cosmos a couple hundred feet up, providing enough light to help low-orbiting celestial bodies shine via night vision. Nine pm was too late for the golden window, and Dean said he thought we wouldn't see anything, but he wanted me to take a gander through the goggles nonetheless. Though I've worked with lesser night vision for years, this was my first time using high-quality third generation equipment.

When I first looked at a clear desert sky through the goggles, it took my breath away. There were a billion points of light. The entire planet seemed almost encrusted with an amazing shell of shiny diamonds. For each star my naked eye could see, perhaps 50 were revealed through the goggles. Simply beholding the space around Earth this way filled me with childlike glee.

Micha Hanks and Joshua P. Warren get ready for a skywatch. They have seen many unidentified craft in the Brown Mountain region of NC famous for its mysterious lights seen for hundreds of years.

After thirty minutes of amazement, we were about to head back to the hotel. And then I saw something that changed my life. At first, I believed it was some kind of weird digital artifact in the goggles. That was the only way my mind could reconcile the image.

Most of the horizon was filled by an incredible "v" shape. I lowered my goggles and could not see it. I lifted them again and there it was: an enormous "v" slowly and silently gliding across the sky, from the southeast to the northwest. There was a smaller, but identical, "v" flying above it. Now, let me clarify something: this was not a series of dots in formation like the Phoenix Lights. This was a vast, sprawling "v." It was like the hand of God had just drawn a huge angle in the sky with a thin, fluorescent marker. I lowered my goggles and turned to the others. "I think something is wrong with my goggles," I said.

"Huh?"

"Well," I replied, "I keep seeing this big 'v' shape."

The others looked in my direction through their goggles. I've never heard such a chorus of "HOLY SHIT!" come from just a handful of guys. They saw it too.

Round Trip to Hell in a Flying Saucer

We all watched this immense thing move across the sky. Dean, ever the scientist, kept saying, "That must be a flock of geese or something. What the . . . ?"

To this day, everyone there, especially Dean, kicks himself for not being prepared to videotape through the goggles. When we went back to the hotel casino, my head spinning, grizzled Ed Grimsley heard our tale. He chuckled sardonically and said he'd seen this "thing" a few times. He claimed it was a formation of advanced human space fighters, defending against aliens, and gave us an elaborate story about why they fly that way. My friend and I sat up all night mulling the experience over and over again. Man, that was freaky. What we saw didn't look – didn't feel – right. It felt like something foreign to anything I have experienced.

The next day, I called all the local colleges and wildlife services. Every expert confirmed that no formation-flying fowl were in the area. It was too cold and late in the season (they'd migrated out of the area), and it would have been too late at night for them to fly that way anyhow. One doctor of biology at the local university chuckled. "Well, don't forget we're near Nellis Air Force Base," he said. "There are lots of strange things in the sky around here."

Since then, I've been in the field many times, from coast to coast and beyond, with third generation night vision equipment. I bought a pair and even went into business helping people find the best goggles at a great price. I have seen so much bizarre stuff zipping around in the sky that my mind has opened quite a bit. For me, that's saying a lot.

I always adhere to Occam's Razor. I do my best to rule out the conventional first. But I swear, after looking into satellites, space junk, optical illusions, etc, I CANNOT explain some of the things I've seen. My team and I have documented lights that stop in mid-air and change direction. I saw two lights come together, sit for a while, then shoot in different directions. And yes, one night in the Nevada desert, I even witnessed one of these dots of light explode and come cascading down in fire. About 10 people all witnessed it, and each person just exclaimed "WHOAH!" It looked almost like the fireball might hit us. Was that an exploded spaceship from a cosmic battle?

The fact of the matter is very simple:

Does NASA have a secret space program to guard us against invading demonic alien forces? Official video taken from the space station shows an aerial battle with unidentified forces.

I can sit here and speculate all day about what the heck we're seeing up there. But I'm just a tiny earthbound spirit, unable to soar up and check it out. So I don't know what the hell is going on here. But I can tell you that something is happening in the space visible over Earth, with third generation night vision, which does not match up with what we're being told about what's happening up there. Are these rampant military exercises with newfangled technology? Are they aliens and humans duking it out? Are they angels and demons in prophesied warfare? I say it's probably all of the above, partially depending on how you define it. The universe is a very complex place, and if we don't acknowledge that it's like pretending we currently have all the answers.

But don't take my word for it. Go see it for yourself. Look long enough at the sky through third generation tech. When someone asks if there are battles happening up there, you'll probably share my sentiment: *Why the hell not?*

To see some amazing examples, visit: www.Paratemporal.com

Joshua P. Warren

Night Vision and the War In Heaven

Micah Hanks knows about "the war" first hand. An avid skywatcher and researcher of the unexplained, Hanks has studied the UFO enigma for nearly two decades, dealing with the subject in his column in **UFO Magazine**, his blog GralienReport.com, and on his weekly radio show *The Micah Hanks Radio Program*. He remains convinced that UFOs--whatever they are--do exist, and that secret documents released by various governing bodies of the world spell it out clearly for us. In addition to his acknowledgement of the reality of UFOs, he's also spent a fair bit of time in the field using various kinds of night vision equipment, hoping to enhance his perception of the skies above as this special report attests.

Whether you subscribe to the notion that a war between the angels of heaven and Satan's minions is literally being waged in the skies above us, it is difficult to rule out the stark consistency of reports of weird things seen in the skies... *really*. I place the necessary emphasis on *really* because it's foolish, at this point, to attempt to dissuade ourselves from the notion that *something* is indeed going on "up there," and that unidentified objects of unknown origin are often seen.

The L.E.M.U.R. team of Warren, Hanks and Mobius have organized skywatches utilizing night vision goggles and have obtained some startling video footage. Josh hosts Speaking Of Strange every Saturday evening. www.WWNC.com

Gazing into the heavens on a clear night and seeing something miraculous is special indeed--whether the object witnessed should turn out to be a bolide streaking across the sky, a satellite catching the sun's rays momentarily in its reflection as it drifts overhead, or in the truest sense, the inexplicable appearance of an unidentified airborne curiosity. But perhaps nothing could make that experience more magical than the enhancement of one's natural visibility that high-quality night vision equipment can provide.

On many occasions, I've stormed desolate ridges and empty fields while wind whipped and thunder cracked in the distance, gazing skyward with elaborate arrays of night vision eye gear. My introduction to this technology was first through my esteemed colleague, paranormalist extraordinaire and entrepreneur Joshua P. Warren, who by virtue of his innate tenacity had undertaken the bold task of financing the purchase of several sets of night vision goggles. I was thusly introduced to one Ed Grimsley, as well as a mutual associate of the two, Dean Warsing; later, Warsing, Warren and I would appear together on the National Geographic Channel's program *Paranatural* employing these devices.

The fascinating thing about night vision technology is that your natural vision is enhanced to the point that things the naked eye normally would be incapable of perceiving become visible--and brilliantly so. Distant lights from commercial aircraft, obscured by mist, fog and clouds, suddenly leap into existence, while the dying embers of a campfire several miles away are lit up like a beacon through the ghostly green illumination of the eyepiece. It is truly a wondrous experience for the avid nighttime skywatcher, and for the UFO buff, it opens the imagination to an entirely new way of thinking.

But with that awesome sense of opportunity, there comes caution, as well: once faint glimmers from passing satellites and speckled streams trailing behind meteorites become vibrant patterns of illumination, it can become easy for the eye to begin playing tricks. In my experience with this technology (little though that may be), I remain unconvinced of the anomalous nature of anything I've personally witnessed. Furthermore, I've attended conferences and lectures where well known researchers and what, essentially, would amount to paranormal "politicians" advocating UFO disclosure, have shown videos of everything from satellites and meteors, to bioluminescent plankton in our coastal waterways, which they adamantly asserted were UFOs trying to communicate with humanity through faint flashes and flickers. Less often is it that what we think we've seen--however enhanced our natural abilities may have been at the time--turns out to be what really exists.

But the brilliant thing about night vision technology, in the hands of the capable researcher, is that by familiarization with the natural phenomenon visible (or invisible, for that matter) in the sky at night, implementation of night vision eyepieces can gradually allow one a greater ability to discern the proverbial "wheat from the chaff." I know with associates like my fellows Warren and Warsing that, while most phenomenon seen at night can be easily explained, sometimes strange things appear that *do* defy rational explanation. I've had both the aforementioned gents describe with enthusiasm strange objects (or better yet, entire arrays of objects) they have witnessed over the Western United States on occasion; I can certainly vouch for the honesty and accuracy of such reports, if nothing else, based on the merit of our friendship, and in spite of whether or not I can attest to having been there to see these things myself. For now, perhaps I can only hope for the next opportunity!

Ultimately, there are far greater mysteries in this world than most of us are comfortable admitting or guessing about; night vision technology, for the time being, seems to provide a window to greater realization of some of those wonders that occasionally drift into the skies overhead.

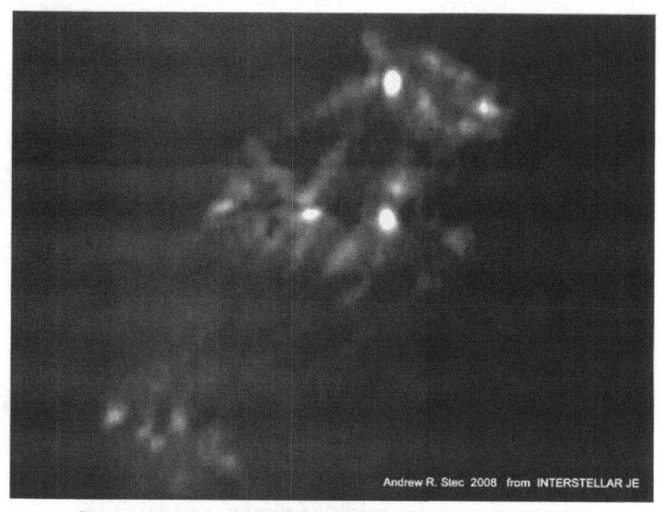

Andrew R. Stec 2008 from INTERSTELLAR JE

Strangest photo ever -- giant craft photographed in deep space seemingly morphs into a humongous demon. From Jose Escamilla's film "Interstellar"

The Authors

SEAN CASTEEL - is a freelance journalist who has written about UFOs, alien abduction and related phenomena since 1989. He has contributed to UFO Magazine, the now-defunct UFO Universe, FATE Magazine and Open Minds Magazine. Sean has also written several books for Global Communications, including UFOs, Prophecy and the End of Time and The Excluded Books of the Bible. He has a website at www.seancasteel.com

TIMOTHY GREEN BECKLEY — has been described as the Hunter Thompson of UFOlogy. Since an early age his life has more or less revolved around the paranormal. The house he was raised in was thought to be haunted. Tim saw his first of three UFOs when he was but ten, and has had two more sightings since — including an attempt to communicate with one of these objects. Tim grew up listening to the only all night talk show in the country that revolved around the strange and unexplained. Long John Nebel's guests included the early UFO contactees who claimed to have visited other planets and built time machines in the desert. Tim was fascinated by everything that went bump in the night — or even in the daylight for that matter.

Over the years he has written over 25 books on everything from rock music to the secret MJ12 papers. He has been a stringer for the national tabloids such as the Enquirer and editor of over 30 different magazines (most of which never lasted more than a couple of issues). His longest running effort was the newsstand publication UFO UNIVERSE which went for 11 years. Today he is the president of Inner Light/Global Communications and editor of the Conspiracy Journal and Bizarre Bazaar.

He is one of the few Americans ever to be invited to speak before closed door meetings on UFOs presided over by the late Earl of Clancarty at the House of Lords in England. The Inner Light Publications and Global Communiations' catalog of books and video titles now number over 200, including the works of Tim Swartz, Sean Casteel, T. Lobsang Rampa, Commander X, Brad Steiger, John Keel, Tracy Twyman, Wendelle Stevens and a host of many other authors. He is also the host of numerous horror films under the moniker of Mr. Creepo.

Send an email for a free subscription to his publications —MRUFO8@hotmail.com

Web Sites: www.ConspiracyJournal.com www.TeslasSecretLab.Com

Our Contributors

NICK REDFERN NICK REDFERN is an author, lecturer and journalist. He has written about a wide range of mysteries, including cryptozoology, UFOs, psychic phenomena, and government conspiracies. He has penned articles for Britain's Daily Express newspaper, Penthouse, and writes regularly for the newsstand publications UFO Magazine; Fate; TAPS Paramagazine; and Fortean Times. His many books include Final Events; Contactees; Science Fiction Secrets; and There's Something in the Woods. Nick has appeared on numerous television shows, including VH1's Legend Hunters; the BBC's Out of this World; the History Channel's Monster Quest and UFO Hunters; the National Geographic Channel's Paranatural; and the SyFy Channel's Proof Positive. Nick Redfern lives in Arlington, Texas and can be contacted at nickredfern@sbcglobal.net. - - www.NickRedfern.com

SCOTT CORRALES became interested in the UFO phenomenon as a result of the heavy UFO activity while he lived in both Mexico and Puerto Rico. He was also influenced by Mexican UFOlogists, Pedro Ferriz and Salvador Freixedo, a former Jesuit priest who advocated a paranormal, inter-dimensional interpretation of the phenomenon. In 1990, Scott began translating the works of Freixedo into English, making the literature and research of experts and journalists available to English-reading audiences everywhere. This led to the creation of the SAMIZDAT journal in 1993 and his collaboration with Mexico's CEFP group, Puerto Rico's PRRG, and the foremost researchers of Spain's so-called third generation of UFO researchers. Books: Chupacabras and Other Mysteries, Flashpoint - High Strangeness In Puerto Rico. Website: Journal of the Institute of Hispanic Ufology. http://inexplicata.blogspot.com/

KENN THOMAS' new book, JFK & UFOs: Military-Industrial Conspiracy and Cover-Up from Maury Island to Dallas, will soon be available from Feral House, on the web at feralhouse.com. His current book, Secret and Suppressed II: Banned Ideas and Hidden History into the 21st Century, is also available from Feral House. Mr. Thomas' other books on JFK, NASA, Nazis and JFK and Mind Control, Oswald and JFK are available from AUP at www.adventuresunlimitedpress.com. Mr. Thomas is available for lectures on conspiracy topics, including "The Parapolitics of UFOlogy and the Origin of the Military Industrial Complex". He is a frequent guest on talk shows worldwide. Website: SteamShovelPress.com Please e-mail k23thomas@yahoo.com.

BRENT RAYNES is the author of Visitors From Hidden Realms (2004) and On The Edge of Reality (2009), and the editor of the popular online magazine Alternate Perceptions (www.mysterious-america.net). Brent has been investigating and researching UFOs since 1967. His interests have included the full spectrum of paranormal phenomena. He's been involved in a good many haunted house investigations, has been doing EVP (Electronic Voice Phenomena) work, as well as cryptozoological studies, plus met many Native American practitioners and been involved in visiting sacred sites and taking part in their ceremonies. In November 2010, Brent was a keynote speaker at the ARE (Association for Research and Enlightenment) in Virginia Beach, Virginia, where a special UFO conference was held. It was called Visitors From Hidden Realms, in honor of Brent's book.

BRAD STEIGER is the author/coauthor of 170 books with over 17 million copies in print. Steiger's first published articles on the unexplained appeared in 1956, and he has now written more than 2,000 articles with UFO or paranormal themes. From 1970-'73, his weekly newspaper column, The Strange World of Brad Steiger, was carried domestically in over 80 newspapers and overseas from Bombay to Tokyo. Among his books are Revelation: The Divine Fire, The Werewolf Book: An Encyclopedia of Shapeshifting Beings; Real Ghosts, Restless Spirits, and Haunted Places; Shadow World, and, with his wife Sherry, UFOs Are Here, UFO Odyssey, The Gale Encyclopedia [three volumes] of the Unusual and Unexplained; Conspiracies and Secret Societies: The Complete Dossier. Sherry is herself the author or coauthor of over 40 books. From the mid-1980s through 2002, they lectured and conducted seminars throughout the United States and overseas. They have two sons, three daughters, and nine grandchildren, eight girls, and one boy. www.BradandSherry.com

Round Trip to Hell in a Flying Saucer

PHILIP J. IMBROGNO is a science educator, and a leading expert on UFOlogy, the paranormal and the stone chambers of New York. With Dr. J. Allen Hynek and Bob Pratt, he co-authored the best-selling Night Siege: The Hudson Valley UFO Sightings (Ballantine Books, 1986), still in print (Llewellyn). He is also the author of Celtic Mysteries in New England and Contact of the Fifth Kind and Interdimensional Universe (all published by Llewellyn.) His fifth and most recent book, Files from the Edge: A Paranormal Investigator's Exploration of High Strangeness (Llewellyn), has remained on the Amazon.com list of top 25 best-selling UFO books since its publication in April, 2010. Also, his next book, Ultraterrestrial Contacts, was published in December of 2010. Phil has also coauthored two books with Rosemary Ellen Guiley: The Vengeful Djinn: Unmasking the Hidden Agenda of the Genie; and Portals Doorways to Another Dimension. Both titles are to be published sometime in 2011 by Llewellyn.

THOMAS HORN is an internationally recognized lecturer, publisher, radio host and best selling author of several books including the newest, Forbidden Gates. His works have been referred to by writers of the Los Angeles Times Syndicate, MSNBC, Christianity Today, New Man Magazine, World Net Daily, News Max, White House Correspondents and dozens of newsmagazines and press agencies around the globe. Thomas has been interviewed by US Congressmen and Senators on his findings as well as featured repeatedly in major media including top-ten talk shows, America's Morning News for The Washington Times, CBN, The Harvest Show, Coast to Coast AM, Prophecy in the News, and the Southwest Radio Church to name a few. Thomas received the highest degree honorary doctorate bestowed in 2007 from legendary professor Dr. I.D.E. Thomas for his research into ancient history, and has been repeatedly endorsed by such national leaders as Dr. James Kennedy. www.raidersnewsupdate.com

WM. MICHAEL MOTT is the author and illustrator of PULP WINDS, the long-awaited collection of short fiction, verse, and Forteana. With introductions by Walter Bosley, Brad Steiger, and Gerald W. Page, these tales will take you from the antediluvian world to lost cities beneath the Earth, onward to other planets around distant stars, and even to the Dark Ages, the Old West and the High Seas. New twists on mythos and madness are intermeshed and presented in these yarns of terror and adventure! In addition to being the author of the new book, he is also the author of the satirical fantasy novel Pulsifer: A Fable and its sequel, Land of Ice, A Velvet Knife (recently re-released in one volume as the Pulsifer Saga Omnibus Edition, from TGS Publishers) as well as the non-fiction books Caverns, Cauldrons, and Concealed Creatures and This Tragic Earth: The Art and World of Richard Sharpe Shaver. Book links, artwork, and audio interviews from a variety of radio shows can be found at www.Mottimorphic.com

T ALLEN H. GREENFIELD (the "T" or "Tau" being a customary title given to an esoteric prelate in the Doinel lineage upon their consecration) is a native of Augusta, Georgia, USA. By the age of sixteen, he had become a world traveler, and has visited many countries all over the globe in the years since, from France to French Polynesia; from Canada to Venezuela; Greece to Grenada; Israel to Indiana. He is a long-time student of esoteric spirituality and Gnosticism, a study he began in 1960. A past (elected) member of the British Society for Psychical Research, the National Investigations Committee on Aerial Phenomena (NICAP) (from 1960), etc., he has twice been the recipient of the "UFOlogist of the Year Award" of the National UFO Conference (1972 and 1992), which has run continuously on an annual basis for 41 years. He is a Borderland Science Research Associate (BSRA). He considers the UFO phenomenon to be a "signal" from the Collective Unconscious that the neglect of a magical spirituality by society as a whole is a cause of emotional plague and social disaster. Works include Secret Cipher of the Saucers, Hermetic Brother Revisited. www.mindspring.com/~hellfire/bishop/

CHRISTOPHER O'BRIEN from 1992 to 2002 has investigated and/or logged hundreds of events reported in the San Luis Valley—located in South-Central Colorado/North Central New Mexico. His ten-plus years of investigation resulted in the three books of his "Mysterious Valley" trilogy, The Mysterious Valley, Enter the Valley, and Secrets of the Mysterious Valley. His field investigation of UFO reports, unexplained livestock deaths, Native American legends, cryptozoology, secret military activity and the folklore found in the world's largest alpine valley, has produced one of the largest databases of unusual occurrences gathered from a single geographic region. His latest book Stalking the Tricksters was recently released by Adventures Unlimited Press and distills his years of field investigation and research into an ingenious unified paranormal field theory that addresses the apparent interrelatedness between divergent paranormal phenomena. He is currently a co-host on the popular weekly GCN Network radio program The Paracast. www.OurStrangePlanet.com

Round Trip to Hell in a Flying Saucer

JOSHUA P. WARREN is an investigator, author, filmmaker, radio host and President of L.E.M.U.R. as well as an internationally-recognized expert on mysterious phenomena, specializing in ghosts. Books include How to Hunt Ghosts, Haunted Asheville, Pet Ghosts, The Wishing Machine Workbook, The Secret Wisdom of Kukulkan & Poor Man's Paranormal. He made the cover of the Electric Space Craft Science Journal, in 2004, for his team's groundbreaking lab experiments on plasma. Joshua is the host of the top-radio Clear Channel show, Speaking of Strange, and often appears on mainstream TV like Discovery, History Channel, National Geographic, SyFy, etc.
See: www.JoshuaPWarren.com and www.Paratemporal.com

MICAH A. HANKS has researched all things strange since a very young age, beginning while he was still in grade school. Since that tender age of discovery, he has grown to work toward documenting the world's bizarre mysteries, having contributed articles and stories to FATE Magazine, Fortean Times, Mysteries Magazine, UFO Magazine, and others. He has also had the pleasure of working with the Travel Channel for their Weird Travels television program, as well as the History Channel's Guts and Bolts during investigations as an investigator with the L.E.M.U.R. Paranormal Research Team. His adventures have taken him to all kinds of amazing places; from snow-capped mountaintops in the middle of July hiking through the Rockies of Montana in search of Bigfoot, to a haunted 19th century jail in historic Charleston, South Carolina. He's studied Martial Artists in Chicago who perform the ancient art of the "Death Touch," and while he was there he also visited Resurrection Cemetery, famous location of "Resurrection Mary", one of America's most enduring hauntings. He's trudged through the mountains of Cherokee, North Carolina in search of "Boojums" and what Cherokee natives described to him as "The Woolly Ones," stomped through the foothills of Tennessee in search of the southern Skunk Ape, and struck the hills in the heart of Amish country in search of Ohio's Grass Man. Visit http://gralienreport.com

TIM R. SWARTZ is an Indiana native and Emmy-Award winning television producer/videographer. Tim is the author of a number of popular books including The Lost Journals of Nikola Tesla, Time Travel: A How-To-Guide, Richard Shaver-Reality of the Inner Earth, Admiral Byrd's Secret Journey Beyond the Poles. He is a contributing writer for: Sir Arthur Conan Doyle: The First Ghostbuster, and Brad Steiger's Real Monsters, Gruesome Critters, and Beasts from the Darkside. As a photojournalist, Tim has traveled extensively and investigated paranormal phenomena and other unusual mysteries from such diverse locations as the Great Pyramid in Egypt to the Great Wall in China. He has worked with television networks such as PBS, ABC, NBC, CBS, CNN, ESPN, Thames-TV and the BBC. His articles have been published in magazines such as Mysteries, FATE, Strange, Atlantis Rising, UFO Universe, Flying Saucer Review, Renaissance, and Unsolved UFO Reports. View his website at: www.conspiracyjournal.com

ADAM GORIGHTLY is a writer, lecturer, musician and erstwhile podcaster. Adam's book titles include The Shadow Over Santa Susana, Black Magic, Mind Control and the Manson Family Mythos, and The Prankster and the Conspiracy: The Story of Kerry Thornley and How He Met Oswald and Inspired the Counterculture. His late, great podcast series, Untamed Dimensions, is archived at http://gorightly.podomatic.com// Adam's first music album, Transmissions From A Dying Planet, is available at amazon.com. Adam has appeared as a guest on numerous radio shows such as Coast To Coast AM, Erskine Overnight, The Richard Syrett Show and the X-Zone with Rob McConnell. He has lectured at various events, such as the Roswell 60th Anniversary Festival and the Retro UFO Conference on such topics as conspiracies, Forteana and UFOs. He has a website at: www.adamgorightly.com

NOTE: The majority of our contributors can also be found on Facebook.

CIA UFO DIARY OF COMMANDER MOORE

"A CHILLING MUST READ FOR ALL CONSPIRACY PRONE UFO ADVOCATES"
TIMOTHY GREEN BECKLEY, EDITOR UFO UNIVERSE

A former Navy Commander and CIA operative's private memoirs involving the retrieval of wreckage from a UFO shot at over the Nation's Capital and how pieces of this craft were stolen from a safe inside a supposedly secure government office building in Washington, D.C.

REVEALED FOR THE FIRST TIME!

· How aliens he defines as *"Skymen"* have been coming to Earth's surface and exploring it for what could number thousands of years!

· Some of these beings possibly have homes in caverns on the moon, Mars, Jupiter, or the asteroids!

· Many more originate much nearer to the Earth's surface, from *"Skyislands"*, or even from within the hollows of our planet, and possibly underwater hangars!

· The *"Skyislands"* are apparently orbiting the Earth in several bands or chains, likely indicated by jet streams!

· *"Skymen"* have kidnapped a multitude of people and skycraft users have long extracted blood from surface animals and humans, and commit mysterious murders!

★ ★

NOW YOU CAN ADD THIS RARE BOOK TO YOUR LIBRARY!

THE SECRET UFO DIARY OF CIA OPERATIVE COMMANDER ALVIN E. MOORE EXPOSES THE EXISTENCE OF THE SKYMEN AND INVISIBLE PLANET X

Read the section in this book about the possibility of invisible worlds — or Sky Islands as Commander Moore called them — then order your copy of the amazing, 275 page, CIA UFO DIARY by Commander Moore for **$16.00 + $5.00 S/H**

Global Communications · Box 753 · New Brunswick, NJ 08903
Credit Cards: 732 602-3407 - Pay Pal: MRUFO8@hotmail.com

Made in the USA
Middletown, DE
28 March 2021